The Buyer's Toolkit

An easy-to-use approach
for effective buying

Jonathan O'Brien

First published in Great Britain and the United States in 2017 by Kogan Page Limited

2nd Floor, 45 Gee Street	c/o Martin P Hill Consulting	4737/23 Ansari Road
London	122 W 27th St, 10th Floor	Daryaganj
EC1V 3RS	New York, NY 10001	New Delhi 110002
United Kingdom	USA	India

© Jonathan O'Brien 2017

The right of Jonathan O'Brien to be identified as the author of this work has been asserted by him in accordance with the Copyright, Designs and Patents Act 1988.

ISBN   978 0 7494 7981 7
E-ISBN   978 0 7494 7982 4

British Library Cataloguing-in-Publication Data

A CIP record for this book is available from the British Library.

Typeset by Integra Software Services, Pondicherry
Print production managed by Jellyfish
Printed and bound in Great Britain by CPI Group (UK) Ltd, Croydon, CR0 4YY

For Elaine, Emily and Hugh

CONTENTS

ABOUT THE AUTHOR

Jonathan O'Brien is CEO and owner of the international procurement consultancy and training provider, Positive Purchasing Ltd (www.positivepurchasing.com). Jonathan has over 27 years' experience working in procurement. He has worked all over the world to help global organizations transform their procurement capability through training, education and working directly with practitioners and executive teams to drive in the adoption of negotiation, category management, supplier relationship management and other strategic procurement methodologies.

Jonathan is an electronics engineer who moved into procurement. His career in engineering soon shifted into supplier quality assurance, and it was the hundreds of supplier audits undertaken involving detailed examination of business practice and process that provided a sound understanding of how organizations work, and thus began the process of working with companies to help them improve. A move to a senior buying role in a large utility company shifted the focus to the commercial aspects of procurement and this career path culminated in a global category director role for an airline business. Jonathan moved to an internal consultant role and helped lead a series of major organizational change programmes. A subsequent move into consultancy, initially with a large global strategic purchasing consultancy and later with his own business provided Jonathan with the opportunity to work with some of the biggest and best-known companies in the world to help improve purchasing capability, gaining a rich experience along the way.

Jonathan holds an MBA from Plymouth University Business School, a Diploma in Marketing and an HNC in Electronics, is a Member of the Chartered Institute of Purchasing (MCIPS), an NLP Master Practitioner and a former registered Lead Assessor of quality management systems.

Jonathan and his team at Positive Purchasing Ltd have developed and created the Red Sheet® negotiation tool, the 5i® Category Management process and the Orchestra of SRM® – providing three of most fundamental strategic approaches to procurement and negotiation now used by companies all over the world.

This is Jonathan's fourth title: the other titles, so far published across eight editions in various languages, have become core texts in the professional buying, procurement and negotiation space. Jonathan continues to write. He is also an accomplished broadcaster and artist and lives with his family in Plymouth, UK.

You can e-mail Jonathan at jonathan@jonathanobrien.co.uk.

LIST OF FIGURES

LIST OF TABLES

PREFACE

Learning how to buy well can make a dramatic difference to our personal and perhaps our professional lives. It can help companies of all shapes and sizes increase their profit, reduce risk and gain competitive advantage. It can help not-for-profit organizations do more with the funds available. Effective buying can save us money – lots of money in some situations! All we need is the ability to understand our situation and apply some simple techniques to maximize our outcomes. This book provides a simple and effective toolkit that will help you do that. However, there is much more to good buying than just securing the best price; in fact, sometimes price may be the least important consideration. Good buying is also about making sure we get everything we need, and perhaps some or all of the things we want as well on the best terms. It is about securing the best value possible. It is about making sure that when we buy, we get the goods or the services we agreed, at the agreed time and to the agreed quality. Sometimes good buying can be about finding new and unique things suppliers can offer that can enrich our lives, or helping the organizations or companies we work for improve what they offer and even gain competitive advantage. This book will help you do all of these things.

Buying is much more than a commercial transaction, it is a practice that offers a wealth of possibilities and advantages simply by having some basic knowledge of the buying process and using some simple tools and techniques that put us in the driving seat. Yet it seems the benefits of learning and instilling good buying practice frequently get overlooked. Good buying skills do not get taught in mainstream education and, unless someone specifically studies the profession of procurement to learn the trade, the skills and techniques involved could remain a best-kept secret! Suppliers love this and the entire world of selling is predicated on the foundation that the seller can easily gain advantage over the buyer, often without us being aware of this. It is no accident that companies invest heavily in brand building, powerful marketing and ensuring their sales teams have all the training to win our business. Professional publications and training on advanced strategic procurement are freely available, but much of this is inaccessible or cannot readily be interpreted for everyday buying scenarios. This book changes that. This book draws on the advanced procurement and negotiation theory and models used by world-leading global companies, re-interpreted and distilled down into a simple set of tools and techniques that we can all understand and apply with ease.

This book provides a simple step-by-step buying approach and toolkit that can be applied with or without prior buying experience but can transform the buying outcomes possible. Whatever your experience, buying situation or need, whether professional or personal, if you want to buy more effectively then this book is for you.

ACKNOWLEDGEMENTS

This book has taken the vast wealth of learning, knowledge and research that formed my first three books and distilled it down into a form that is simple to access and use. It was born out a need I identified several years ago when a friend of mine remarked on how her boss had all of a sudden asked her to go and figure out how to buy a new major piece of equipment that the organization had found funds for. There was no one she could ask, no one had much experience of buying such things before, most avoided such tasks and all I could offer were advanced procurement or negotiation solutions aimed at big global organizations. She soon figured it out, but the need for a simple 'buyer's toolkit' aimed at anyone who buys, which doesn't need any prior experience to use, kept coming back to mind. I subsequently floated this to many people who might have some use for such a thing or who ran a business of some sort. The response was always the same – when can I have it? I remember chatting to our accountants who remarked: 'The receptionist does all our buying, she probably spends about half a million pounds each year but we've never given her any training in how to do this... Perhaps we should?' So I must begin by acknowledging all the people I came across who helped me see the real need for something simple that can help anyone buy really well. Thanks also to all the people who helped make my first three books the great global success stories they are today, because each and every one of you has contributed to this book indirectly. Thanks to Nick Dobney for the thought download that led to the commercial print example. Thanks to the team at Positive Purchasing for the ongoing support and belief in this book and to those who helped proofread figures and some text. Thanks to all who have inspired some of the examples found in this book. Once again thanks to my family for putting up with a bit less of me while I wrote this, something they are quite familiar with by now. Finally thank you for buying and/or reading this book. I hope it helps and I hope that it changes how you buy, puts you more in control and helps you secure significantly better buying outcomes whenever you buy.

INTRODUCTION

Using the book

This book is written for anyone who buys. This book does not assume any prior knowledge of buying and is suitable for all individuals whether buying personally or as part of a job or for an organization. This book contains a wealth of simple, effective, practical and highly accessible tools and techniques that will change how you buy from this point on. It is suitable for the individual who wants to buy a new car, for the administrative assistant tasked with buying office supplies, for the small company that is trying to figure out how to better manage their spend and suppliers, for the headmaster who wants to buy new playground equipment, for the medium-sized company who wants to take the first step towards improving and having a buying function that adds value to the business, or for the person working in a large corporate who wants to take the first step towards understanding what the procurement function does. If you buy and read this book you will buy better, secure the best value or deal and be in control of the process throughout.

PATHWAY QUESTIONS

This book is organized so as to lead you through an exploration of what good buying is, the benefits and impact this can bring and how to go about making it happen. The book is compiled around the *Power Buying Process* – a systematic, step-by-step approach to highly effective buying of anything, anywhere, by anyone. It also provides guidance on where next and how to transition to a more strategic approach to procurement. The book seeks to provide answers to 20 key or 'pathway' questions. If you can answer all of these questions with confidence then you're in great shape and you are already a *Power Buyer*. The reality is that, for most, reflecting on these questions highlights the gap between current buying practice and being really good at buying. This book will not only help answer these questions but provide practical tools and approaches that enable you to buy with confidence and secure better outcomes.

Pathway questions addressed in this book:

1 What is buying?

2 What shapes how we can buy well?

3 What benefits are possible with effective buying?

4 What stops us being good at buying?

5 What are the steps to effective buying?

6 How do we define what we need and want?

7 How do we discover the strength of our position and power, if any?

8 How can we get behind the supplier's price?

9 How can we boost our buying power?

10 Who could we buy from?

11 How do we understand the market?

12 How will we buy to secure the best outcome?

13 What supplier (or solution) should we choose and how do we decide?

14 Should we negotiate? If so how do we go about doing this?

15 What sort of contract do we need? What do we need to do to agree the contract?

16 How do we ensure the buying arrangements we have agreed happen in practice?

17 Do we need to manage the supplier? If so, how?

18 Do I need to check that the supplier performs as agreed? If so, how?

19 What do I do when things go wrong or if I need to drive improvement with a supplier?

20 How do I make Power Buying a success and continue the journey as a power buying professional?

Using the 5D Power Buying Process

This book provides 15 templates relating to the 5D Power Buying Process, given in the appendix (and explained in Chapters 5 to 9) to help you buy. The 5D Power Buying Process was developed by Positive Purchasing Ltd and is © Positive Purchasing Ltd, reproduced under licence in this book.

How to buy really well

This chapter explores what buying is and the components of good buying as an individual or for an organization. It begins to lay the groundwork for our buyer's toolkit and explains some of the core concepts that define modern buying around the world.

Pathway questions addressed in this chapter

1 What is buying?
2 What shapes how we can buy well?

We are all buyers

We all buy things, whether it's a trip to the supermarket, a new car, a house, securing the services of a builder or perhaps swapping possessions with a friend; buying is an integral part of our personal daily lives. For some it is also part of our professional lives, whether our job formally includes responsibility for buying and committing expenditure on behalf of an organization or whether we just end up doing this.

It's really not that complicated

Have we made buying more complicated than it needs to be? Perhaps. The practice of buying is nothing new and is part of the framework of commerce that has enabled mankind to build the world we live in today. Buying in today's global marketplace may appear daunting to the uninitiated, requiring specialist knowledge and approaches, yet the basic principles have not changed since our ancestors bartered turnips for potatoes or would haggle to buy a small pig for three groats.

Buying is an exchange of 'something for something', most often involving money. It can involve some negotiation and perhaps some sort of relationship with the seller, but not always.

We are all buyers yet few of us ever receive any sort of training about how to do it well. It is one of those life skills we learn, and most of us think we are good at it if we manage to get what we set out to get – but are we really good at it? How might we know, or is this how the supplier wants to make us feel? What does good look like? And what if we could buy better? How could we improve our outcomes and by how much? How does buying change when we buy on behalf of an organization? This book sets out to answer these questions and many more besides.

Buying is really not that complicated, and it is a process we can easily be in full control of and become highly effective at. The secret is understanding the basic things that are at play when we buy and applying some simple tools and techniques to manage our approach.

Buying as individuals

Our daily routines depend upon us buying the goods and services we need in our lives. In most cases this is second nature, built around convenience and organized in a familiar and accessible manner. The degree to which we can influence outcomes can be limited. Trying to negotiate a cost reduction for the contents of our shopping basket at the checkout or suggesting the gas station gives us discount because we want to commit to buy all our gas there for the next year are unlikely to get us very far! Yet there are personal buying situations, generally when we are spending greater sums of money, where there is scope to buy better and secure a greater outcome just by following some simple steps. Whilst this is a book about developing buying skills, I am confident that you, together with most people I know, are already pretty good at buying. It something we learn to do, especially if we need to ensure our limited cash goes as far as we can. As shoppers we love bargains and will know or search out who offers the best deal. Perhaps we might check things out thoroughly before committing and weigh up the pros and cons, perhaps we will ask the opinion of others who have already bought the thing we are considering, or check the reviews online. These are all good buying techniques and this book will build on and help further develop this capability whilst providing some useful tools to better structure our thinking.

Buying as a profession

Companies and organizations need to buy all sorts of things in order to function. Whether raw materials, equipment, essential supplies, services to keep things going or contractors to do the work, buying is part of every business, school, hospital, institute, society, club or institution. For most organizations, especially smaller concerns, buying tends to be something organized solely to obtain the goods and services the company needs when it needs them. Perhaps buying is a part of someone's overall job – tradesmen might simply go and buy the building supplies needed for a construction job from a merchant. The administrator at a school might be responsible for, amongst other duties, buying the supplies the school needs from its suppliers or a small- to medium-sized manufacturing business may have one or more dedicated buyers tasked with managing the spend of the business.

In larger companies buying becomes more of a core function and tends to be referred to as 'procurement', 'purchasing' or 'sourcing'. There is much debate about these labels and what they suggest in terms of how strategic the buying is within the business; however, the reality is there is no universally accepted definition and the meaning of these words changes with industry and geography. In this book I shall refer to the professional end of buying as 'procurement'.

In small- to medium-sized enterprises buying tends to be quite tactical – reacting and responding to what the enterprise needs and sourcing it in order to satisfy those needs. In larger enterprises, a similar tactical approach to buying was, for many years, standard practice; however, over the past 30 years or so there has been dramatic shift in the world of corporate buying and for many big organizations procurement is now a strategic function. What does this mean? Well, strategic procurement is less reactive, but rather considers the overall aims and goals of the organization and what it is trying to achieve and then determines how the supply base can best help realize this. A strategic procurement function will work to understand what needs to be sourced, looking as far into the future as possible, and then figure out the best way to source the goods and services, and how to secure the greatest value, least risk, lowest price and most innovation according to what the organization needs and wants. Modern global organizations recognize the important contribution procurement can make to the business and are increasingly giving procurement board-level representation, with the 'Chief Procurement Officer' or CPO being commonplace in today's more progressive organizations. We will return to the modern strategic procurement function in Chapter 10.

The buying spectrum

Buying is not one single thing, but many different approaches to acquire the goods or services we need. There is a spectrum of buying (Figure 1.1). At one end there is basic buying where, put simply, we buy what we need when we need it. This end of the buying spectrum is highly tactical and reactive, but as we move through the spectrum the amount of buyer intervention to enable and bring value to the transaction increases. Buying 'deals' are not just bought as presented by the seller but there is some sort of interaction between parties to discuss, determine, agree and perhaps negotiate aspects of the purchase such as price, specification, terms, timing, etc. Beyond this we find a managed approach to procurement, looking beyond single transactions but putting arrangements in place for entire areas of spend, some may even be long term. At the other extreme of our buying spectrum is strategic procurement, where how things get purchased and from whom is carefully managed so the organization can realize its overall goals. Here key suppliers are not arm's-length providers but become an extension of the business perhaps even working collaboratively with the business to create new competitive advantage.

The five factors that shape how *we buy*

The skill behind effective buying, is determining *how* we should buy for any given requirement or situation. Sometimes the transaction is a one-off, sometimes we need to look longer term where there will be many transactions along the way. We must consider where we might buy from, and how we will determine and define exactly what we need and want as well as the most effective way to satisfy this. We must also consider what relationship with suppliers, if any, might be necessary, and how the contract

Figure 1.1 The buying spectrum

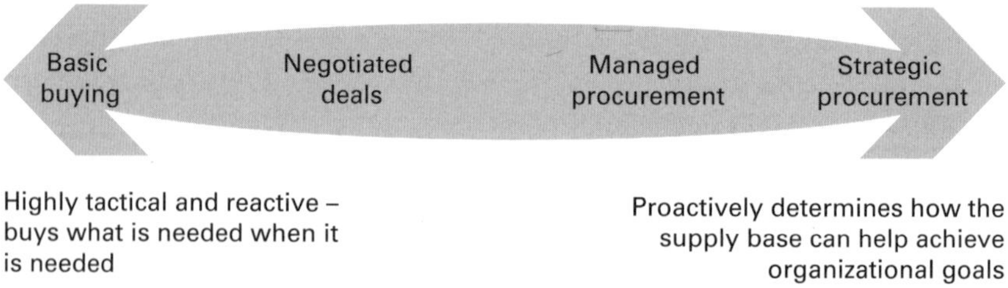

| Basic buying | Negotiated deals | Managed procurement | Strategic procurement |

Highly tactical and reactive – buys what is needed when it is needed

Proactively determines how the supply base can help achieve organizational goals will be established. Together these factors make up our buying approach. Sometimes we have the freedom to decide this approach, sometimes not, but if we do this determination can only be in response to an assessment of our situation, the market, our options or how much power we hold, and how exactly we do this is what this book is about.

The rest of this chapter is therefore concerned with determining our buying approach or *how* we will buy. There are five considerations here, which I shall expand in turn:

1 *value* – the value of what we are buying;

2 *risk, complexity and difficulty* – the risk and complexity or what we are buying along with the difficulty we might encounter in buying it;

3 *choice* – what choice we have, or don't have, around how we buy;

4 *relationship* – the nature of the relationship we need or want with the seller, and;

5 *contract* – how we will contract for the goods or services

The value of chickens

It's all about value! Whilst buying is usually the exchange of goods or services for money, it is in fact the exchange of value that lies at the heart of buying. Exchange of value has been part of human life since we learned to walk upright. Before money our forefathers would determine just how many chickens a single goat was worth and when the concept of money began it linked an exchange to a physical amount of grain held in a secure store, which had a set value. Today there are still transactions without currency, for example community cooperatives are springing up where those with skills or trades exchange their time for other trades without a single bank-note changing hands. Yet for most transactions, currency is the medium of the exchange of value enabling us to assign a monetary value to the things we seek to acquire, and even gauge the relative value of the acquisition within the currency or relative to others. Obvious stuff, although it is worth reflecting on buying as a value exchange because that perspective helps us understand how to be good at buying, and specifically how to ensure that we acquire all the value we need and want from a deal (we will return to this in Chapter 5). The first consideration that shapes *how* to buy is the value of exchange (either as a single transaction or across multiple transactions). The greater the value, the more we have at stake and so the more we need arrangements to protect ourselves, preserve cash flow and, where appropriate, maximize the value either for our benefit or to benefit both parties according to the situation.

The risk of nuclear submarines

The second key consideration that shapes how we buy is concerned with understanding the risk and complexity associated with what we are buying together with the difficulty we might encounter in trying to buy it. Going to a store to buy groceries does not tend to be fraught with risk or difficulty, nor is there anything complex we need to think about when specifying a loaf of bread. The seller has pretty much taken care of all the difficult bits and presents us with the options we are most likely to want. The same simplicity exists for an organization buying simple supplies and the only difference might be how the transaction happens, perhaps involving a purchase order or some sort of corporate account. Yet if our organization was setting out to buy a nuclear submarine, things might be different. Such things don't tend to make it onto Amazon.com, nor will there be a product catalogue we can order from, and even if there were, raising a purchase order might not adequately articulate our needs. It is not just the risk associated with what we are buying that we are concerned about here; after all, a nuclear submarine could be considered a 'risky thing', but also the risk of poor buying to acquire it. This would not only mean we did a bad deal, but could mean we had failed to make the necessary provision or planning needed to acquire a nuclear submarine, which could in turn expose us to many other risks. This is the risk associated with delivery failure or lateness, not getting the right thing or not to the required quality or standard and not providing for the right interaction between buyer and seller. So whilst some purchases are simple others are much more complex and require specialist procurement approaches to manage the associated risk and difficulty.

The risk/complexity/difficulty associated with what we are buying is therefore the second consideration that shapes *how* we should buy. If we map this against the degree of value being acquired for different purchases we can begin to relate these to the different buying approaches on our spectrum. Figure 1.2 plots some examples.

Cutthroat or caring?

Cutthroat or caring buying? Perhaps you have already made up your mind which camp you side with merely from the title of this section, because as individuals we can and do make choices around how we want to buy according to our personal beliefs and values. For example, if we believe we should pay more because our purchase promotes local producers, we have this choice and can exercise it if we wish. Within organizations, we also have a choice as to how we buy. The choices we make can have a

Figure 1.2 Examples of different types of buying according to value and risk/complexity/difficulty

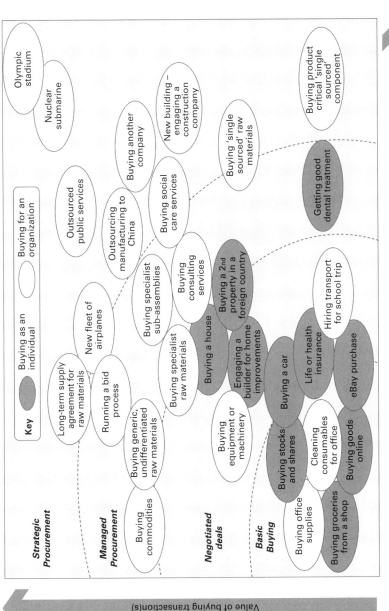

significant impact assuming the firm can organize itself to make informed choices. Every buying scenario is different and so there is a range of possibilities. Perhaps *how* we buy may be determined by our understanding of the marketplace, suppliers, future needs, and how important specific suppliers might be to us both short and longer term. Organizations may wish buying choices to be aligned with and driven by corporate goals and policy informed by corporate values. For example, if the organization's brand is predicated on certain environmental or ethical principles then it follows that what, where and how it buys must align with these, if for no other reason than to protect the brand against the risk of its buying practices becoming public knowledge.

The choice dimension to buying is the third primary consideration that determines how we buy. Thirty years ago, this was not something buyers paid much attention to, and arguably was less relevant as buying was generally more tactical (the remit of procurement was little more than to buy things), less international and there were fewer giant concentrations of huge buying power. Yet today, ignoring the relevance of what choices we make around how we buy can have significant negative consequences.

As we have seen, buying is about the exchange of value. It is the way this exchange is made, and the different choices and possibilities here that give rise to the choice dimension within buying (Figure 1.3). This is supported by Granovetter (1985) who suggests that the business decisions we take as individuals are influenced by both sociological and economic concerns and that how we approach a business decision exists somewhere on a continuum between these two. At one extreme, and outside the range of normal buying is theft, an involuntary one-sided exchange. Next, the rawest form of exchange is cutthroat buying, where one party has the ability to exercise its power over the other and drive the deal to the extreme and seize the best outcome purely on their terms. I have heard it argued that good at buying means being cutthroat to secure the best deal! Well, perhaps, but at this extreme cutthroat buying can also be associated with parties prepared to 'do anything' to get what they want without care for the other party. This approach to buying tends to be driven purely by business decisions made at an individual not company level (and therefore how they act in the relationship), and are totally influenced by economic concerns, perhaps motivated by personal gain. As such this drives self-interest behaviour that is not only cutthroat but can also be dishonest, opportunistic or involve wrongdoing. Whilst cutthroat buying can deliver short-term wins to maximize profit and returns, Granovetter (1985) suggests individuals operating at this extreme tend to fail

Figure 1.3   Our choice around how we buy

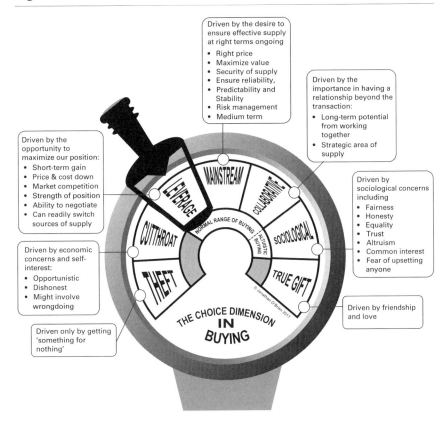

Driven by the desire to ensure effective supply at right terms ongoing
- Right price
- Maximize value
- Security of supply
- Ensure reliability,
- Predictability and Stability
- Risk management
- Medium term

Driven by the importance in having a relationship beyond the transaction:
- Long-term potential from working together
- Strategic area of supply

Driven by the opportunity to maximize our position:
- Short-term gain
- Price & cost down
- Market competition
- Strength of position
- Ability to negotiate
- Can readily switch sources of supply

Driven by sociological concerns including
- Fairness
- Honesty
- Equality
- Trust
- Altruism
- Common interest
- Fear of upsetting anyone

Driven by economic concerns and self-interest:
- Opportunistic
- Dishonest
- Might involve wrongdoing

Driven only by getting 'something for nothing'

Driven by friendship and love

because they struggle to win or retain support. Granovetter (1985) also points out that it is most likely they will have no or few friends – something that would be essential to maintain any sort of ongoing buying relationship if one is needed. So a cutthroat buying approach tends to be outside the normal range of professional buying. It is typically a once only, one-sided approach that is ineffective in the medium term and one that can work against us – increasing risk of jeopardizing supply and creating an unsustainable situation.

However, move one notch on and we enter the range of professional buying with *leverage* buying - an approach that *is* entirely appropriate. If we are in a position of power and we are buying a generic product, in a mass market with many providers vying for our business, then playing 'buying hardball' and leveraging our power may be exactly the right approach. Where cutthroat stops and leverage starts can be blurred line and one that is about recognizing the responsibility that comes with having buying power.

A powerful retailer might be able to demand a low price point from a small struggling producer in a developing country and secure a short-term gain, but the price point may be unsustainable long term if the producer is unable to invest in the equipment needed for the medium term. Is this cutthroat buying or good leverage buying and how far should we go? This very 21st century question is increasingly the subject of debate in modern large companies and as has led to an emergence of buying policies and changes in practice by many firms in recent years.

Effective buying is about understanding our position and what power we might have before we buy. There is a vast range of *mainstream* buying scenarios where we find ourselves either in a position where the supplier holds all the power, and our choice or alternatives are limited, or where the power between us and the seller is reasonably balanced. Sellers work hard to place themselves in a strong position and maximize the strength of this position. Sometimes this is real and sometimes they may work to hide an actual weak position. We will explore this more fully later. In mainstream buying, our choice of *how* we buy is driven by what we need to do to put the right sort of buying or supply arrangements in place so we get everything we need and want and that security of supply is assured. Whilst in this buying scenario we might not hold the power to leverage an outcome completely on our terms, our aim becomes to secure the best or right price with as much additional value as possible whilst understanding and making provision to manage any risk that might exist. As such, good buying here will typically look beyond a single transaction and seek to agree arrangements for buying over the medium term. This would also shape our negotiation approach.

At the high end of normal professional buying is where short-term economic concerns are replaced with joint working in the pursuit of long term goals that benefit both buyer and seller. Collaborative buying has in recent decades become highly important to organizations which have looked to establish relationships with strategic suppliers who could provide innovation or take over running core functions of the business. Here, *how* we buy looks very different to traditional or everyday buying and is more concerned about how the right operations and relationships can exist between parties.

Moving one notch on again and starting to exceed what is the normal range of buying for many firms, we enter a growing world of altruistic buying – a conscious decision and choice by firms or individuals to go beyond the traditional range of buying and to operate based upon sociological concerns. Here, the individual or the organization is motivated by concerns such as fairness, honesty, equality, trust, altruism and common interest and that these then drive business decisions (Granovetter, 1985).

Sociological buying by individuals is increasingly visible all around us and there would seem to be a correlation between increasing disposable income and the choice by some to pay more for something that goes a step further than satisfying the need. For example, choosing to pay more for a Fairtrade certified product over one that is not because we want to ensure the farmers get a better deal is sociological buying – consumers would have given little thought to how their cup of coffee got there 20 years ago. At a company level, sociological buying underpins the modern sustainable buying or CSR (Corporate Social Responsibility) movement. One company that I work with buys huge volumes of tea, but instead of buying the tea at a public tea auction in the usual way, where the price finds the lowest market level, the company deliberately bid higher than market price for the tea from specific plantations they are working with. This ensures that producers receive a premium price to enable them to invest and grow. We will return to this theme and examine sustainable buying in Chapter 10.

Beyond sociological buying we have a true gift, which is not really buying at all but rather giving something, motivated by friendship and love. Crucially here, the true gift holds no expectation that the gesture will be reciprocated. The dynamic of reciprocity is a component across the entire choice dimension to buying and one worth reflecting on for a moment. Away from gifts made out of true love and friendship, when something is given it tends to create a debt and obligation within the other which remains until the gift is reciprocated. The degree to which this happens depends upon the individual. Within the normal range of buying no debt is created because there is a reciprocal exchange of value. Sometimes this is immediate and sometimes delayed, eg until an invoice gets paid. Cutthroat buying creates a debt by taking, but one that is unlikely to get repaid. Sociological buying however, also creates a debt by giving and one where there is no expectation to be repaid. However such buying can instill in the seller a sense of loyalty and wanting to do the best possible to repay the additional support. In a similar vein, this same dynamic of giving something to create obligation is something that sellers frequently attempt to use with buyers to gain advantage. We will return to this in Chapter 10 when we consider how to manage personal ethics when buying.

So the third consideration for *how* we buy is choice, and increasingly this is an important consideration in determining our buying approach. It is therefore important to understand both the strength of our position and what choices we have available to us to determine the most appropriate buying approach, which may well vary according to either our or the supply base circumstances. We will explore specific tools to help do this in coming chapters.

Trust me, I'm here to help! Our relationship with the seller

Whenever we buy there is almost always some sort of relationship with the seller and often a social exchange that accompanies the transaction. This happens more than we might think. If I, as an individual, go to buy a car, or engage a contractor to do some building work, there will be some sort of discussion, interaction, exchange, agreement of specification and perhaps negotiation with the seller. In the service sector the relationship is obvious – a meal in a restaurant will involve social exchange with the waitress with a direct correlation between how friendly they make the experience and the tip they receive. Stopping to buy petrol might appear to be 'relationship free' but it will most likely involve some small talk with the person at the checkout, and an eBay purchase concludes with a bit of feedback about the how the seller has performed. Buying a can of Coca Cola from a vending machine doesn't involve any direct human interaction, yet the Coca Cola company wants us to have a relationship with their brand and puts lots of effort into doing so with the hope we will reselect their product in future. Relationships can be found in professional buying and are, in fact, essential in many instances. Significant areas of spend are serviced by sales people or key account managers who both sell and look after us: closing the deal, making sure we get what we want and working to keep us from wanting to go anywhere else. As we have seen already, complex, critical or strategic, high-value and high-risk buying demands even more of a relationship and one that enables collaboration and joint working. Signing up a new technology partner who will combine their know-how with our operations in pursuit of a new offering will only work with a close relationship and our people and their people working hand-in-hand to make it happen.

Understanding and managing the relationship dimension within buying is an important consideration. Sellers will seek to cultivate some sort of relationship with us; how this happens can range from instilling brand loyalty through to close personal relationships. The driver behind this is simple – good relationships build familiarity, confidence and trust. They can create a sense of obligation and need to reciprocate back to the seller through the apparent gift of friendship. All this ultimately helps the seller to sell to us and keep us interested for the future.

Good buying means determining the sort of relationship we want or need with the supplier and managing this on our terms rather than being seduced by gestures that appear to be cultivating friendship but are really cultivating sales. That said, if we remain in control, then we can cultivate relationships with the seller to support what we are trying to achieve. Because of the risk of relationship bias, buyers are typically trained and conditioned to keep suppliers at arm's length. For a junior buyer, unfamiliar with how suppliers operate, this is good advice and keeps things manageable. Yet there are scenarios where a relationship can really help us and improve our buying outcomes so we must unlearn the arm's length principle and get closer, but not too close. The point here is the fourth consideration around *how* we buy, which is that we must know and decide what sort of relationship is useful and appropriate and when to cultivate this and manage it on our terms. We will return to this also in Chapter 10.

Sign here! Making a contract

The final consideration for *how* we buy is the way we will contract with the supplier for the goods or services. When we buy we are almost always making a contract with the seller, which is legally binding. As consumers, this does not tend to be something that figures in our thinking when we pop into the 7/11 for some milk or tick the 'I agree to the terms and conditions' to complete checkout online for a new outfit. Indeed, for most everyday buying there appears to be no or little formality to the contract (eg it is established through what we say, our actions and custom and practice), or we find ourselves having little alternative but to have to sign or accept online the supplier's terms which not only formalize the contract between us, but also ensure we agree to some additional conditions that the seller may require. As consumers buying from a big brand company this is a one-way process and our choice here is to accept or walk away. Most people I know, myself included, blindly accept the supplier's terms because they are difficult to understand, we have no power to change them and we put our trust in the company we are buying from – believing and hoping that the goodness of their brand extends to ensuring customers are treated fairly. In addition, in many countries we also have statutory rights – laws and common law that protects consumers.

For other buying scenarios, typically when the buyer holds more power with the seller, or the value, risk and complexity of the purchase is much greater, then buyers and sellers may agree a formal contract for the exchange, using one of a multitude of contractual mechanisms and perhaps even one created specifically for the exchange by teams of lawyers with terms and conditions negotiated and agreed by each party. If we are to be good at buying, then a basic understanding of how contracts work and are established is important. We will return to this later, in Chapter 9.

Shaping how *we buy across the buying spectrum*

These five considerations that shape *how* we buy help us begin to determine the most suitable buying approach within the buying spectrum for what we are attempting to buy. These considerations also help determine the specific things we might need to do to support our buying approach, which typically change across the buying spectrum. How things typically change is given in Figure 1.4.

From here we will consider what is possible through effective buying, what stops us from doing this and we will begin to look at the power buying process and toolkit that will help us for all forms of buying, and that is the subject of the next few chapters.

Figure 1.4 The buying spectrum expanded

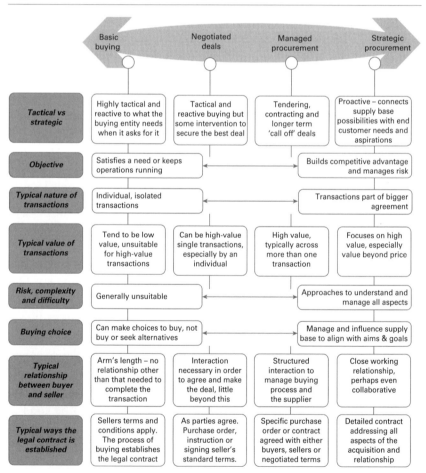

	Basic buying	Negotiated deals	Managed procurement	Strategic procurement
Tactical vs strategic	Highly tactical and reactive to what the buying entity needs when it asks for it	Tactical and reactive buying but some intervention to secure the best deal	Tendering, contracting and longer term 'call off' deals	Proactive – connects supply base possibilities with end customer needs and aspirations
Objective	Satisfies a need or keeps operations running			Builds competitive advantage and manages risk
Typical nature of transactions	Individual, isolated transactions			Transactions part of bigger agreement
Typical value of transactions	Tend to be low value, unsuitable for high-value transactions	Can be high-value single transactions, especially by an individual	High value, typically across more than one transaction	Focuses on high value, especially value beyond price
Risk, complexity and difficulty	Generally unsuitable			Approaches to understand and manage all aspects
Buying choice	Can make choices to buy, not buy or seek alternatives			Manage and influence supply base to align with aims & goals
Typical relationship between buyer and seller	Arm's length – no relationship other than that needed to complete the transaction	Interaction necessary in order to agree and make the deal, little beyond this	Structured interaction to manage buying process and the supplier	Close working relationship, perhaps even collaborative
Typical ways the legal contract is established	Sellers terms and conditions apply. The process of buying establishes the legal contract	As parties agree. Purchase order, instruction or signing seller's standard terms.	Specific purchase order or contract agreed with either buyers, sellers or negotiated terms	Detailed contract addressing all aspects of the acquisition and relationship

Summary

The key learning points from this chapter:

1 We are all buyers, whether personally or professionally!

2 Good buying is really not that difficult with the right knowledge and by following some simple steps.

3 Buying is not one single thing but rather a broad spectrum of different buying approaches ranging from simple buying to strategic procurement.

4 There are five considerations that shape how we buy effectively and the most suitable appropriate to use. These are:

- the value of what we are buying;
- the risk and complexity or what we are buying along with the difficulty we might encounter in buying it;
- what choice we have, or don't have, around how we buy;
- the nature of the relationship we need or want with the seller, and;
- how we will contract for the goods or services.

The size of the prize

02

> This chapter considers why a more effective buying approach is worthwhile and the nature and scale of different benefits it can bring.
>
> **Pathway question addressed in this chapter**
>
> **3** What benefits are possible with effective buying?

Why do anything differently if things seem to work OK when we buy? After all, people and organizations seem to buy just fine without any sort of special intervention. Goods turn up, services get delivered, the organization continues to function, so do we really need to change? For basic buying scenarios, the answer might be no, but beyond this a wealth of worthwhile benefits are available to us just by making small changes in our approach to buying. To answer *why* we should consider a new approach we first must appreciate the size of the prize.

Significant and even game-changing benefits are possible as a direct result of good buying practice. It is possible to dramatically increase the profit of the organization or create greater competitive advantage and brand value through a modern, more strategic approach to how the organization buys. At a personal level, good buying can help us secure more of what we want on our terms. The degree to which these benefits are possible depends of course on our situation, whether such benefits matter to us and if so how we organize ourselves to secure them.

Global organizations that recognize the contribution good buying can bring have long since established procurement teams, comprising the best talented practitioners and positioned as a strategic contributor to business success. When best practice procurement approaches are embedded, these organizations are achieving advantage by having a lower cost base than competitors (typically between 10 per cent and 20 per cent), by accessing and incorporating new ideas, technologies and processes from its suppliers into its products or services and by being faster to market and less exposed to events or circumstances that could harm brand, reputation or ability to its service customers.

The five benefits of effective buying

Once understood, the size of the prize is difficult to ignore. It is not enough to just buy a little bit better, negotiate a bit harder, or do better deals; for an organization to realize this it must drive in and embed an effective company-wide, aligned, modern best practice procurement approach – we will return to what this means in Chapter 10. At a personal level, and for small businesses, the size of the prize is equally worthwhile, with great benefit possible through an effective approach to buying, yet, as you might expect, on a smaller scale and limited in part by the degree of leverage we might hold in any given buying scenario – we will explore how to understand this later.

There are five key benefits that effective buying can deliver, these are as follows and are expanded in Table 2.1 and the next two sections;

1 Reduced price or total cost;

2 Securing greater value from the supplier or the supply base;

3 Reduced risk;

4 Innovation;

5 Improved internal effectiveness.

Table 2.1 The different types of benefit possible with effective buying

The benefits possible with effective buying		
Benefit theme	**What this includes**	**Types of benefit possible**
Reduced price or total cost	Benefits around lower acquisition price or the total cost of ownership (cost to acquire, use and dispose of) for goods or service	• Reduced acquisition price • Lower total cost of ownership • Rebate, kick-back or signing bonus • Reduced penalty payments • Avoiding price increases • Savings through exchange rate fluctuations

(continued)

Table 2.1 *(Continued)*

The benefits possible with effective buying		
Benefit theme	**What this includes**	**Types of benefit possible**
Securing greater value from the supplier or supply base	Additional benefits beyond or aside from lower price or total cost that can bring us value or be worthwhile to us	• Securing additional products, services, features or functionality at no additional charge • Improved efficiency (eg in process improvement) • Reduction in inventory • Sharing resources • Simplification of ordering process and transactions • Reduced time to supply • Value from working together with a supplier to achieve a common goal
Innovation	Benefit we can realize as a result of accessing innovation from the supply base or by working together with a supplier to achieve a new, mutually beneficial goal	• Access or exclusive access to supplier ideas, technology and process (to create new products or allow new markets to be reached) • Access to new markets • Supplier driven enhancements or improvements to current products • Synergy by working together with suppliers • Benefits from association with a supplier's brand • Business growth linked to supplier initiatives • Supplier supported new product development • Competitive advantage or differentiation from supplier initiatives
Reduced risk	Reducing, removing or being ready for risk that could hurt us, cost us or damage our brand and reputation	• Supply failure or delays • Brand or reputation damage • Loss of competitive advantage • Price or cost hikes or higher outturn costs • Poor quality, quality failures or latent defects

(continued)

Table 2.1 *(Continued)*

The benefits possible with effective buying		
Benefit theme	**What this includes**	**Types of benefit possible**
Improved effectiveness	The benefits to us and our entire organization that a more effective approach to buying brings	• Better meeting customer needs, want and aspirations (by aligning buying and supply base possibilities to support this) • Improved or protected cash flow • Common language and ways of working around buying

Securing lower price and total cost

Before we go any further, we must first distinguish between price and total cost. Price is what we pay for the goods or service. Total cost is both the price and all the other costs we have to pay over the life to acquire, use and finally dispose of the goods or service. This is often referred to as *total cost of ownership*. For example, if we buy a car, we can consider not only the price but factors such as servicing costs, fuel consumption, likely reliability and so on. Considering total cost as well as price alone can help inform our buying decision.

Buying for less than you might otherwise pay tends to be the most sought after benefit for individuals and businesses; after all, if we can buy for less we have more to spend on other things! Obvious stuff, but let's stop for a moment to consider what this means to a business. Figure 2.1 shows a simple view of where the money generated from sales or income goes; there is the cost of the people who work in the business, the overheads (facilities, buildings, equipment, etc) as well the goods or services the company needs to buy in order to operate. In a commercial business the hope is that a proportion of the income or sales turnover is retained as profit, and even in a not-for-profit organization this slice is usually still pursued, but instead of profit given to shareholders it becomes the surplus for reinvestment. The size of the slice for bought-in goods and services varies according to what the business does. Figure 2.1 puts this at around 45 per cent of sales turnover, which is typical for a manufacturing business. However in an automotive business this slice would be 70–80 per cent, whereas in a firm of consultants or lawyers where the main business is about people providing expertise the proportion of spend against sales turnover drops to around 15–25 per cent.

Figure 2.1   Where the money from sales goes

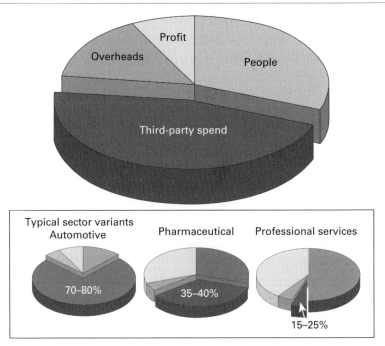

Maximizing profit (or surplus) is more often than not a primary objective for organizations and one that is actively pursued. Considering our pie in Figure 2.1, and taking a simplistic view, we can achieve this by first increasing the 'size of the pie' ie by increasing sales (Figure 2.2) or, second, by reducing the size of other segments, ie reduce costs.

Increasing sales should increase profit and this is of course the remit of sales and marketing functions the world over. However, in order to increase profit by increasing sales we need to buy more, add more overheads and increase the number of people, so it takes a lot of effort and a lot more sales just to yield a small incremental improvement in profit. Alternatively, reducing costs can be much more efficient, although limited by the overall size of sales or income and the degree of opportunity for cost reduction that might exist. With the pie staying the same size, we can increase the size of the profit (or surplus) price by reducing the size of any other slice. Most organizations have given much attention to cost reduction in recent years. 'People' has probably received the most attention, with restructuring, head-count reductions or where there has been wholesale outsourcing of large areas of the business to low-cost labour geographies. Overheads too have been tackled by a vast range of efficiency-improvement initiatives – modern

Figure 2.2   Ways to improve profit (or surplus)

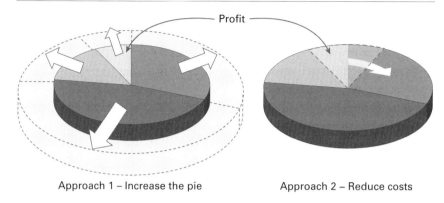

Approach 1 – Increase the pie   Approach 2 – Reduce costs

organizations are a lean affair with increased use of IT, increased automation, more open-plan working environments, home working, hot-desking, and making production or service as efficient as it can be.

Yet, if we look back over the last 20–30 years what is spent on bought-in goods and services has, in relative terms, received the least attention. There are many reasons for this but primarily this has been due to the fact that organizations have been slow to develop good buying capability or to move away from tactical buying approaches to something more strategic. It is also because the suppliers have done a remarkably good job at convincing us we've been getting the best deal possible: I'll return to this theme in the next chapter. However, where the largest expenditure is that spent upon bought-in goods and services then this presents the biggest opportunity to increase our profit (or surplus). All we need to do is to figure out what to do to realize this.

Whilst our eagerness to buy for less will undoubtedly drive much of what we do, there has, in recent times, been a shift away from price as the primary consideration for some buying scenarios, especially in the world of professional procurement. As the world has become more volatile and more unpredictable, and the supply base has become more global, the primary consideration for many large global businesses has in fact become more directed towards securing assurance of supply and accessing new innovation from suppliers who can help bring competitive advantage. At an individual level where disposable incomes have increased, the price we pay becomes less important and other factors come to the fore. So price, and lowest cost, may not necessarily be our primary concern but, as ever, it all depends upon circumstance and what objectives we are seeking to satisfy.

What about the non-financial benefits?

Remember that buying is the exchange of value, so if we are focusing on value, and not price or cost alone, we can widen our perspective and open up new possibilities to maximize the value we can secure when we buy. Value is therefore all of the benefits we might be able to realize when we buy. Buyers pursuing lower price can sometimes be blind to the additional value benefits, some of which may even be more advantageous for us than chasing a lower price or total cost, especially if there is little we can do to influence price. For example, when organizations buy mobile/cell phone provision for the workforce, a large company might be able to negotiate a good set of rates. However the giant providers in this space will only go so far and will hold firm on price points, meaning even the biggest of companies only have so much buying power – CEOs of cell phone companies don't lose sleep if we take our business elsewhere. Here, greater benefit can often be achieved through the pursuit of additional value such as handset upgrades or enhanced network packages and so on.

Furthermore, if we can improve our efficiency, reduce the need to hold inventory or simplify how we order and acquire the goods then we have added value. Similarly, if we can secure the goods or services faster so we can respond to our customers faster, we have added value. For the handful of suppliers that are really important to us, if we can find ways to work together with these suppliers we can create new or enhanced products, features or services that stimulate new or increased demand from our customers and become mutually beneficial to both us and our supplier, creating joint value.

Joint working with key suppliers can also unlock new innovation that could ultimately help improve our business and brand proposition. A company may be able to discover 'the next great thing' from within, but the supply base is home to a much greater wealth of potential – suppliers working on beating their competition and hungry to grow their businesses. Innovation opportunities frequently get missed by companies who wait for innovation to be offered, assuming the supplier will propose something when they are ready, or worse, having a supplier offer a new thing but not being equipped or able to do anything with it. Companies that are unreceptive, unprepared for, or refuse to reward supply base innovation risk it going to competitors! After all, if a supplier has something great they want to find a route to market and generate revenue, so they will want to work with the customer best placed to make this happen. The leading companies don't wait for the supplier to come up with something, but rather figure out who might hold the process, capability, potential and know-how to create a certain, considered and defined piece of innovation. When Steve Jobs sought to invent the iPod, he didn't wait until a supplier popped in with just the thing he needed: instead Apple worked with the suppliers who held the greatest potential and asked: 'How might we do this?' The rest is history. Good buying can therefore unlock innovation from the supply base and in doing so unlock great value for both us and the supplier we chose to work with to make this happen.

The value of reduced risk can also be overlooked. It is easy to assume that everything will always go well, yet failing to consider the risk associated with what and how we buy can have dire consequences. If we order something online and it turns up damaged or late, then this is probably a minor inconvenience. Yet if we are buying a critical component for a factory and it fails to show up causing the entire production line to grind to a halt while teams of workers down tools and await the arrival of the component, then the impact and cost to the organization is severe. Quality problems caused by what we source impact our final product or service, or increase the cost of rework and rectification, perhaps damaging our reputation if the customer gets a bad experience. Our ability to consider supply-side risk and act to prevent or be prepared adds value to our organization by prevention of problems. In some cases there is much more at stake than an inconvenience or even a production line stoppage. There are many notable examples of giant brands who have been publically exposed for poor practice such as child labour, poor working conditions or environmental damage. A single newspaper article by a hungry investigative journalist can cause deep and long-lasting brand damage or can even bring a giant corporate to its knees, especially if such practice is at odds with publically stated brand values. Good buying also adds value to the organization by working to ensure what we buy, and from whom and where and how we buy it are aligned with the values of the organization and don't hold the potential to damage the firm's reputation. This is no easy task and one that the biggest firms on the planet struggle to do well. We will return to this in Chapter 10.

Finally, good buying can bring great internal value to the organization. Firms tend to have a buying or procurement function of one type or another – tactical procurement functions buy things, strategic procurement functions connect supply base possibilities with corporate strategy and customer needs. Yet in each case, buying is one of those things that is in fact more of an organization-wide concern. R&D, marketing, operations and other functions typically have some sort of interface and relationship with suppliers – and suppliers will need no encouragement to cement their position by building relationships far and wide in a business. Operational staff might liaise with suppliers about day-to-day matters, R&D or marketing might want the supplier to help with new product development, and all this might happen with or without the buying or procurement function being involved. It is not uncommon for a technical team to have worked with a supplier and taken decisions around specifying a component without considering how the firm should actually buy the part, diluting any leverage or opportunity for commercial advantage with the supplier in the process. This happens because functions outside of buying or procurement rarely receive any sort of training or instruction on how to buy well. Effective buying also adds value through internal communication, cross-functional engagement and working and alignment of needs, wants and expectations. A standard buying process or approach brings common language and ways of working and this in turn accelerates that retained knowledge and capability of the firm to buy well and avoids common mistakes or inadvertently giving the supplier the advantage.

The prize of many forms of value

If we are to realize the full value that effective buying can yield, then we need to be open to all the forms of value that we might need or indeed might be possible. Historically companies have measured the performance of buying in purely financial terms, with measures such as overall cost, savings achieved, inventory costs, shipping and delivery costs being those typically employed. Judging buying effectiveness through financial measures alone, or indeed rewarding buyers based upon savings performance, can be self-defeating, drive a lowest cost mentality and blindness to the full spectrum of possible benefits. Modern progressive organizations recognize and measure the effectiveness of its buying function by both financial and non-financial measures – actively demonstrating and providing commentary on how the buying function is contributing to the overall success of the organization through buying initiatives.

Summary

The key learning points from this chapter:

1 Effective buying can bring significant benefits including:

- reduced price or total cost;
- securing greater value from the supplier or the supply base;
- reduced risk;
- innovation; and
- improved internal effectiveness.

What stops us being good at this?

This chapter explores the various factors that stand in our way or stop us being good at buying, and sets the scene for what we need to do in order to buy effectively.

Pathway question addressed in this chapter

4 What stops us being good at buying?

It is clear that great benefits are possible if we can buy well! Yet organizations, and we as individuals, frequently fail to realize these to the full degree possible for any given buying scenario, so what is standing in our way here? The answer, and why suppliers gain advantage over the buyer, is two-fold and given in Figure 3.1. First, on the buyer side, inadequate homework, the skills gap and how organizations continue to view buying as a tactical, reactive function are all factors that work against us. However, these are things that we can change. Secondly, suppliers will work to seize advantage through the power of relationships, through conditioning and by making their offering as proprietary as possible, and these are things that we can counter. I will explore each of these factors in turn throughout this chapter as this sets the scene for a buying approach that gets past these things.

Not doing the homework

It is easy to assume that we know what we need and the best way to get it, especially if we have lots of experience around what we are buying. Maybe we do, but this single assumption can often close off opportunities.

Figure 3.1 How suppliers gain advantage

How suppliers gain advantage

BUYER SITUATION

SUPPLIER-DRIVEN

The factors that prevent the buyer from securing the best deal or realizing the range and extent of benefits possible through effective buying

These are things we can counter

Relationships
- Personal relationships with buyer
- Divide and conquer across the buyer's organization
- Create obligation

Conditioning
- Promoting 'You've got the best deal here'
- Creating 'immovable' pricing policies – 'The most I can do...'
- Preparing us and softening the impact for future disadvantage

Proprietary
- Branding
- Differentiation
- Added value
- Bundling (to make the complete offer unique)

These are things we can change

Poor homework
- Failing to asses or understand our position
- Poor market knowledge
- Inadequate planning for negotiations or supplier engagements

Skills gap
- Typically and historically buyers have had little access to training and tools they need
- Sales teams well trained and resourced (on average 10x more training buyers)

Structure
- Tactical, reactive buying
- Multiple, uncontrolled and poorly aligned interfaces with suppliers
- Lack of cross-functional engagement for buying

© Jonathan O'Brien

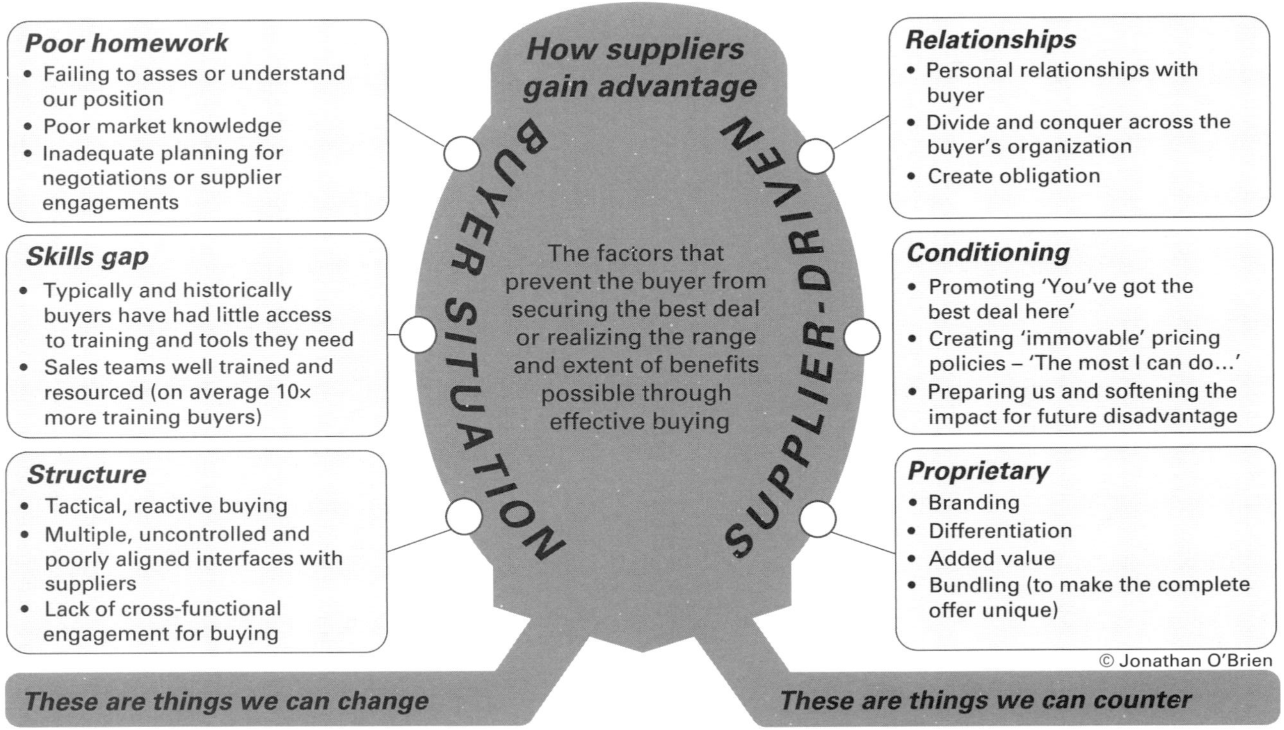

Furthermore, if we are buying something new, high value or complex, then we are unlikely to do this well with only a bit casual research. Possibly the single most important thing we can do to buy effectively is to do our homework beforehand. Good homework opens up potential opportunities to buy better and secure greater results, as well as putting us in control of the buying process. Sometimes we need a simple bit of research, sometimes a fuller 'deep-dive' fact find depending upon the scenario, but in any case we are seeking to establish what we need and want, who might be able to supply it, what is happening in the marketplace, what strength of position we might have and ultimately what we might do differently to buy better.

The thing about homework, and the reason why it is easy to assume we don't need to do it because we have all the knowledge we need, is 'you don't know what you don't know'. It is only through spending good time gathering information around internal needs, suppliers and the market that we begin to discover our true position and what might be possible. Thankfully we can easily fix this disadvantage by simply doing the homework: we will look at tools that help in coming chapters.

A very capable opponent

Surely buying is easy, so why do we need any special skills? It is true that tactical buying is easy and something we all do, and of course our suppliers will work hard to make it easy for us to buy. However, and as we move up the buying spectrum, effective buying requires a more sophisticated approach, but with it come much better outcomes. Historically, companies all over the world have been slow to recognize this and remained content with buying functions that were transactional and reactive. Happily, this is changing and the world of modern strategic procurement can boast many best practice examples delivered by highly talented procurement practitioners that bring great benefit to the company. Despite this, there remains a distinct imbalance in terms of buyer's skills and resources when compared with the supplier's sales and marketing teams.

It is the supplier's job to get the best deal! Obvious of course, but stop for a minute to consider how those in selling roles within our suppliers compare to buyers. Suppliers need to win and retain business and their survival and future growth depend upon being able to do this successfully. Having a high-performing sales team is top priority for most companies and will direct huge resource at making this happen. Those in sales roles receive, on average, 10 times more training than the buyers they interface with. They will typically receive extensive sales and product training, and perhaps even training in softer skills that help get the deal, such as psychology training, negotiation, NLP (neuro-linguistic programming), training in body language and anything else that might help build a relationship, better connect with the buyer and win trust. Such skills would also be of great benefit the buyer, yet it is rare for buyers to receive such training.

It is not only the skills gap that can work against us but availability of time and resources. Professional buyers are busy people and a meeting or negotiation with a supplier might be just one thing within a busy day. Yet, for a significant sales opportunity, it is not uncommon for the seller's sales team to have many people spending many hours preparing for a single meeting. Sales teams will plan how they are going to sell to the buyer, and may even put effort into researching the buyer and figuring out the best way to build a relationship. Sales teams usually have some sort of CRM (customer relationship management) system to track and coordinate every interaction they have with you. It is no coincidence that the sales person remembers your kid's names or the vacation you went on last year. All this is to gain an advantage, build a relationship and clinch the sale. If as buyer we fail to appreciate how the game works then we can be at a disadvantage. Thankfully we can fix this disadvantage by our capability in the face of a strong opponent – reading this book is the first step towards this.

We're simply not organized for great buying

So why have companies all over the world been slow to recognize the benefits of effective buying? The answer is simply that in many companies these benefits have remained hidden, with executive teams failing to see the opportunity. Indeed, and for many years, there was a commonly held view that the supply base presented little opportunity – if there was, 'someone would have spotted it'. Worse, as we have seen, if the organization has only ever considered buying as a tactical, reactive function, then that is all it will ever be, perhaps boasting extensive experience at running tender or bid exercises and agreeing new contracts with suppliers yet, despite this, operating tactically.

As we saw in Chapter 1, the shift away from tactical buying towards a more strategic procurement approach has been firmly on the agenda for global companies within recent years or at least within those who have recognized the potential. Achieving this has demanded much more than new ways of working: a fundamental rethink of the supplier intervention the organization needs and how the entire organization engages with its supply base. It has also required organizations to dramatically uplift their capability and drive in new best practice ways of working around procurement. Those companies who have made the leap to great buying have had to restructure themselves to do so and make buying a business-wide concern. If we are buying in a firm that has not made this leap, our ability to buy effectively is hampered by the way the organization views purchasing. Not only will our internal misalignment be self-defeating, but suppliers will be quick to take advantage by establishing relationships and influencing all those across the entire business who might hold some sway in the buying decision.

Thankfully, the disadvantage of structure can of course be fixed, starting with recognition that there is a better way and the resolve to go after it. This shift rarely happens organically, but requires the executive team to drive in such a change. In many cases the executive team first need to have their eyes opened to the possibilities as, in my experience, it is common for those running the firm to be blind to the hidden potential and believe their buying function is adequate or is not a priority for business investment.

Your supplier wants you! The advantage through relationships

Suppliers like to have relationships with buyers and in Chapter 1 we began to explore how the relationship we might want with the supplier shapes *how* we buy. This is simply because if we do not understand the dynamics or if we are not in control of the relationship then we can find ourselves at a disadvantage.

As we have already seen, when we buy there is almost always some sort of relationship and social exchange with the seller. By sellers establishing and building a relationship with the buyer, the supplier increases the likelihood of making the sale or retaining a client. Relationships take many forms, ranging from strong personal social interaction between key individuals on both sides where a friendly engagement accompanies all business, down to brand building where marketing teams work hard to have some sort of 'relationship' with all its customers through the brand. We typically end up having some sort of relationship with suppliers when we buy, either as individuals or professionally. Crucially however, and in both cases, these relationships exist between individuals (ie companies don't have relationships with companies but the individuals within those companies have relationships with each other). Relationships can disadvantage the buyer in three ways if we are not in control of things.

The power of personal relationships

Relationships can be hugely powerful and their potential should never be underestimated. Having the confidence that when we buy we are making the best choice with the most suited supplier who will deliver on what we agreed, all whilst securing the right value for money, is difficult enough, especially if we really don't know enough about what we are trying to do! If we have some sort of relationship with the seller, where we have come to have a degree of trust and familiarity with the seller, perhaps based upon past experience or how we perceive the brand proposition, then it makes a difficult choice a lot easier. It is therefore not just the supplier who seeks a relationship with buyer, but buyers often want a relationship with the seller also. It can be like swimming in deep water and finding someone you can cling to. Where the supplier can have a personal interface with the buyer, and where it matters to them, it is their job to build the relationship and even become an apparent friend – the reason why sales people are recruited for their 'instant like' qualities and ability to build rapport. That said, depending upon the individuals involved, real, genuine and strong relationships and even friendships with trust at the core can emerge in buyer/seller relationships. This is most often seen with entrepreneurs or those running small businesses where long-term supplier relationships emerge and become key enablers of success. Large companies, and indeed modern good junior buying practice, work to prevent such relationships at anything less than the most senior individuals by introducing processes or removing the opportunity for any sort of relationship, eg through the use of e-bidding and eAuction type tools. Why? Well despite the examples of positive, balanced, mutually beneficial buyer/supplier relationships, a skilled and highly likable seller may also be able to cultivate the illusion of a relationship of trust, support and friendship to secure a sale and repeat business. Maybe you've experienced a supplier saying something like, 'In the spirit of our working relationship',or, 'We're partners here, right?' or similar phrases designed make us believe we are part of a relationship. Preventing an imbalanced situation where the supplier gains advantage through a relationship requires us to be skilled at judging what is happening and indeed the need for a relationship.

Divide and conquer

How the buyer sees the supplier is key here and this will be one of five mindsets given in Figure 3.2. These mindsets arise based upon role, history, personal agendas, degree of understanding of buying and how the individual level views their role. Individuals may be certain their mindset is right, yet it may in fact be working against the organization's overall procurement effectiveness. Different mindsets can cause conflict between those in procurement and the rest of the business. Whilst procurement might be maintaining arm's-length relationships, those in technical or operational functions may well view the supplier as 'my friend' or 'can really help me,' or even 'I really need them' – eager to pull on any help and support a supplier might offer. Suppliers selling to a large company will be quick to exploit and reinforce these mindsets and will work to establish multiple relationships across the business to do so. A supplier supporting technical teams or those working on research and development might be able to get their product or service specified and incorporated in the design specification so that nothing else can be bought. If a healthcare supplies company can establish a preference amongst clinicians and physicians for their brand of surgical glove, then these individuals will insist on it – it is no accident that training hospitals get given lots of free kit! By the time the procurement team gets involved with the supplier the deal may not have been done, but the product or service may have already been decided with no scope to consider alternatives, and therefore no leverage. This divide and conquer approach by suppliers is very common. At the heart of it is a series of relationships, deliberately cultivated by the supplier in a coordinated way to achieve an overall single objective. It works because, and can be hard to counter so long as, functions are blind to the detrimental impact associated with a series of individual, non-aligned interfaces with a supplier.

Creating obligation

Another way suppliers gain advantage in relationships is by creating obligation. 'There's no such thing as a free lunch' is a phrase that first seems to have appeared during the 1930s, referring to the practice in American bars of offering an apparent free lunch in order to entice customers in to drink (Safire, 1993). It communicates the idea that it is impossible to get something for nothing. It is a concept that is core to economics (Gwartney et al, 2005) and even became the title of the economist

Milton Friedman's 1975 book. A supplier trying to win a sizeable sale might like to provide some sort of gift designed to help build the relationship. This may be as simple as buying us lunch, but could also extend to invitations to corporate golf days or networking events, or 'thank you for your business' gifts at the end of the year. These days, most medium to large companies in the US, EU and UK have strict policies on acceptance or non-acceptance of gifts. In other parts of the world gifts can be a fundamental part of how business is done. Anything that a supplier provides that is something more than we have contracted for can be a gift. Gifts help suppliers build relationships and can disadvantage the buyer because of the simple human fact that when someone gives us something then we become obliged to that individual and it may instill a feeling of needing to reciprocate. In his classic work *The Gift*, Marcel Mauss (1925) suggested that when a gift is given it is never free but rather gives rise to reciprocity. Mauss proposed that the giver does not just give an object or something of value but also gives part of himself, for the object is indissolubly tied to the giver. There is a bond between giver and gift that then creates a social bond within the process of exchange and thus creates an obligation to reciprocate on the part of the recipient. In short, if a supplier can create obligation within the buyer, the buyer may be more disposed to favour the supplier and award them the business. We will return to this in Chapter 10.

Relationships where the supplier has the upper hand can disadvantage the buyer, but sometimes a relationship with the supplier is a good thing, is important and perhaps even essential, but here they must be more balanced. For example, if we strike a partnership with a technology provider because we can see great potential by combining their innovation into what we do, then we will need to work together with them to make this happen. This won't be an arm's-length relationship, but one of partnership, where key staff on each side work together and celebrate achievements. A small building company might have relationships with certain trusted contractors who have proved to be reliable and deliver a high standard of workmanship. We may want to get to know and build a relationship with the only gardener in the area who can pick or choose so he or she may feel more inclined to ensure we received good attention.

The relevance or importance of relationships with suppliers also changes with culture. In Western culture we don't need a relationship with a supplier, yet we may choose to have one, but in some Eastern and Middle Eastern cultures business will not be done unless there is a relationship, and one where individuals have come to trust each other.

Figure 3.2   The five mindsets of supplier engagement

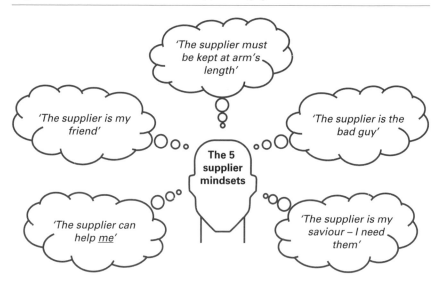

Relationship bias can be countered simply by working to decide where we do and do not need a relationship and cultivate it either on our terms or in a way that works for us. This is not something we can do alone, but together with the rest of the organization. In addition, no matter how close a supplier relationship might be for good reason, there must always be a competitive tension, perhaps with the means to exit if things go sour.

Don't believe the hype!

The final way in which the buyer ends up disadvantaged is simply by coming to believe and accept that the deal in front of them is the best possible and that all the benefits have already been secured. This is not confined to individual perceptions: entire companies from the top down can get lulled into believing their buying is as effective as it could be. I have sat in front of one sceptical CEO who couldn't see the need to invest in developing her buying function and said: 'If we could get more benefit by buying better we would have done it years ago.' So why don't people notice if our suppliers have been outwitting us?

One of the reasons is due to buyer conditioning – where the seller gets the buyer to believe they have the best possible deal. Suppliers do this all the time, it is part of the selling and negotiation process and something suppliers tend to be very good at. It is also something an unwitting or inexperienced buyer, or those outside of the procurement function, may be blind to.

If we buy something, and walk away feeling like we got a great deal, but later find out we paid too much and we could have sourced the same thing much cheaper, then we are suddenly left with a bitter aftertaste over our purchase. When this happens it can leave us feeling a bit stupid and can create bad feeling towards the seller we had previously felt good about. It can make us feel like we've been duped in some way, and perhaps might make us not want to go back to that seller again. Suppliers can't afford to let us feel like this as it fast becomes very bad for business, so it's the supplier's job to make you feel like you got the best deal. At the heart of this is not the deal we do, but how we feel about it, and the entire sales process is geared to creating the right feeling in the buyer. Experienced sellers and negotiators work hard to leave us believing that we are getting a great deal and one that can't really be bettered. The seller will maintain a position to ensure we have to work for any negotiated saving, thus increasing how we value the win, and they may be quick to condition us around how far they are going and how difficult this is for them. In a recent negotiation with an experienced tradesman to do some work on my house, when asked if he could improve his price, he made an elaborate show of how difficult this would be, how exceptional my request was, how he would need to be careful he wasn't cutting his own throat to get the work and then, once he was done with the frowns and sharp intakes of breath, offered 10 per cent, followed by another 5 per cent. An impressive and well-polished routine.

Suppliers will work to manage how we feel about the deal so that we believe we have the best possible. Sometimes this may be the case, however often we are blind to our true position. Yet with good homework and research we may be able to be better informed, which means we can work past any conditioning the supplier might put our way.

There are other ways that suppliers condition. One approach adopted by powerful brands the world over is to create apparent immovable prices driven by strict pricing policies. It is a common tactic when negotiating for a supplier to say something like, 'the most I am authorized to give is...' or 'we have a strict pricing policy set by head office' and so on. Sometimes we are powerless to get beyond this, sometimes this is a tactic designed to discourage us and can be countered. Another way is to prepare us for a possible change to our situation such as a future price rise. If a supplier regularly supplies something to us, and one day informs us that the price has increased then there is a good chance we might question this and even try to reject it. Instead suppliers tend to use conditioning to soften the impact in advance and might say something like: 'We are facing cost increases for our import costs and currently we are doing our best to prevent having to pass this on to you.' This is more subtle and something designed to prepare the buyer for a cost increase and reduce the possibility of a future cost increase being challenged. These are usually clever tactics used by suppliers as part of a planned approach to apply a cost increase, which may or may not have any sound basis. Of course, we can counter this by challenge the reason and seeking facts and data about the exact cost impact. We can also counter-condition the supplier regarding our expectations.

Buy me! The buyer's problem with proprietary

When a supplier creates a position where we are compelled to buy their product or service over a competitor's then they have created the ultimate advantage over us and perhaps the marketplace. When the supplier has this advantage it removes or dilutes our ability to negotiate on price or secure additional value. The supplier can effectively say 'take it or leave it'. This might sound like a rare situation, yet it is in fact an everyday and common place buying scenario that we find ourselves it, we just might not quite appreciate what is happening.

Suppliers will, if they can, work to make what they supply proprietary in some way, and companies spend billions of dollars each year pursuing this. Proprietary can take many forms but is fundamentally about creating a situation where we can only buy what we want or need from them. Suppliers do this in one of four ways:

1 **Branding** – it is hard to go anywhere without seeing some sort of supplier's brand or advertisement. In the UK, companies spend around £20bn on advertising: the figure in the US is about seven times this. Brands create a shortcut for us, often using names, images, symbols, colours and so on to anchor us back, all designed to get us to a position where we go and chose brand B over brand A. If we set out to buy something generic that many can supply we have choice, options and

potential to take advantage of competition between suppliers to secure the best deal. If we set out to buy a single brand we have limited the marketplace to one, and removed any leverage we might have otherwise had.

2 **Differentiation** – often accompanies a brand to become a unique selling point, but not always. Differentiation is where a product has some sort of uniqueness over competitors that we might want so much we are prepared to choose a product or service that has it. For example, if a garden product used to kill weeds on a driveway is positioned as having a higher concentration of the active ingredient than other products, and therefore likely to perform more effectively, this differentiation might be enough to compel us to select this product on this basis.

3 **Added value** – similar to differentiation, but not necessarily unique. Here the supplier seeks to enhance what they supply by providing additional things of value within the purchase that makes the overall package more attractive. If the garage that services our car provides the added value option to collect and drop back our car then that might make using them more compelling than others. If we come to rely on this added value then we become locked in to that supplier.

4 **Bundling** – this is when the supplier bundles several forms of additional services or added value in with the core thing we are buying. If the bundle becomes a unique mix of offerings that we come to need or rely upon in that bundled form then the supplier has locked us in by virtue of the bundle we are buying.

We can, in many cases, counter the impact of buying proprietary simply be moving away from proprietary. There are some situations where we have no choice and must buy proprietary, yet here we can still improve our position by developing the right relationship with the supplier and seeking as much added value as possible. In many cases, when we challenge 'why we buy it like that' we find that we don't in fact need to be buying proprietary or we have somehow ended up doing this. It is here where the game-changing benefits can be found and in Chapter 6 we will explore how we check if we are setting out to buy proprietary, and options to break out of this using the *Power Check* tool.

Summary

The key learning points from this chapter:

1 There are a number of factors that stand in our way to realizing the benefits of effective buying and so can disadvantage the buyer. These include:

- factors concerned with the buyer's situation:

    a failing to do adequate homework;

    b the skills gap between buyer and seller's sales person;

    c organizational structure – positioning buying only as tactical and reactive; and

- factors that are supplier driven:

    a bias from relationships suppliers build with the buyer;

    b conditioning the buyer that we have the best outcome possible; and

    c making the area of supply too proprietary.

The 5D Power Buying Process

04

This chapter responds to the challenges buyers face and reveals the power buying process – a structured approach for effective buying that defines the journey for the rest of this book.

Pathway questions addressed in this chapter

5 What are the steps to effective buying?

Introducing the 5D Power Buying Process

Now we come to the 5D Power Buying Process (Figure 4.1), a simple but highly effective toolkit that will help anyone buy anything much more effectively. As we have seen, there are great benefits available through good buying and there are also a number of ways we as buyers can find ourselves disadvantaged. If applied well, the 5D Power Buying Process will enable you to secure many of these benefits and will help you overcome the things that hold you back.

The 5D Power Buying Process is a five-step model with three simple tools at each step. The approach is based upon best practice business improvement and is equally suitable for driving effective buying for simple everyday one-off buying or more complex, high value, supply arrangements. It features the essential and well-proven components from the world of strategic procurement where key tools from category management and supplier relationship management have been incorporated in a more simplified, but highly effective, form.

Buying effectively is simply a case of working through the 5D Power Buying Process. Each tool comprises either an action or means to better understand our situation. By working through the 15 tools in sequence, the 5D Power Buying Process can help secure the best possible outcomes. At first, using the process may seem overwhelming, especially for simple buying scenarios. However, with practice and familiarity the approach becomes second nature. Furthermore, the degree or thoroughness with which each tool should be used or applies depends upon the buying scenario.

Throughout the next five chapters we will move through a detailed explanation of each of the 15 tools. Templates are provided at the end of the book in the appendix. You can find detail of how you may use these templates at start of the appendix.

How each tool is used and when it is needed is explained at the start of each tool section, with each section then going on to provide detailed explanation and instruction for this step should it be needed. For example, tool number 11 is *Negotiation*, which could be a major undertaking in its own right requiring good planning, or our buying situation may mean that there can be no negotiation. It all depends upon our situation and the early tools in the process help inform us as to how to proceed. As you become proficient at applying the 5D power buying process you will come to know what to use, what to leave out and when.

The five steps

The five steps in the 5D power buying process are: *Define, Discover, Determine, Deal* and *Deliver*. Our first step is to *define* what we are setting out to buy and our specific needs and wants. If others are involved, affected or impacted then it is here that we engage with them. Step 2 – *Discover* – is concerned with understanding our position and specifically what, if any, power or potential to leverage new benefit we might have and therefore what things we would need to do in order to realize it. As we move into step 3 – *Determine* – we complete our fact finding and therefore we have a good understanding of the market and potential supply base. From here we can determine how we are going to buy and what sort of arrangements we might need to put in place. Step 4 – *Deal* – is about which suppliers we are going to use or how we are subsequently going to select them (if we don't already know). We also conduct any negotiation we may want or need and then put in place the necessary arrangements to contract with the supplier in whatever form is most appropriate. Finally, in step 5 – *Deliver* – we implement the necessary actions and changes to put the new buying arrangements into

Figure 4.1 The 5D power buying process

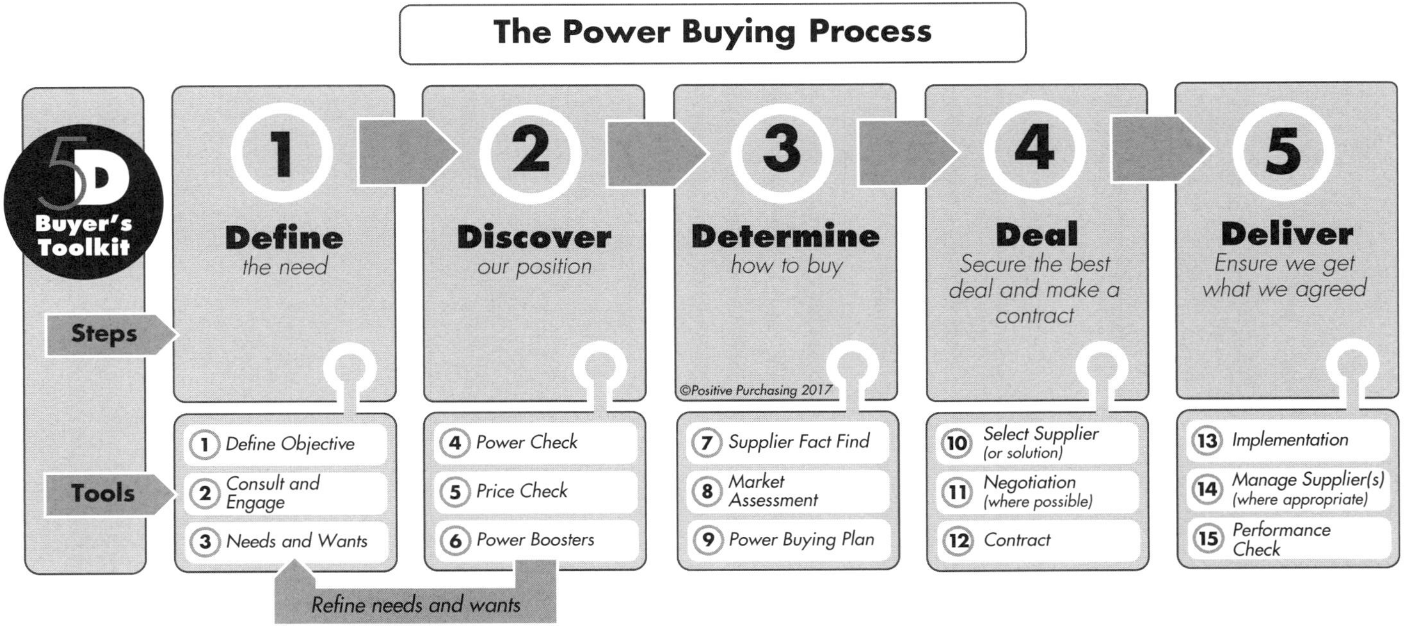

The Power Buying Process

5D Buyer's Toolkit

Steps

| 1 Define the need | 2 Discover our position | 3 Determine how to buy | 4 Deal Secure the best deal and make a contract | 5 Deliver Ensure we get what we agreed |

Tools

1 Define the need
- ① Define Objective
- ② Consult and Engage
- ③ Needs and Wants

2 Discover our position
- ④ Power Check
- ⑤ Price Check
- ⑥ Power Boosters

3 Determine how to buy
- ⑦ Supplier Fact Find
- ⑧ Market Assessment
- ⑨ Power Buying Plan

4 Deal
- ⑩ Select Supplier (or solution)
- ⑪ Negotiation (where possible)
- ⑫ Contract

5 Deliver
- ⑬ Implementation
- ⑭ Manage Supplier(s) (where appropriate)
- ⑮ Performance Check

Refine needs and wants

©Positive Purchasing 2017

practice. Good buying doesn't stop when we have done the deal, but instead we work to ensure that we get that which we have agreed. The supplier may need to be managed on an ongoing basis, perhaps even with arrangements to monitor their performance and review how things are going with them from time to time.

Together, these steps form best practice buying and if well executed will enable any buyer to secure great benefit. Making this happen for real is about becoming highly familiar with the 15 tools and being able to apply them as appropriate to all buying scenarios, and that is the subject of the rest of this book.

Summary

The key learning points from this chapter:

1 It is possible to change or counter the things that disadvantage the buyer and the 5D Power buying process helps to do this

2 The 5D Power buying process is a five-step, 15-tool approach that enables effective buying in any situation. It is based upon best practice business improvement and incorporates key tools from the world of strategic procurement.

Step 1 – define the need 05

This chapter explores step 1 of the 5D power buying process and is concerned with clarifying and then defining the need behind what we are setting out to buy. It covers the three tools contained in step 1 – *Define* – and examines the start of any buying exercise with a simple tool to understand any overarching objectives that we must meet and clarify the degree to which we can influence the purchase. We will look at how good buying requires us to consult and engage with others and finally we will explore how we reach a final, agreed definition of our needs, and wants which will form the basis to guide what and how we buy.

Pathway question addressed in this chapter

6 How do we define what we need and want?

Buying is fundamentally about satisfying a need, and maybe some wants through the exchange of value. For example, imagine we set out to buy a pair of shoes because our old ones have worn out and we need a new pair because we have an important interview coming up. The need is clear and the value is not having to turn up in bare feet and hopefully making a great first impression. Or maybe we might not need a pair of shoes as we have many already, but instead harbour a desire or want for yet another new pair of shoes by our favourite designer that we have just spotted in a shop window. The degree to which this is a need or want might be a conversation with ourselves, supported by lots of self-justification and later the subject of a domestic debate with a loved one. Nevertheless, owning and wearing the latest designer shoes might bring value by engendering confidence and lofty feelings of success and betterment that makes it all worthwhile.

Just buying shoes might be something we do without any conscious thought that our choice and action might be driven by formulation of needs and wants in our minds, but this will undoubtedly be happening in order to reach our decision. It is this fact that drives the world of marketing and selling to convince us of our need, even where we weren't previously aware it existed.

Needs, wants and the value we get when we buy are specific to the purchase and our situation, but there may also be background factors that drive how we make our buying decision. For example, if we have little money, but need shoes for an interview, then our driving objective will be only to get shoes that are smart enough at the lowest cost, but if money is not really a constraint and instead making a fashion statement every time we walk outside is our goal, then our guiding objective will be different.

Finally, our buying decision might be one where we need to engage others before we buy. Others may need a say in what gets bought or could provide helpful advice and knowledge to help us. Buying a new pair of shoes might seem a solitary pursuit, and perhaps so, but if they are new school shoes being bought by a parent then there may be an expectation that the shoes would be appropriate for school. The child may find he or she has some choice, but only amongst the styles the parent deems acceptable. Here, both the child and parent have their own individual needs and wants, and expectations of value they are seeking, for the purchase. These may not be one and the same. The child desiring a pair of bright yellow steel toe capped boots in order to look different might find this being tempered by a more conforming parent. What gets bought in the end is born out of discussion, debate, challenge and ultimately a merging, alignment and agreement of new 'consolidated needs and wants', eg black shoes that are a bit 'boot-like'. All of this is about meeting the overall objective, which might be 'best value for money'.

Perhaps this may sound familiar but I wonder if you have ever stopped to think about all the things that happen when we buy shoes and how we arrive at our buying choice. Shoes are a personal example, but the dynamics behind our buying are the same for both personal and corporate buying. When we buy for an organization there are needs and wants to be satisfied, with many interested parties, each of which will hold opinions, perhaps about what we should buy and from whom, as well as overall objectives of the organization that need to be satisfied.

Good buying is therefore about being able to navigate through this to define the need and not just the need we start out thinking we have, but the need we come to finally determine as the right one (eg *black* boot-like shoes, not yellow). Step 1 of the power buying process contains the three key tools that work in concert to do this (see Figure 5.1), which are to clarify and define the objective, consult and engage, and finally define a single, consolidated and agreed definition of the specific needs and wants for our purchase.

A core thread that runs through step 1 is the degree to which we are able to question and challenge exactly what the underlying need is, to influence our guiding objectives and perhaps change the preconceptions of those who have an interest in what we buy. This can open up alternative and greater value, adding possibilities around what and how we buy. Organizations that buy what they always bought in the way they always bought it, will always get what they've always got!

The opportunity for better buying often lies in something as simple as asking: 'Why?' Recently, and back to our shoe example, I found myself in a shoe shop having a discussion about what I felt was the real need my teenage son should be focusing on. While attempting to find new ways to try and make my point understood, I overheard another father making it very clear he wanted a traditional shoe for his son and anything using modern materials was rejected immediately. The assistant attempted to suggest that some of the synthetic materials were more mainstream and provided better and safer grip, were more durable and water resistant but this didn't seem to land with the father who insisted 'that's what I've always had so that's what we want', while his disengaged son stared into the distance. Right there is one of the main culprits behind poor buying. 'Because that is what we have always bought', along with 'because the drawing or specification says so', 'because someone said so', 'I didn't know there was another way' and

Figure 5.1   Step 1 – Define

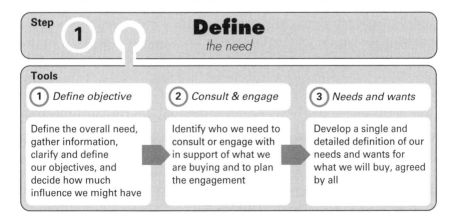

'I didn't really think about it' are all beliefs or states of mind that can stand in our way. Add to this the fact that if there are lots of people who have an interest in what we are buying, they may have different agendas, ideas and interests – whether obvious or not. Finance people might prefer lowest cost, engineers might gravitate towards the best specification, and so on.

Therefore, the theme that runs through the three tools in this chapter, and indeed the entire process, is considering how we might do it differently, secure more value and take others with us on that journey. To be good at buying, you need to be ready to challenge. If you can do that you will be able to buy really well.

Tool 1 – define objective

Purpose – to determine the overall need, to gather background information around what we are setting out to buy, to clarify and define our objectives, and help us determine from the outset the degree to which we might be able to influence what or how we buy and buy better.

How to use it – the first step for any buying activity. Use in concert with the other tools in step 1 to form a full final definition of what we are going to buy.

When needed – highly recommended step in corporate buying in order to gain initial clarity, especially where multiple people are involved or where sourcing complex, high-value goods/services. Less essential, but still useful or something we may just do as part of our thought processes for more everyday buying.

Whether buying for a company, or setting out to buy as an individual, taking a moment to consider what we are setting out to buy and the overall objectives that lie behind the purchase is a vital, but often missed, initial first step. Tool 1 provides a simple structure to not only gather and clarify vital information about the required or intended purchase, but also help prepare us to define our needs and wants and it prompts us to ask some important initial questions that could open up new possibilities for what or how we might buy.

The degree to which this tool, in its fullest form, is useful depends upon the situation. If there is no precise certainty or definition of exactly what we need to buy, then it is obvious how this tool helps. However, there are many buying situations where there is a clear definition of the need and what is to be purchased. A company may specify the product and perhaps even supplier and part number, say in some sort of specification, drawing or internal job management system. There may also be complete clarity regarding the objectives the company wants to satisfy, eg deliver on time, in full, at lowest price. So it would seem that this initial step is redundant. Perhaps so. Perhaps our job as a buyer is to simply do what we are told and buy what we are instructed to buy. Yet we may be able to secure greater value by challenging what we are setting out to buy, how it should be bought and therefore by judging when challenge is appropriate or even possible. In doing this we may also find ourselves coming up against firmly held preconceptions, beliefs and views and our ability to navigate through this is what can make a difference.

CASE STUDY Fifty shades of battleship grey

A defence procurement team considered ways it could help reduce the cost of building and maintaining the nation's fleet of warships. Amongst the many initiatives, one multi-million spend area was the huge annual volume of grey paint used to paint and regularly repaint warships. The paint had, for many years, been procured to its own ancient defence specification, a document written many years previously and widely specified on drawings and in maintenance schedules. The history of this unique specification was unknown, but it seemed it had been written to reflect exactly one particular supplier's standard specification at the time and with a colour with its own unique name, having the inspired name of 'battleship grey'. The paint colour was in fact identical to a standard, readily available, off-the-shelf shade of grey with its own internationally recognized RAL number (the colour specifying and matching system used in Europe). The only difference it seemed was the unique labelling and, as the supplier was quick to point out, special production, packaging and labelling, segregated storage and different checking regimes. The price for the unique battleship grey was in fact three times that of the standard product, with little interest from suppliers to work to improve this. An internal challenge eventually led to an amendment to the internal specification to define only the generic paint and colour number. Huge savings soon followed and the taxpayer benefited from money being available to be spent in other, more needed areas.

Using the tool

The *Define objective* template 1 is provided in the appendix. In practice we would develop and use this tool together with tools 2 and 3, and Table 5.2 includes some questions we can use with others to help us define the objective. Use this tool to define the objective as follows:

1 **Define the need** – consider and define the overall need we are trying to satisfy. This should be as generic as possible so as retain options for different ways to meet the need. For example a need to buy some Anacin (or Annadin in the UK) might seem clear, but there is only one way to satisfy that need and only one brand we can buy. Instead, if our need is to by aspirin, already we open up choice and potential to buy cheaper. Furthermore, if our need becomes to buy painkillers, then we widen our choice further. If our need is to get rid of a headache, then there are even more possibilities, including drinking water, head massage, etc. Therefore, consider the basic need we are trying to satisfy and work to see what ways we might be able to satisfy this need, even if that is different to that which is expected.

2 **Define the purchase** – next, and with our need in mind, define what we are going to buy. Again, keep as generic as possible eg *pain killers or treatment for headache.*

3 **List what we know** about the purchase including:

   ● How much, how many, how often, by when, to where, etc?

   ● Have we bought this or something similar before?

   ● If yes, what do we know about this (eg from whom, what exactly did we buy, was it a success, might we repeat this, etc)?

4 **Specification or preferences** – is there a specification or any preferences for what we need to buy? If so what is this? The specification may be clear, but preferences can take a variety of forms ranging from an idea of a specific supplier, brand, product we could buy, to a firm conviction about that which must be bought. These may be our preferences or that of others. With the idea of challenge in mind, at this stage we should note details of preferences.

5 **Identify key risks** – list any key risks associated with this purchase, particularly if we get this wrong ie if what we bought was wrong, if it underperformed, if the supplier failed to deliver, etc. This is important as if there is significant risk then we may wish to buy in a way so as to prevent or minimize the risk.

6 **One off or repeat?** – consider if this is a single, one-off purchase or if we will, or are likely to, repeat this purchase in future. Knowledge of future repeat purchase will be useful to us in any negotiation with the supplier.

7 **Ways to pay** – establish how we will want to pay for this, eg invoice, on account, credit card or other method. This will help us to understand any cash flow impact and could help in a future negotiation.

8 **Primary objectives** – establish all the primary objectives behind this purchase. These may not be obvious or apparent but it is important to understand what the driving forces are. The primary objectives may be a clear direction set by the company or someone in authority; otherwise we may need to ask questions to establish this. This step might seem unnecessary but there can easily be a mismatch of expectations unless the guiding objectives are clarified. It also provides the basis for challenge and consideration of alternatives, especially if there is a mismatch between preferences and objectives (eg buy a leading brand, premium product but make sure it is lowest price). Deciding to buy something is easy, the objective behind it is rarely thought about, yet essential to understand as it will certainly surface later if we get it wrong. If the objectives are less than clear then establish what they are by asking 'what must this purchase deliver?' Possibilities here might include:

- lowest price/cost;
- best value for money;
- best quality or service;
- just to buy the specified goods/brand or service;
- to source from the specified supplier; and
- certainty of supply or lowest risk.

It is also good to note what is driving these objectives such as:

- our own assessment;
- company policy;
- instruction by others; and
- its specified (eg on a drawing, specification, etc).

9 **Budget or cost objectives** – establish if there any budget or cost objectives or aspirations that we must meet?

10 **Scope for alternatives** – based upon everything we have found out so far, decide if there is scope to consider alternative solutions, products, suppliers or ways to fulfil the need. This is a key step and it is here where we determine if we may be able to add value in what and how we buy and indeed if it is worth considering alternatives. There are clear situations where there is no scope and our only choice is to buy what is specified, eg it is a specified make and part number in a product or process that has been qualified or certified in some way based upon a known and defined component part. So a question here we can ask is: 'What must happen in order to buy differently?' Our answer to this question tells us whether we can add value in our buying approach. There will be many scenarios where there is clearly no scope, but if the answer is around having to convince someone or change 'because we've always done it that way', then we may in fact have scope to drive change. This is one of the most important steps within our buying process and our initial assessment of how we might be able to add value. Our scope to consider alternatives to that which we are to buy may be very clear, or we may not know for sure at this stage and this will become clear as we move through the 5D power buying process

11 **Sustainability objectives** – finally, consider what, if any, sustainability objectives exist for this purchase. Decide this by reference to any stated company policy or rules, through discussing with others involved or, in the case where it is for us to decide, our personal values. Sustainability objectives range across the following:

- none;
- nice to have but only if there is no or only marginal additional cost to do so;
- this is something we want even if we have to pay for it but providing only a small uplift in cost; and
- this is our essential and primary objective.

Tool 2 – consult and engage

Purpose – to identify all the individuals where we must, or it would help us if we were to, consult or engage with in support of what we are buying and to plan our actions accordingly.

How to use it – part of our initial step for the buying activity. Use in concert with the other tools in step 1 to form a full final definition of what we are going to buy.

When needed – essential where others will use or be supported by what is being purchased, or have some sort of interest in what gets bought, and useful where others can help us in making key decisions about what and how we buy.

Buying is rarely a solitary pursuit, more often than not others are involved or it is helpful to us to involve others. Whether we are buying personally or professionally, there are often people who have some sort of interest in the purchase or who might be able to help us ensure we buy well. Typically, these are people who:

- are users of the goods or services;
- will have their own needs or wants regarding what gets purchased;
- will be impacted or affected by the purchase in some way;
- will be paying for it or hold the budget;
- are in charge or are accountable in some way;
- stand to gain or lose as a result of the buying choice or decision;
- could stand in our way, prevent us buying or impose their will on the purchase;
- could help us, especially if we are challenging what should be bought and suggesting alternative approaches;
- have knowledge, expertise or insight into the goods/services and how best to source them; and/or
- might need to be kept informed, eg if they need to know about changes to what gets purchased.

This body of individuals, or our stakeholders, could represent a wide and diverse group within an organization. If we fail to consider who these people might be or fail to engage with them, then not only do we risk not buying the right thing in the right way but we could miss out on support from those who could help us; and those who are not supportive could impede progress to buy well. Imagine a scenario in a big business where something an individual uses in their day-to-day work, and is very familiar with, suddenly gets changed for an alternative supplier's product as a result of a change made by someone in a head office function. Whilst the new product might perform the same function, the lack of familiarity and indeed subtle changes that have taken the worker by surprise might be enough to create performance or quality problems. However, more damaging can be how that individual feels about having the change imposed without any sort of involvement or even being kept informed. Some may simply respond and do their best to make the change to the new product, but more likely there will be resistance to the change from an unwilling individual with no motivation to support the change and maybe even a will to find reasons to make it fail or at least disrupt it (we will return to this in Chapter 9). This may seem like an extreme response, but in fact resistance to change in organizations is frequently the single biggest reason why new initiatives fail. If we are seeking to buy professionally, and challenge what has gone before then to be successful we must take people with us on that journey. In order to do this we first need to identify who the people that have some sort of interest are and then proactively engage and consult with them. This process is often referred to as 'stakeholder mapping' and is essentially is a three-step process.

Using the tool

The *consult and engage* template 2 in the appendix provides a means to execute the following steps:

1 **Make a list** – identify and make a list of all the people or groups of people who have some sort of interest.

2 **Determine interest** – for each determine why they are interested. To help we can classify them according to whether they are the decision maker, the budget holder or the user for what we are buying, or if they are an expert who could help us, or if they might need to be kept informed, eg to keep them supportive and help prevent resistance in relation to what is being purchased. Here we can use RACI analysis (Figure 5.2 gives an example), a stakeholder classification used by companies all over the world, where we determine the nature of those involved according to whether they are:

 • *Responsible* for doing the work, completing the task, achieving the outcomes and therefore will use the goods/services we are buying;

 • *Accountable* for the outcomes, what happens and therefore what those who are *Responsible* do. *Accountable* also for the cost and therefore the likely budget holder or will be paying the bill;

 • Individuals who are neither users nor accountable, but with whom we should *Consult* and engage in a two-way dialogue. This may be to secure their opinion and expertise as well as their help and support, for example if we are to consider moving from a known source/product/service to an alternative; and

- Individuals we must *inform* and keep informed about what we are doing and perhaps why and what gets achieved.

3 **Decide how to consult and engage** – with each person or group. What we will do here depends upon who they are and the nature of their interest (from our RACI assessment). For example, users of the goods or service we are about to buy will have specific needs and wants that we should understand, and so we will need to engage with them to understand these (tool 3 below provides a framework to do this), perhaps in a meeting or e-mailing them some questions, etc. We may need a different sort of engagement with those who have knowledge or expertise that might help us and so on. There is a further dimension here, because it doesn't follow that just because we engage with someone (or a group) that they will be supportive or will cooperate. Some will, but some may be vehemently opposed, especially if we might be suggesting buying an alternative to that which they want. Some may be able to help us, others may not care. In deciding how we might consult and engage, we should also consider how supportive or not the people or groups might be and determine our actions accordingly. We may need to win some people over, or our attempts to find the best buying solution might be met with resistance, which could stop us. We are, in fact, developing a mini-plan for the specific actions we are going to take for each interested person or group.

4 **Make it happen** –– finally we then need to go and put the plan into action and consult and engage with the people or groups who have an interest. In the example in Figure 5.2 we have noted some actions and we could strengthen these by assigning owners and agreeing timescales if necessary. Consult and engage is not a once only activity but good buying may demand an ongoing dialogue throughout the buying process in order to secure the right outcome with the right degree of support for this outcome.

One final note for this tool is that we should keep it confidential. This is especially important if we are noting opinions that certain individuals might not be supportive in determining our actions. If they got to see this in print it could be counter-productive to what we are attempting to do here.

Figure 5.2 An example of the consult and engage tool

People to consult with and engage – New Plastic fittings project

List the people (or groups) we should engage with	Interest/engagement needed				How we will consult and engage
	R	A	C	I	
1 Mike Fuller – Operations manager		✓			Meet to understand what he needs/wants
2 Dirk Janssens – Area supervisor		✓			Meet to understand needs/wants and ask them to help
3 Hugh Manear – Area supervisor		✓			Against any change – meet and work to get on board
4 Susan Garcia – Technical manager			✓		Ask for help to evaluate suitability of new alternative products
5 Deepak Bhagwat – Done this before elsewhere			✓		Meet so he can share his experience
6 Operatives and users	✓				Canvass opinion and input, retrain them and keep informed
7 Store manager	✓				Work with them to understand inventory needs and change over
8 Rest of business				✓	Article in monthly newsletter
9					
10					

Tool 3 –needs and wants

Purpose – to apply a proven structure to develop a single and detailed definition of all the specific needs and wants for what we will buy, developed and consolidated following consultation and engagement with others.

How to use it – part of our initial step for the buying activity. Use in concert with the other tools in step 1 to form a full final definition of what we are going to buy.

When needed – essential for every buying scenario and, when complete, forms the basis to drive the rest of the buying process.

A well thought through and agreed definition of our needs and wants for what we are setting out to buy is essential for effective buying. *Well thought through* because it should ideally be precise but not constrict or narrow our buying possibilities, and *agreed* so it synthesizes, challenges, aligns and finalizes all of the different needs and wants of all those who have an interest.

Imagine you are with a supplier talking about what you are about to buy, and the supplier says: 'Tell us what you need from us and how we can help.' You might respond by describing the product you require, its specification, the required lead-time and how it must be delivered, and you might even have a target price that must be satisfied. In its simplest form the process of defining needs and wants – also called 'business requirements' – is just this, but it is about having a predetermined answer to this question as opposed to letting the supplier propose what they can sell. Crucially, however, this must be a consolidated and aligned definition of what the entire business needs and wants.

To be effective, our final definition of needs and wants must also be about what is right for the business. This may seem obvious, but often companies end up buying a particular grade, nature and type of goods or services as a result of historical factors or what the supplier said was needed, as a result of preferences from technical or marketing functions, or for a variety of other reasons. Worse, if that preference or a named supplier gets defined within company specifications or drawings then it can become firmly established. Sometimes there is good reason to do this, but sometimes not. As we saw at the start of this chapter, if we are to buy effectively it is important to challenge established ways whenever possible; it is also important to make a distinction between what individuals might want or believe they need and what the business needs. Great opportunities can often be found simply by focusing on the business need rather than accommodating what individuals want. The process to get there may involve pain of conflict between functions, especially if the company is not used to individuals tasked with buying questioning things, but this should not put off a determined buyer from working to determine a single, appropriate and agreed definition of needs and wants.

This tool 3 is a simplified version of the RAQSCI business requirements tool used by companies worldwide and expanded in full in my other books.

We need good coffee!

Imagine you are tasked with buying coffee and hot/cold beverage facilities for a large office building. There are many possible options and types of equipment you could choose from: you could buy or lease self-vend/self-service equipment or even outsource the provision and have a small permanently manned coffee outlet with no shortage of suppliers who are ready to help with whatever option is chosen. The company has some objectives to guide you, which centre around good value for the budget set, some ongoing subsidization and a quality solution that keeps the workforce content. The primary need is to find a solution that helps retain staff by making them feel good about where they work whilst removing the need for staff to leave the office to go and get coffee.

With this in mind the first step might be to engage with those who work in the building to understand what they need and want, and then to process these inputs into a final consolidated and agreed definition that we can use to engage suppliers with. To do this we could send out a questionnaire, walk around the office and canvass opinion or appoint a small team to work with, who will represent the wider company. If we ask a question like 'what do you need in terms of refreshment facilities', then it is possible we could be overwhelmed by responses firmly stating needs for the finest freshly ground bean to cup barista outlet, quality teas, take-away cups, full service operation, completely free and so on. Going one step further and asking why this is needed might even produce some very convincing arguments.

This is a common buying challenge. Asking what people need will harvest a myriad of personal wants. These shouldn't be ignored, but rather considered against a broader context of the overall business need. Our job is to determine business need, and even some business wants, and to do this we need to do some detective work and gather, analyse and synthesize, and perhaps challenge, information and ideas from multiple sources, including:

- corporate strategy, aims and objectives, eg if the brand positioning and values of the business place a strong emphasis on acting in an ethical and sustainable way, then it might be important that coffee served at company sites is fair trade;

- company specifications, drawings, standards or anything that stipulates specifics such as named manufacturer, supplier, part or product number, etc;

- what we have bought before, the experience and knowledge around this, what worked well and where things could be improved;

- specific business targets we must meet, or constraints or parameters we need to work within, such as available budget or timelines;

- the needs, expectations, aspirations and desires of our end customer, patient, student, etc, whether stated, assumed or yet unrealized; and

- the needs and wants of those within our business.

Must have, nice to have

The needs and wants tool helps us define simple statements under five key themes or headings as shown in Figure 5.3. These have a sequence or hierarchy, and for this reason the model is shown as a staircase. With a staircase you have to step on the first step, then the second and the third before you can get to the fourth. In the same way with needs and wants, it is pointless considering lowest *price* or best *quality* if we cannot satisfy a fundamental *must have* requirement around being certain the goods will turn up or that what we are buying is legal. This hierarchy is crucial as it refocuses attention in a prioritized order on what is important. It helps disarm concerns from colleagues and suppliers. I often hear, 'You buyers are only interested in lowest price!' to which I reply, 'Actually, no, price is way down on the list; there are other needs that must be met first. 'Consequently, as we start to use the model to define statements of our requirements under each of the headings, we find that our true needs tend to be mostly under the first few headings (the first steps on our staircase) with our wants under the latter headings (the higher steps).

Our most important requirements or our 'must haves,' and the first stair on the needs and wants staircase, are the things that must be secured above everything else without compromise – excluding any suppliers that cannot meet any of these. This might include specific legal requirements (or regulatory requirements in a regulated industry), eg a food producer must comply

Figure 5.3 The needs and wants staircase

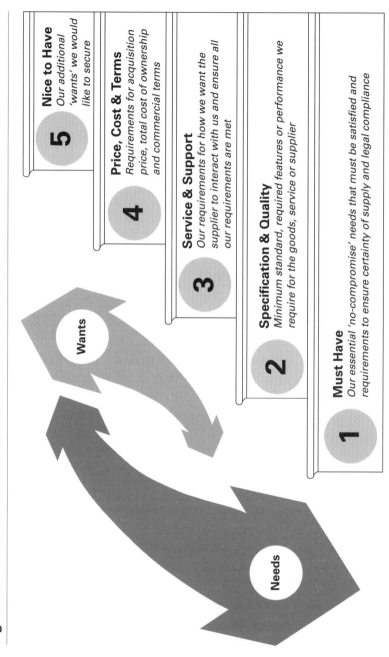

1 Must Have
Our essential 'no-compromise' needs that must be satisfied and requirements to ensure certainty of supply and legal compliance

2 Specification & Quality
Minimum standard, required features or performance we require for the goods, service or supplier

3 Service & Support
Our requirements for how we want the supplier to interact with us and ensure all our requirements are met

4 Price, Cost & Terms
Requirements for acquisition price, total cost of ownership and commercial terms

5 Nice to Have
Our additional 'wants' we would like to secure

Needs

Wants

with food safety and hygiene regulations. It might also include mandatory obligations for compliance with company policies and procedures in areas such as health and safety or sustainability CSR.

If the 'must haves' can be satisfied then our next needs, and perhaps some wants, are those concerned with specification any definitions of quality for the goods or service. Quality definitions might reference a standard that must be met or could be a statement of the required reliability, consistency or repeatability, eg 'must run for minimum of 10,000 hours,' etc. Here we would include any requirements for the supplier to work to a management system such as ISO9001, ISO14001, ISO18001 or other standards. It is this area where we should look closely to determine what scope exists to buy differently. Perhaps the definition of specification is fixed and firm, the product of much thought and deliberation by others, and our job is to buy it, or perhaps not so. Asking 'Why does it need to be like that?' can sometimes help us refine our needs. This is especially relevant in any situations where a specific make, model, brand or supplier is being stipulated but other suppliers exist and offer apparently similar products/service or where other generic alternatives are available. If you go to the supermarket to buy Mr Muscle Toilet Power bleach in gel form then our choice is limited from the outset. However, setting out to buy a sodium hypochlorite based bleach in gel form immediately opens up new buying possibilities. Considering carefully how we state our needs and wants here can make a big difference.

Under 'service and support' we define any specific aspects or levels of service we want or need. This might include lead times, inventory holding by the supplier, how they will manage our account and interact with us, any training we might need from them, supporting information to be provided. Defining these needs and wants is easily missed, partly because many aspects of support happen after the goods have been received or are ongoing. It also means we need to think about how our relationship with the supplier needs to play out to ensure we secure the best support. Discussion with interested parties is key to defining what we need and want here.

Price, cost and terms concern not only the acquisition price, but the total cost we will incur to acquire, use, implement any change (eg switching to a new supplier or product) and ultimately dispose of the goods/service. We may or may not know what is possible or realistic here, or may require research and negotiation we haven't yet done to inform us. We may be working within a strict budget or have future needs for cost reduction. Here the difference between needs and wants becomes particularly relevant – demanding a degree of certainty regarding what we can realistically state in terms of needs, and realistic or semi-informed aspirations for wants. It would be easy to state the impossible here and be disappointed when we try to source it. What we define must be realistic, seeking to balance the 'lower stairs' with the 'upper stairs' and perhaps being ready to go back and review some 'lower stair needs' if we find our expectations are unrealistic. We might also require certain terms or conditions. One important area here is payments terms – something that is easily overlooked or assumed to be 'what the supplier stipulates' – yet attempting to negotiate and secure advantageous terms can have a great impact to us. How quickly we have to pay directly impacts our cash flow. The longer we can take to pay, the more cash we retain in our organization. The difference between agreeing payment after 30 days or 60 days, for example, might seem small, but across the total spend of an organization this can be significant. Suppliers will of course seek to get payment as early as possible, but payment terms can be as negotiable as the price itself, so considering our 'wants' here can help set us up for a subsequent negotiation.

Finally, and once we have defined all other needs and wants, there may be some additional 'nice to haves' we would, ideally, like to secure. This might include additional features, functionality, capabilities, services, support, innovation or other benefit such as accelerated timescales or some sort of priority over other customers. The 'nice to haves' tend to emerge in discussion with interested parties and by considering what we want in the future. Simply calling them 'nice to haves' can easily dilute their importance, making us quick to let them fall by the wayside, but such things can play a key role in any future negotiation with a supplier as bargaining chips to secure the best possible outcome for us.

Developing our definition of needs and wants is a bit like putting together a jigsaw, made difficult because all the pieces are scattered far and wide. We may need to refer to company documents and talk to all the interested parties, canvass opinion and check many points of reference. Here the three tools within stage 1 of the buying process are used in concert to arrive at our definition of needs and wants. Table 5.1 expands the 'needs and wants' staircase and shows possible sources for each heading. We may find ourselves working with others in positions of power and influence with firm views or established precedents and asking 'Why do we need it like that?' It is here where we need to work to establish certainty around what is truly a need, and what is a want. If we know this, it opens up greater opportunities to find new value in the way we buy. Figure 5.4 gives an example of the 'needs and wants' tool for our coffee example above. There is one final dimension here, which is whether our statements centre around our immediate needs or wants or whether any are future requirements. We may have certain things we must ensure are provided for at some time later: these should be referenced as future needs or wants.

Table 5.1 Examples of the different types of need and want at each level and potential sources of information

Requirement	Might include	Potential information sources
Must have *Our essential 'no-compromise' needs that must be satisfied and requirements to ensure certainty of supply and legal compliance*	• Compliance with legislation • Compliance with any regulatory obligations • Compliance with mandatory company policy or procedures (eg health and safety, or sustainably buying/ CSR 'must haves') • Insurances or certifications required • Assurance of supply (eg must be sourced from suppliers who are financially stable, have capacity, geographical coverage, no significant risks etc)	• Relative legislation • Company policies and standards • Company strategy, aims and objectives • Our brand values (and what this means for what/how we buy) • End customer expectations • Regulatory obligations (if in a regulated environment) • Non-negotiable needs of internal users and those with an interest **Consult and engage with:** • All users • Marketing
Specification and quality *Minimum standard, required features or performance we require for the goods, service or supplier*	• Specification • Quality standards • Specific quality, reliability or consistency measures that must be satisfied (eg 98% defect free etc) • Quality management systems the supplier must meet (eg ISO9001)	• Company standards • Company or industry specifications • Drawings • History, expectations of users, known issues or problems • Needs and wants based upon experience and expectations of users and those with an interest **Consult and engage with:** • Users • Technical functions • Quality assurance

(continued)

Table 5.1 *(Continued)*

Requirement	Might include	Potential information sources
Service and support *Our requirements for how we want the supplier to interact with us and ensure all our requirements are met*	• Maximum lead time • Delivery requirements • Logistics, inventory holding, staging, allocating etc • Processes and procedures the supplier must follow (eg delivery rules/ preferred times) • Ongoing support and response times (eg help desk, hotline number etc) • Maintenance or other ongoing support • Requirements around how the supplier will manage our account, communication and the relationship ongoing • Supporting information to be provided/ available • Training and education (eg for our staff on what is being provided)	• Historic or expected practice • What those involved need or want in order to do their job effectively • Processes and procedures **Consult and engage with:** • Users • Sales and Marketing • Operations service providers • Procurement • Logistics and supply chain
Price, cost and terms *Requirements for acquisition price, total cost of ownership and commercial terms*	• Acquisition price within budget or stated target (stated value or relative to something eg lowest benchmarked market cost) • Maximum implementation costs or cost of change	• Historic pricing (what we paid before) and total cost • Research around market pricing and market trends • Budget information • Cost breakdown (what it should cost/we should pay)

(continued)

Table 5.1   *(Continued)*

Requirement	Might include	Potential information sources
	• Continuous improvement (future cost, cost reduction targets, cost avoidance) • Payment terms and requirements for cash retention in the business • Other terms and conditions • Charging methodology (what is chargeable, what is not) • How we will transact	• Standard terms and conditions • Procurement procedures • The needs and wants of those who hold the budget or seek to we are legally protected **Consult and engage with:** • Finance • Legal
Nice to have *Our additional 'wants' we would like to secure*	• Additional features, functions, capability, service, support or benefit we would like • Access to current or future innovation • Use of emerging technology • Accelerated timescales • Getting priority over other customers	• What users or interested parties would like and want over and above what is needed. • Future aims and objectives **Consult and engage with:** • Users • Sales and Marketing

Ask the audience

In order to define all our needs and wants we need to ask those who have an interest or can help and this is part of *consult and engage* (tool 2). As we have seen, asking 'What do you need?' can be counter-productive to good buying, yet it can be difficult to know what to ask beyond this. Here it can help to use a range of questions that seek to build a picture of what individuals might want and truly need, without necessarily asking them these direct questions, and then figure out how to extract the common business needs and wants from the responses.

Figure 5.4 Example 'needs and wants tool 3'

	List each of our requirements	Is it a need?	Or a want?
1 Needs **Must Have**	1 Must demonstrate compliance to food safety/hygiene standards	✓	
	2 Must be financially stable, experienced operator with proven track record	✓	
	3 All supplier staff on-site to have full criminal records checks	✓	
	4 Supplier must hold full insurances to our contractor specification	✓	
2 **Specification & Quality**	1 Front of house 'customer service trained' uniformed staff	✓	
	2 Premium beverage offering (Barrista coffee and fine teas etc)	✓	
	3 Agreed range of light take away hot and cold snacks throughout the day		✓
3 **Service & Support**	1 Attended counter service 7am-3pm M-F. Out of hours managed vending	✓	
	2 Supplier to refit area and supply own equipment	✓	
	3 Dedicated on-site manager and point of contact		✓
4 **Price, Cost & Terms**	1 Managed retail pricing formula – must be less expensive than high street		✓
	2 Rental of space and facilities at market rates + metered service charges		✓
	3 3 year agreement, extendable by mutual agreement		✓
5 **Nice to have** Wants	1 Customer satisfaction surveys quarterly		✓
	2 Facility for staff to order and pay via an app and collect more quickly		✓
	3 Cashless vending		✓
	4 Deli style made to order baguettes and sandwiches available lunchtime		✓

Learning how to ask the right questions is a skill that can be developed but is key to learning how to be good at buying. Remember, if we are able to challenge what others believe we should be setting out to buy, or established definitions, then this can help us shift from tactical buying to buying that adds value to the organization. Table 5.2 provides some questions we can use in different situations. At the heart of many of these questions is that simple word: 'Why?' It's a word children use early on, and keep using to get to the heart of things they don't understand. We can learn from this, and whilst we might not want to be childlike, adopting an inquisitive, suitably persistent questioning style can help here.

Table 5.2 Questions to help build needs and wants

Purpose	Questions to ask
General questions that can help establish all the needs and wants and define the overall objective (Tool #1)	• What have we bought in the past and how much have we bought? • What do we need to buy in the future and how much will we need? • Who buys this and why? • How does this get used? • What influence will this purchase have on you, or your department's performance? • What about this purchase is most important to you? • What do others buy in this situation? • If you had the power to change anything about what we are buying, what would it be and why?
To establish the 'must haves'	• Is there any current or future legislation we must comply with? • Do we need to comply with any industry, customer or company policies, standards or guidelines (including sustainable buying/CSR)? • What are the biggest risks with this purchase if we get it wrong? • Have you previously ever been without the product/service when required? Why?
To establish quality and specification needs and wants	• What industry, customer or company specifications are relevant here? • Are there any minimum levels of performance that must be achieved? • Who are the worst suppliers and why?

(continued)

Table 5.2   *(Continued)*

Purpose	Questions to ask
	• Who are the best available suppliers in the market? Are we using them? How can we be sure? • Are there expectations around what level of quality or other management systems suppliers should be able to demonstrate? Why do we need this?
To establish service and support needs and wants	• What levels of service are important? • What are the factors associated with this purchase that could stop us being effective or consume too much time and resources? • What supplier support, information or activities would enable you to work effectively? Why? • What frustrates you about the way your suppliers service the account? • Rate your supplier's personnel? • How do your suppliers perceive us?
To establish price, cost and terms needs and wants	• Is there a budget or cost target for this purchase? • What cost pressures are you under with regard to this purchase? • What is more important – the price or the total cost of ownership? Why is that? • How have your suppliers helped you to drive down costs? • What contractual terms are needed for this purchase?
Questions to establish the 'nice to haves'	• What would help us be more competitive, perform even better or exceed targets? • Do you think the supplier could bring new innovation, technology, process improvements etc that would be really beneficial to us? If so what and why? • How much of your supplier's goods or service capabilities are you using? • If we could have anything … what would it look like?
Questions to challenge (if appropriate)	• Why do we need to buy that? • How does buying X with Y help us? • If we changed Z how would that work? • How did we arrive at that specification or definition of what we want? Could we consider alternatives? • Which standards or specifications do you agree and disagree with? Why? • Which standards or specifications do suppliers find it hardest to deliver consistently? Why?

Using the tool

The *needs and wants* template 3 in the appendix is compiled as follows:

1 **Gather information** about what we are to buy. Refer back to what we established at the outset, using the *Define Objective* tool 1 together with relevant internal or external policies, procedures, drawings, specifications or other relevant documentation.

2 **Consult and engage** with those who have an interest within the organization (tool 2) and perhaps even outside of it. Discuss the purchase with them, use questioning and challenge as appropriate (refer to Table 5.2)

3 **Create statements** – once understood or agreed, turn each requirement into a series of statements of need or want under the relevant headings. Compile statements as a precise definition of what must be fulfilled so that you could know or test when it had been met, eg 'Comply with specification A124,' or 'Maximum emergency response time of four hours', etc. Build up all the statements to arrive at a complete definition. If any are requirements for the future then identify this within the statement.

4 **Need or want** – for each statement, decide if it is a need or want and tick the relevant column in the tool. 'Must haves' will always be needs and 'Nice to haves' will always be wants.

5 **Align, refine and update** the set of definitions, discussing conflicting areas, negotiating around the true need with those who are involved to arrive at a refined, complete definition.

6 **Share and secure agreement** from those involved for the final definition.

7 **Keep it fresh** – it's not a one-time thing, but needs and wants might change over time. Revisit the definition from time to time for repeat purchases.

Summary

The key learning points from this chapter:

1 Step 1 *Define* contains three tools that work in concert to create a comprehensive definition of what we need to buy.

2 Buying is about satisfying a need. Good buying is about being really clear what the true needs and wants for the organization are, and separating these out from individual's needs, wants and preferences.

3 Arriving at the right definition of needs and wants might require us to carefully challenge what has gone before or others in the organization.

4 Tool 1 – *Define Objective* – is applied at the start of any buying exercise to help gather information, understand any overarching objectives that we must meet and clarify the degree to which we can influence the purchase.

5 Tool 2 – *Consult and Engage* – provides a means to identify those who have an interest in what we are buying or could help us, and to develop a planned approach to consult or engage with them.

6 Tool 3 – *Needs and Wants* – provides a hierarchical framework to build a set of statements under key headings that collectively form the definition of our needs and wants. With challenge where appropriate, discussion, alignment and agreement with interested parties, we can arrive at a final, agreed definition of our needs and wants, which will form the basis to guide what and how we buy.

Step 2 – discover 06 our position

This chapter explores step 2 of the 5D power buying process and is concerned with discovering the strength of our position as well as getting behind the supplier's price. We will then explore ways to respond to these assessments to determine what leverage we might hold, and the specific ways we might be able to secure greater value from our buying approach.

Pathway questions addressed in this chapter

7 How do we discover the strength of our position and power, if any?

8 How can we get behind the supplier's price?

9 How can we boost our buying power?

Step 2 – *Discover* – is so called because it is about arriving at a point where we see something new and significant. Great discoveries don't tend to fall into our laps, but require much effort to go and find them. This step of the process is no different and it is where we begin to do our homework that leads us to a much better buying outcome. How well you buy depends upon the rigour you put into these early steps of the process. There are buying scenarios where the strength of our position (or not) along with what options we might have are obvious. For example, if you want to buy the fragrance from Chanel that your loved one adores, then embark on an exercise to determine all the individual components and costs that make up a bottle of Chanel, and what they each should cost, and therefore the actual cost of a bottle of Chanel, followed by attempts to negotiate based on this, then you are unlikely to get very far. Clearly here we have no power and the most we can do is find out the cheapest place to get it and which currency to buy it in. Many buying scenarios are less obvious and it is easy to fail to see what power we actually have. Add to this all the factors that stop us buying effectively (Chapter 3) and things can become quite foggy.

Figure 6.1 Step 2 – Discover

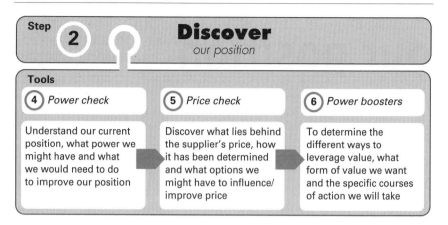

We therefore need to assess the position we are in and understand what options are open to us, if any, to buy effectively. Step 2 contains three tools to do this (Figure 6.1) and we will look at each in turn.

Tool 4 – power check

Purpose – to understand our current position, what power we might have and what we would need to do to improve our position.

How to use it – apply early on to gain an understanding of our position. It can be worked by an individual, but there is benefit in working it in a group with interested parties.

When needed – essential in every buying scenario, but might be applied by rote (in your head) with experience.

The *Power Check* tool (Figure 6.2) incorporates, and is based upon, a tool called *Day One Analysis,* which is used by procurement professionals worldwide, so called because it is one of the first tools to be used. This tool has been incorporated into a more comprehensive template given in at the end of this chapter, specifically designed to help guide us towards the right course of action.

The power check tool helps provide a quick and very simple assessment of our current position regarding what we are buying or about to buy in order to determine what power we have or, more crucially, what we would need to change in order to strengthen our buying position. To use the tool, we classify the product, (or groups of similar products), into one of the four quadrants according to the number of suppliers there are in the marketplace that supply, or could supply, the goods/services (ignoring any constraints we might have imposed that limit this), against the number of buyers or customers who buy this, of which we are one. The axes within the power check tool need to be understood clearly. They are not sliding scales. We must decide if there is either one supplier or buyer (which would be us) or more than one supplier or buyer, but there is no middle ground. It can help to work this tool in a group, as this will typically spark discussions regarding differences in outcomes or positioning, depending on how people view the goods or services we are attempting to buy. This discussion is good and differences will often reveal insights into what is happening. Figure 6.2 gives and explains the power position in each quadrant and the potential responses are detailed in the full template of this tool at the end of this chapter but explained here:

- **Generic** (many suppliers, many buyers). In this quadrant we have the greatest choice and ability to switch supplier; so we have the power. Suppliers will be 'one of many' and therefore seeking to beat their competitors. If we are in *Generic* we should be able to easily find the best deal.

- **Tailored** (many suppliers, one buyer). Here the products and services are made uniquely for us. This might include anything that is branded or made to our own, unique specification or drawing. The supplier's focus is on selling its process and capability, and because of this we may need some sort of relationship with the supplier, perhaps to facilitate day-to-day interactions between companies that support the tailored goods/services. As there is more than one supplier, we hold the power here too, so in theory we have choice and can switch suppliers or find the best deal. However, our power is slightly less than that in *Generic* as the supplier will have to make unique provision for our requirements, perhaps unique tooling or getting acquainted with our specific needs. If we are already using the supplier then switching to another may involve some work to support the transition.

- **Custom** (only one supplier and only one buyer). As the name suggests, this quadrant features the things that are custom-made for us only by only one supplier. Here, only this supplier can provide the goods/service (eg because they have something unique, patented or no one else could do this) and only we buy this particular product or service (eg because it is unique to our requirements, to our specification, or we hold the patent, etc) so it can only be made/supplied to us. In *Custom,* power should be balanced as we need the supplier as much as the supplier needs us. Here we will most typically need some sort of relationship with the supplier, perhaps even a close, collaborative and long-term relationship depending upon what we are buying. Where this is the case it is essential we manage this relationship to ensure it remains balanced and equal as it is likely the supplier will accumulate certain know-how regarding what they provide to us, thus increasing our dependency on them. This is OK providing things remain balanced between us, but if we fail to manage the relationship the supplier can accumulate power over us which could work against us.

- *Proprietary* (one supplier, many buyers). This is where suppliers want you to be, as it gives them the power and a degree of control. They are very clever and will work to identify ways in which you can only come to them for their products. It is here, when we used the power check tool, that we discover if indeed we are in a *proprietary* situation, and if so how the supplier has this advantage. Where this is the case, our ultimate aim in order to buy effectively is to discover how we might be able to move out of *Proprietary,* usually into *Generic.* This may or may not be possible and depends upon why we are in *Proprietary* and our circumstances. In Chapter 3 we explored the buyer's problem with proprietary and the ways suppliers gain advantage which are through branding, differentiation, added value or bundling. In establishing we are in *Proprietary* we must also establish why. This helps us determine what we might do to buy more effectively and our potential responses here are given in Table 6.1. In *Proprietary,* the supplier does not need a relationship with us, but may cultivate a superficial relationship to secure their position. If we have no choice but to remain in *Proprietary* then we may also seek to establish a superficial relationship to maximize our position and secure the best terms as much as possible.

Figure 6.2 The *Power Check* tool

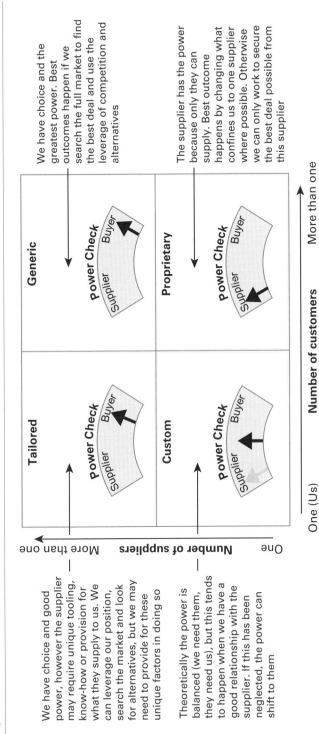

Tailored

We have choice and good power, however the supplier may require unique tooling, know-how or provision for what they supply to us. We can leverage our position, search the market and look for alternatives, but we may need to provide for these unique factors in doing so

Custom

Theoretically the power is balanced (we need them, they need us), but this tends to happen when we have a good relationship with the supplier. If this has been neglected, the power can shift to them

Generic

We have choice and the greatest power. Best outcomes happen if we search the full market to find the best deal and use the leverage of competition and alternatives

Proprietary

The supplier has the power because only they can supply. Best outcome happens by changing what confines us to one supplier where possible. Otherwise we can only work to secure the best deal possible from this supplier

Number of suppliers

More than one

One

Number of customers

One (Us)

More than one

Power Check — Supplier / Buyer

Table 6.1   Our potential responses where the *Power Check* tool reveals
we are in *Proprietary*

How the supplier has gained advantage	Potential responses
Branding	• Can we switch to a *Generic* product or service? • If the supplier/product/service is specified, eg in a company specification or drawing, can it be challenged? – use facts and data arguments to show the savings possible with a switch. • Focus on the overall need being fulfilled – are there other ways to satisfy this need to negate having to buy this particular brand?
Differentiation	• Identify what the differentiator is and determine if this is something we want or need, if so, are there alternative ways we can satisfy this need? • What exactly would happen if we switched to a *Generic* product/service? – quantify the difference, challenge the need and check if we can function without it.
Added value	• Establish what is the added value. Why is it important? Who is asking for it and why or is it something the supplier has just done and has been blindly accepted? • Put a value to the added value elements – estimate how much does that bit costs or ask the supplier to quantify it. • Challenge if there really is a need for the added value components based upon the facts around the added cost. • If the added value components are required, establish if this can this be sourced separately and more effectively.
Bundling	• Establish the individual components that have been bundled together and if these can be unbundled to ideally create a collection of individual *Generic* products/services that can be bought more effectively separately, or use the threat of this to secure leverage with the supplier. • Where the supplier has gained control over one critical component of the bundle explore options to remove this dependency. • Re-bundling is OK once you are in control – ensure you make provision, say within a contract, to exit later should you need to (eg the supplier cannot accumulate any unique know-how or facilities that give them an advantage).

Using the tool

The *Power Check Tool* template 4 is provided in the appendix and is a step-by-step assessment of our position which then guides the user to potential courses of action. Use as follows:

1 **How many suppliers there are** – consider all the suppliers who are currently available in the marketplace for the goods or service we are buying.

2 **How many customers or buyers there are** – we are one buyer, but does anyone else buy this?

3 **Classify the goods/service** – based upon 1 and 2, decide what quadrant the goods/service would sit in.

4 **Determine the response** – decide what we can or need to do according to the classification (the template provides guidance here). Where the Power Check tool reveals our buying may be sub-optimum, or we lack power, decide what we can do about his, challenge if we can and identify courses of action that might improve our position. If in *Proprietary* consider the responses given in Table 6.1.

Tool 5 – price check

Purpose – to discover what lies behind the supplier's price, how it has been determined and what options we might have to influence or improve price.

How to use it – apply together with the Power Check tool to gain a full insight into our position. Apply to the extent that is possible or relevant according to the buying scenario (the tool will guide you to do this).

When needed – not essential, buy very helpful to identify where there is opportunity in buying scenarios where we can influence price.

Have you ever stopped to think about where 'price' comes from when we buy? Is it a number determined by some mathematical formula linked back to universal constants, is it derived from market forces and what we are prepared to pay, or is it simply a number made up by someone in the supplier's marketing department? The answer is it depends, although we can be sure that 'price' is not a real number, it is a determination based upon various factors. 'Cost', however, and specifically the supplier's cost to produce or supply the goods or service before adding their profit margin, is a real number. We can influence cost, eg by improving efficiency, yet it still remains a real and determinable part of what we pay. So if we can understand how much it costs the supplier to do what they do, then surely it follows that we can know if the price they are proposing if fair? Well, again it depends. If we are buying the services of a contractor to paint a house, we could check the price by considering how many hours will be worked, and by how many people, at what hourly rate (and how this compares in the market) and by considering the cost of materials. It would be relatively easy to check if we are getting a good deal or not, and if not we might negotiate or exercise our choice to find another contractor. In this situation getting behind price can be really useful. However, if we are buying a branded smartphone, with a $700 price tag, attempts to understand the supplier's cost would not only be a very difficult undertaking, but would also be pointless. Confronting the retailer with a demand for a much better price as the analysis suggests that the cost to make the phone is only a little over $100 is unlikely to secure much more than some mild amusement.

As we saw in the previous chapter, suppliers prefer to be able to differentiate their products in some way so that we can only buy from them. In the supplier's marketing department, as a new product is being developed, we might hear people ask, 'What can we sell this for?' or 'What price will the market stand?' To answer these questions, suppliers commission extensive research to see how consumers react to different price points. The aim of this is to determine the price that will maximize both sales and profit.

If more proof is needed that 'price' is not a real number, then consider how often you hear phrases such as 'Buy one, get one free', or '30 per cent off our published list price'. If price was a real number, these offers would not be possible.

Why is 'price' so powerful? Well, simply because suppliers want to maximize their revenues. They therefore put huge amounts of effort into conditioning us that their price is the right price for what we are buying. A walk around a supermarket reveals many items where the price bears little relation to the actual cost of the goods. This means that we are all overpaying for our groceries every day, even though we may be buying at the best price possible. So how can we tell? Understandably suppliers are opposed to customers getting to know the true costs for what they supply. Sometimes we can do some detective work and figure it out, and then only if the effort is worthwhile. However, first we must understand how the price was determined.

There are in fact six ways that price gets determined (referred to as *Price Model*). These are greed, value, budget, cost plus, market and target pricing and these are explained in Figure 6.3. Each relates to a different relationship between price, cost and a third component – value. In Chapter 1 we explored how buying is the exchange of value. Value can take many forms and it can mean many different things, at different times. How value is seen also depends upon the perspective of the beneficiary. Our perception of value therefore depends upon our circumstances. In a developing country, getting access to the basic utilities might represent great value to those who live there, yet for the rest of us our expectations have long since far exceeded this and instead value might be desirable brands, latest fashion, cutting-edge technology and so on. Suppliers will, of course, seek to find fresh sources of value or even perceived value that they can get us interested in.

When we buy, value is not necessarily limited to the goods or service but could include the wider supply experience. For example, if we buy insurance, then the low price of the premium is one source of value, but the real value might come from a 'no quibble' payout or from good call centre support. Indeed, these value areas may be more important than the premium cost itself.

When we buy, the price we pay or are being asked to pay, will be determined in one of the six ways given in Figure 6.3. Most of these, but not all, are 'supplier determined', ie based on what the customer is prepared to pay for some sort of value or, in some cases, based on what the supplier can get away with. Some pricing approaches are 'buyer determined' or even 'market determined', both giving the buyer the advantage of power over the supplier. If we are faced with supplier determined pricing then this helps us to consider if we might want to challenge or question what we are buying versus the need we are trying to satisfy. For example, and back to our house painting example, if he decide to buy the paint, then we have a range of *Value Pricing* options from the retailer's own brand product to the premium brand we have experience of. We might decide to go with what we know and pay the premium for the value of knowing we only need to have the house painted once, or we might check out online reviews of the non-brand paint with a view to acquiring an adequate product at greatly reduced price.

Tool 5 (at the end of this chapter) gives each of the six ways price can be determined and provides some potential responses for each. This tool should be used together with the Power Check tool to decide how we might move forward. If what we buy is in *Proprietary* then how price is determined is irrelevant so long as we remain in *Proprietary*. If we are in *Tailored* and, to a lesser extent *Custom*, then we may also be able to get behind price by developing a

Figure 6.3 The six ways price can be determined (aka *Price Model*)

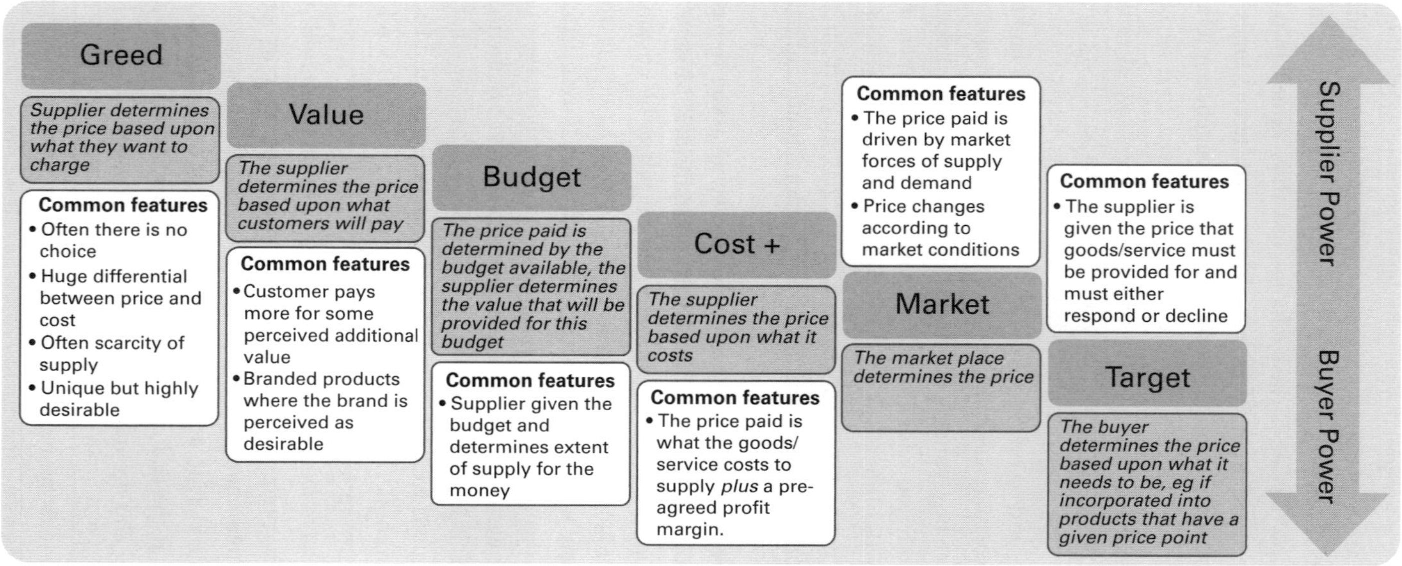

Supplier Power ← → **Buyer Power**

Greed

Supplier determines the price based upon what they want to charge

Common features
- Often there is no choice
- Huge differential between price and cost
- Often scarcity of supply
- Unique but highly desirable

Value

The supplier determines the price based upon what customers will pay

Common features
- Customer pays more for some perceived additional value
- Branded products where the brand is perceived as desirable

Budget

The price paid is determined by the budget available, the supplier determines the value that will be provided for this budget

Common features
- Supplier given the budget and determines extent of supply for the money

Cost +

The supplier determines the price based upon what it costs

Common features
- The price paid is what the goods/ service costs to supply plus a pre- agreed profit margin.

Market

The market place determines the price

Common features
- The price paid is driven by market forces of supply and demand
- Price changes according to market conditions

Target

The buyer determines the price based upon what it needs to be, eg if incorporated into products that have a given price point

Common features
- The supplier is given the price that goods/service must be provided for and must either respond or decline

cost breakdown. A cost breakdown in *Generic* is rarely useful as, in theory, the market should determine price and we can switch, although there are occasions when it can help, even if only to validate pricing. A cost breakdown, also known as *Purchase Price Cost Analysis (PPCA)* or *Should Cost Analysis*, is suitable for non-complex goods and services and is essentially the process of identifying all the associated elements or component parts, deciding what each 'should cost' and then building up an idea of what the complete goods or service 'should cost'. Where there is a vast difference between this figure and the price, we may have uncovered an opportunity, along with the required facts and data needed, to negotiate a better price, or at least help inform the argument and compel a supplier to clarify where additional cost might lie. A cost breakdown can therefore be very helpful if simple to do, and so long as we are in an appropriate Power Check tool quadrant. Such a breakdown can be useful to help inform us for a single purchase, but they can also be used ongoing as a dynamic tool to monitor price and know when to renegotiate. For example, if a product is largely commodity based, then it follows there should be a relationship between current market price for the commodity or commodities. Suppliers are quick to raise prices when commodity prices rise, but less quick to offer a reduction when they fall. A dynamic cost model can help us monitor and be in control of this, using published commodity pricing information to help us. Furthermore, where we need to agree to price increases it can help us understand by how much. For example, if 20 per cent of the cost of a product is copper and the cost of copper on world markets rises by 10 per cent, it doesn't follow that the supplier's product should also rise by 10 per cent. The actual cost impact is 10 per cent of 20 per cent of the direct cost of materials less overheads (say a 50 per cent of the complete price), which equates to a more realistic price increase of 1 per cent. It is worth being able to appreciate this subtlety and how the maths works here, as it is all too easy to accommodate supplier's price increases too willingly.

Using the tool

The *Price Check Tool* – Template 5 in the appendix – is a step-by-step assessment of how price is determined with the option of developing a simple cost breakdown and which then guides the user to potential courses of action. Use as follows:

1 Establish price – what is the price we are paying or being asked to pay?

2 How does this compare – determine how this price sits in the marketplace. If this is not known, conduct some simple research to find out.

Decide where it sits between 'cheapest in the market' and 'most expensive'. Did this research highlight any new opportunities?

3 **How is price determined?** – decide which of the six pricing models are being used.

4 **Determine the response** – decide what we can or need to do according to the classification (the template provides guidance here). Where the Power Check tool reveals our buying may be sub-optimal, or we lack power, decide what we can do about this, challenge if we can and identify courses of action that might improve our position. If in *Proprietary* consider the responses given in Table 6.1.

5 **Maybe… do a cost breakdown** – relevant and useful for non-complex purchases in *Tailored, Custom* and occasionally in *Generic* (to verify the price that the market should determine). Identify all the individual components, activities and costs that go into making up the goods or service. If it's a product, take it apart if possible and look at all the bits it contains. For a service, list all the different activities that happen, any materials used and any expenses incurred. Estimate the cost of each cost element or component – Check the size, weight, length and so on of raw materials used – what would each cost? How many hours work is involved, by whom, and what hourly rate might they earn? Don't forget to include any shipping, transportation or delivery costs. Make estimates, do research, ask those who know and do other detective work to arrive at an idea of cost for all the 'direct cost' elements. It doesn't need to be precise, just approximate. Finally add on the other costs which the supplier has – their overheads to run the business, their costs of sales and marketing, whether they do research and development. If so, that has a cost. It can be possible to establish the percentage of the supplier's annual sales turnover (and therefore of the price you pay) that gets spent on such things from their annual accounts. Advanced cost breakdowns will use such information, for a simple breakdown then a rule of thumb that is reasonably accurate is to take 50 per cent of the total of all the direct cost elements and add it on. Total all the costs to give an approximate 'should cost' figure. Compare this with the price being paid/proposed and look at the difference. If the calculations are sound, this difference represents the supplier's profit – decide if it is reasonable or use this information as the basis for a negotiation. If the supplier rejects it, ask them to present the correct analysis. It will, at the very least, open up the debate.

Tool 6 – power boosters

Purpose – to determine the different ways we could boost our power and leverage value (based upon our *Power Check* and *Price Check* situation), what form of value we want and the specific courses of action we will take.

How to use it – use in conjunction with the *Power Check* and *Price Check* in order to determine potential courses of action, subject to understanding what might be possible in the market or with potential suppliers.

When needed – essential in every buying scenario, but might be applied by rote 'in the head' with experience.

Remember that buying is the exchange of value, and clearly when we buy we want to ensure that this exchange maximizes the value we get from the transaction. Both the *Power Check* and *Price Check* tools within step 3 of our *Power Buying Process* help us understand the strength of our position and each points towards specific way forward according to our circumstances. Tool 6 – *Power Boosters* – is a means to conclude this and determine potential courses of action we could take to leverage greater value and therefore increase the overall power we have as a buyer and maximize our buying outcomes. These *Power Boosters* are also known as 'Value Levers' (you can find a more expanded model in *Category Management in Purchasing,* published by Kogan Page).

How we can secure greater power and value depends upon the buying scenario and on applying different types of intervention with what we are attempting to buy, how we will buy it, with the market or with one or more suppliers. We can take advantage of competition between suppliers in a marketplace by finding the best deal, perhaps even making suppliers compete to win our business. Sometimes we might be able to secure better pricing by combining all our spend for a particular requirement together and maybe giving a commitment for the future also. This aggregated requirement increases our attractiveness to the supplier and gives us leverage to negotiate better pricing and the potential to find the best deal in the market, but not always. If we are buying in *Proprietary* in the *Power Check* tool then our aggregation of demand or a competitive bid process will carry little weight with the supplier. If we want to work with a named architect for our new company headquarters, aggregating spend or driving competition will be counter-productive: instead, here leverage with the supplier comes by building a relationship and working to make us more attractive, perhaps agreeing to pay good rates and pay promptly. Here also, what we are leveraging is unlikely to be price but rather attentiveness, being a priority customer, getting the best package of support for our money, etc. Value therefore takes many forms and is secured in different ways. When we buy we must decide what value is possible, what we will pursue (and what we should not attempt to pursue) and the specific power boosters or courses of action we will apply in order to leverage our power.

There are eight power boosters, as follows and also in Figure 6.4. These are competition, aggregation, manage demand, change specification, improve or build a relationship with the supplier, incentivization (of the supplier), improving process efficiency and analysing where cost is introduced and identifying ways to remove/reduce it. Table 6.2 gives different courses of action that might be required in practice to use each power booster.

We could choose to select the power booster(s) that we feel would be most appropriate for the situation, and this would most likely be just fine, but our position within the *Power Check* tool and *Price Check* tool can better help us decide which power boosters would hold the most potential for us. There is a natural alignment of some (but not all) of the power boosters with quadrants within the *Power Check* tool or specific price models in use within the *Price Check* tool. This is given in Figure 6.4. Therefore, all of the tools within step 3 of the *Power Buying Process* should be used in concert to begin to identify our buying approach.

Different forms of value are secured from the different power boosters, for example, competition and aggregation tend to help secure a lower price, process efficiency and analysing and removing cost tend to help create the value of being more cost effective and working on our relationship with a supplier can make us more attractive to them and so reduce risk or pursue innovation, etc. Therefore, the power boosters we will end up applying should be those that will help us achieve our overall buying objective(s) that we identified back at Tool 1. At this point, the purpose of this tool is to decide which power boosters may be useful or possible, then – and only once we fully understand our power position, the marketplace and potential suppliers – we can finalize our decision around which power boosters we will use along with the specific actions

Figure 6.4   The eight power boosters aligned with the *Power Check* tool and *Price Check* tool

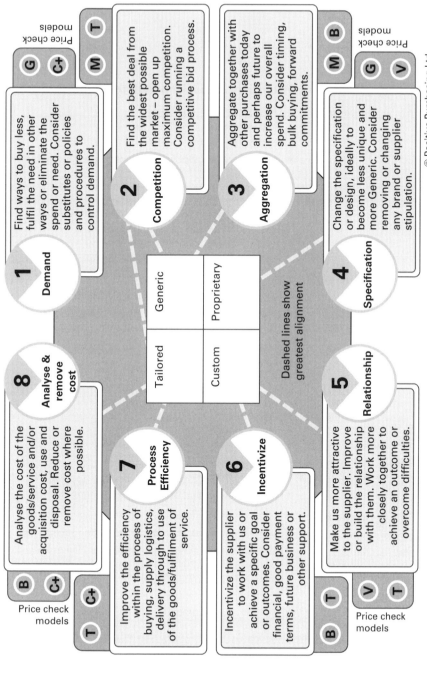

© Positive Purchasing Ltd

we will take to do this. This in turn helps determine how we will buy. The *Power Buying Plan* (Tool 9) covered in the next chapter brings all of this together.

Table 6.2 Potential courses of action to apply each of the eight power boosters

Power Booster	Potential courses of action to realize this value
1 *Demand*	• Reduce need or buy less • Eliminate need and don't buy • Find other ways or substitutes to fulfil need • Introduce/change policy to manage demand and drive compliance
2 *Competition*	• Switch suppliers • Run a tender or competitive market exercise • Use eAuctions or competitive bidding • Look beyond current market – if we buy from one region, can we look globally or at low-cost country suppliers?
3 *Aggregation*	• Aggregate spend or demand for same or similar goods/services across the organization • Aggregate spend for different goods/services with the same supplier and 'buy together' • Bulk buy • Consolidate volumes • Commit to forward volumes or future spend • Consortia buying with partners
4 *Specification*	• Change, consolidate or standardize specifications • Make generic • Add/remove some feature or function to remove uniqueness • Review 'fitness for purpose' or value-engineer • Remove any brand or supplier stipulation
5 *Relationship*	• Make us more attractive to the supplier • Change, improve, develop or build the relationship • Agree a structure for how the relationship works • Manager supplier interfaces better • Joint working and collaboration to drive joint improvements • Drive in shared objectives and values with common aim and purpose

(continued)

Table 6.2 *(Continued)*

Power Booster	Potential courses of action to realize this value
6 *Incentivize supplier*	• Offer contractual commitment to specified volumes, spend or length of contract • Promise of future volumes of spend • Introduce pricing mechanism to protect supplier against price hikes in the cost of materials • Offer improved payment terms • Offer stage payment • Prompt settlement discount • Financial reward or bonus if key agreed goal is achieved • Help the supplier improve their route to market through your organization • Provide other forms of support to the supplier that will help them
7 *Improve process efficiency*	• Understand and drive in improved efficiencies in the supply chain • Improve capability (process, and skills of people) • Reduce or eliminate waste • Eliminate unnecessary steps • Make the buying transaction more effective • Optimize packaging, logistics and supply
8 *Analyze and remove cost*	• Understand the total cost of ownership • Understand and where cost is introduced in the supply and value chain • Identify and pursue improvement objectives to tackle specific cost areas and reduce or remove cost

Using the tool

The *Power Boosters* tool – template 6 in the appendix – is a means to determine the potential actions we could take so to leverage the most value when we buy and in turn begins to shape how we will buy. Use as follows:

1 **Review the position for *Power Check* and *Price Check* tools** – note the power check quadrant and price check model in the centre of the template.

2 **Select power boosters** – check which power boosters we might be able to use based upon those that most align with the *Power Check* quadrant and the *Price Check* model in use (as referenced on the template). Tick those that we will use.

3 How we could apply this power booster – for each potential power booster determine how it might be applied and the courses of action required (use Table 6.2 to help).

Summary

The key learning points from this chapter:

1 Step 2 *Discover* contains three tools that work in concert to discover our current position, what power we may or may not hold and the potential courses of action we would need to take in order to secure greater value when we buy.

2 Supplier's seek to reduce our choice and lock us in by making what they provide proprietary in some way and then convincing us to buy and keep buying this.

3 Tool 4 – The *Power Check* tool – enables us to decide what power we hold based upon the number of buyers for the goods or services (of which we are one) and the number of suppliers who can fulfil our needs. It also helps us identify what action we would need to take in order to improve our buying power.

4 Tool 5 – The *Price Check* tool enables us to identify the way price is being determined for what we buy, and therefore what options we might have to influence it or what we would need to do in order to buy better.

5 Tool 6 – *Power Boosters* – are the eight ways that different types of value can be leveraged. We can apply one or more power booster to improve how we buy. The boosters we are able to use depend upon our power and price position (*Power Check* and *Price Check* tools). Power boosters can secure different forms of value depending upon our circumstances and we need to be clear what we want to pursue, eg reduced price, lower cost, improved efficiency, reduced risk, etc.

Step 3 – determine how to buy

This chapter explores the three tools associated with determining how to buy, including supplier fact find to determine who we might buy from, how we will buy based upon market conditions and a means to create a simple buying plan.

Pathway questions addressed in this chapter

10 Who could we buy from?

11 How do we understand the market?

12 How will we buy to secure the best outcome?

There are many ways to buy

By this stage in the power buying process we understand our overall buying objectives as well as the overall need we are attempting to fulfil. We have detailed our needs and wants, perhaps with some challenge and refining along the way, and we have some understanding of what power we might hold and what power boosters might help us. We are now ready to buy the goods or service, but who should we buy from and do we need to understand the marketplace we are sourcing from in order to secure the best outcome? Step 3 – *Determine how to buy* – helps us answer these questions and includes three tools (Figure 7.1). We will look at each in turn.

Figure 7.1   Step 3 – Determine

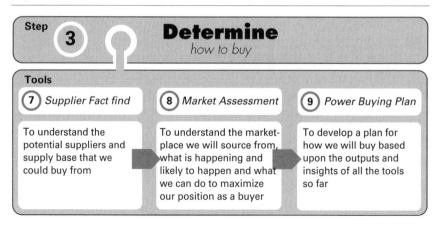

The value of good information

Effective buying demands quality information across four key areas: internal, product/service, suppliers and the marketplace. Gathering information is not unique to this step; in fact, the first of these has already been addressed within step 1 where we gathered information about our internal requirements, our objectives and the needs and wants we are trying fulfil (about the product or service we are buying). This step covers the final two.

It is the depth and quality of our understanding of these four areas that can make the difference between poor and great buying effectiveness. One common mistake here is to assume we already know enough to make a good buying decision. The reason for this is we are very good at knowing what we know (ie the suppliers we know or have used before) – we may even know something about where our knowledge is incomplete and therefore where we need to go and do our homework. However, it can be difficult to contemplate what we don't know we don't know. The problem here is there is nothing tangible for us to grab onto and so it is very easy to overlook the possibility that there could be more knowledge out there that could help. In my experience, it is in the 'unknown unknowns' where we typically find new ways to source that will deliver huge benefits. Finding these is simply about being open to the idea that there is more knowledge out there and keeping on looking.

Good supplier fact-finding and market assessment should look beyond what we know or the gaps we are aware of. If you've ever been involved in research, perhaps for a dissertation or for a project, then the concept of exploring the unknown will not be new. Perhaps you've experienced this in other ways such as contemplating a new bathroom or kitchen. At the outset, there may be a clear idea of what is wanted and where to get it from, but searching online might throw up new possibilities: different configuration options, new materials, different ways to fulfil the need, suppliers you had not previously known about and so on. In fact, the final solution and supplier may well be completely different from that which was initially considered – all resulting from good fact-finding!

The process of fact-finding rarely has structure, and there is no sequence of places to visit to find information, but instead it is a case of some detective work – searching out relevant pieces of information. Each new discovery might open a door to another new idea, which suggests searching for sites about this new idea, which then lead to a new door to open and yet another idea, so on. There is no way of knowing when we have found out enough information. The process may take different forms ranging from online searches to reviewing reports, spreadsheets, technical papers and so on. Doing extensive research doesn't mean we must end up drowning in data and information. Instead it is about being confident we have examined a particular area to a good depth, and we know enough to make a good buying decision, avoiding the temptation to assume we already know. It is also about being able to understand in simple terms what has been discovered. If we are able to articulate a summary of what we have found, as if having to brief someone else in less than one minute, we are doing well. Therefore, as we accumulate insights, asking 'So what does this tell me?' can help build a useful summary as we go.

Getting good at research

There are many different types of research and sources of information we can use and deciding what we need depends upon our situation. We may end up doing a variety of fact-find activities. Today good research is within the reach of us all and the internet is a fantastic source of information, much of it free, if we know where and how to look. The basics of internet searching are known to almost everybody these days; however, it is important to remember that popular search engines can present results that they want us to have – perhaps those listings determined by companies paying to get there or as a result of the prevailing algorithms determined by the search engine to limit website designers from gaining a free advantage through incorporating too many search engine optimization features. This means the internet searches we all know may not be good enough for effective research and so it is worth developing an advanced skill here and learning how to access information of a greater quality, often for free. There is no right or wrong way to carry out internet searches and experimentation is the best approach. Ten tips for advanced internet research are provided below to help here (incorporating suggestions adapted from the Open University Information Literacy Toolkit, 2009). Furthermore, it is worth considering using a selection of search engines and desktop search tools that access the internet, especially those focused on business such as www.copernic.com or www.hoovers.com The rest is down to clarity of search terms and thinking about all the potential sources of the information needed.

Ten tips for advanced internet research

(incorporating tips adapted from Information Literacy Toolkit, 2009).

1   Get familiar with several search engines: different search engines will return different results for the same search term so read the online help files for the search engines – they contain great detail about how to search effectively.

2   Think carefully about the search terms you use, and repeat searches using alternative words or phrases that hold the same meaning, eg purchasing, procurement, sourcing, buying, etc.

3   Limit results for a given search using the search options feature within the search engine (refer to the online help files to find out how).

4   Double quotation marks – use to find phrases or terms in the exact order specified and so limit results.

5   AND (+) – use the plus sign to combine search terms so only results featuring both keywords will be returned, eg *cleaning+chemicals*.

6   NOT (–) – use the minus sign to limit a search so as to exclude a concept, issue or person, eg *syringe–medical*.

7   OR – use OR (in capital letters) to find related words or synonyms, eg supplier OR vendor.

8   Truncation – use to search for different endings to a specific word, eg buy, buy-ing, buy-er. Some engines do this automatically, others might require the use of a 'wild character' to indicate different possible endings to the word, eg buy*.

9   Geographical limits – many search engines are set by default to first return results relevant to the country you are in, which may be unhelpful for global research. Use advanced search options to widen or lessen the scope here.

10 Check the number of hits for your results to see whether you are getting more or less information relative to the highest-ranking result.

Tool 7 – supplier fact find

Purpose – to determine the potential suppliers and supply base that we could buy from.

How to use it – conduct supplier fact-finding once we know what we are going to buy, ie once steps 1 and 2 are complete (in practice we may end up doing some of this prior to this point). Don't rely on old knowledge or thinking – ensure the understanding is fresh.

When needed – essential in every buying scenario.

Supplier fact find

Supplier fact find is about answering three key questions:

1 Who are all the suppliers who could do this?

2 Which ones might be suitable?

3 What do we know about them?

Deciding 'who' the suppliers that could do this are might seem straightforward, and perhaps we believe we already know this. However, remember that preconceptions around our supply base limit our options – the more potential suppliers we have who can satisfy our needs and wants, the more choice we have and so the more power we have to secure a great buying outcome (*Generic* or *Tailored* quadrants in the Power Check tool). If our buying situation is such that there is only one supplier we can use (*Proprietary* in the Power Check tool) then our power will be limited by this very fact unless we can change what is driving the single source scenario.

Good supplier fact find should therefore attempt to identify as many potential suppliers as possible who might be able to provide what we need – from here we can then select who to approach. We do this through research around who is out there (Table 7.1) but here it is important to widen our thinking as much as we can by focusing on the overall need we are trying to fulfil (from tool 1). For example, if there is a film I would like to see I could go online and buy a DVD, or I could even do it the old-fashioned way and walk into an actual outlet. However, this assumes the need is fulfilled by buying a physical DVD – true if I want to own a collector's edition but if the need is simply to watch the film, then I can probably fulfil this need by streaming the video using one of the suppliers from a different marketplace; I could even simply borrow a DVD.

Assuming we are not constrained by being in *Proprietary*, good supplier fact find is about identifying as many potential suppliers as possible for what we want to buy, and possibly even other suppliers who could fulfil the need in a different way. Not every supplier we find will necessarily be suitable so we may need to apply some pre-qualification.

Supplier pre-qualification

Supplier pre-qualification is the process of applying some simple criteria to sieve out those suppliers we don't want to consider any further so as to avoid being overwhelmed or wasting time researching suppliers who are unsuitable. Supplier pre-qualification is not about selecting suppliers (that is covered in tool 10), but rather about excluding unsuitable suppliers to end up with a short list of suppliers we can then research in detail. Pre-selection criteria that might be applied here include:

- geographical location or ability to service;
- capability;
- supplier's size or capacity;
- supplier's financial position, eg by running a check using a specialist company such as Dunn & Bradstreet;
- recognized accreditations such as ISO9001;
- favourable references or recommendations; and
- checking whether their company registration records check out.

Table 7.1 lists possible information to collect and potential sources we can use.

When we carry out pre-qualification we must balance identifying the widest possible marketplace to give us the most choice with being able to do make progress. For example, imagine we were seeking to find a partner to take care of all our facilities management across all UK sites. The number of facilities management maintenance contractors in the UK is around 17,000 (British Institute of Facilities Management, 2015). This figure probably doesn't include many of the 'one man and his van' type companies, so the actual number may well be around 30,000. If we were seeking to appoint a supplier, then finding out something about each one would clearly be impractical, so instead we need a shortlist. This shortlist may consider only those who have nationwide capacity, are of a given size and standing (say with an annual sales turnover of £1bn+), and hold suitable accreditations. This would reduce the potential number to just six, and if this is too constrictive we could widen our search to companies with annual sales turnover of £300m+, to give us 15 potential candidates (www.building.co.uk, 2017).

Once we have excluded suppliers we know we won't use, we can carry out full fact find about the short-listed suppliers. Our aim here is to find out as much as we can and what we discover will then help us to select our suppliers (part of tool 10, covered later in this chapter). However, in deciding the potential suppliers we could source from, we also need to understand the marketplace they form and that is our next area of focus.

Looking globally

It is easy to assume that the only practical supply base is the one most local to us that we know. However, we might be able to open up opportunities by considering suppliers in other geographical locations. Today, the world is a much smaller place with a global market open for business. Once, sourcing from distant parts of the world was something reserved for a handful of specialists, but today this is an everyday thing for business and also for us as consumers. eBay offers no shortage of goods comparable with that we know but at a fraction of the price, shipped from China to our door in less than a week.

In the UK, marketplaces for bulky items such as bulk chemicals and building products were for many years nicely closed. However, as European and more recently Eastern European suppliers attempted to gain a foothold, new opportunities opened up, changing market dynamics. The idea of hauling heavy bulk products can easily get rejected as unworkable based on the assumption that the increased cost of freight would offset any price advantage. However, we live in a world where things are being shipped all around it all of the time. Global freight is in fact not as costly as you might think. It costs around £6 to ship something the size of a washing machine from China to the UK.

Having said all of this, sourcing from distant suppliers introduces new complexities and risk, including heightened CSR challenges. Increasingly, however, leading companies manage to overcome these problems to make global sourcing a viable option. We will return to global buying in Chapter 10.

Using the tool

The *Supplier Fact Find* tool – template 7 in the appendix – provides a means to capture key outputs from our supplier fact find activity. Use as follows:

1 **Who is out there?** – begin with high-level research to determine as many potential suppliers who could do this as possible, listing them on the template if practical to do so (eg if there are fewer than 10).

2 **Pre-qualification criteria** – where there are many potential suppliers, determine one or more criterion and apply to exclude those suppliers who are unsuitable.

3 **Research potential suppliers** – identify those who could do this, then research them to find out as much as possible about each one and note findings. (Table 7.1 provides details of possible information to collect and sources to use.)

Table 7.1 Supplier fact find

Type of supplier fact find	Information to collect	Potential sources
Who are the suppliers that could do this? *(research about the supply base)*	• Who could supply the specific product/service we are buying (current and other suppliers)? • Who else is out there who could fulfil the need in other ways? • Are there suppliers in other geographies that we could consider? • Are there any suppliers who don't currently do this, but could adapt?	• Internet research • Tradeshows • Supplier's literature • Industry publications • Ask those who know • Physical encounter (eg at a trade fair, networking events)

(continued)

Table 7.1 *(Continued)*

Type of supplier fact find	Information to collect	Potential sources
What do we know about them? *(research about specific suppliers)*	• Where are they located? • What do we know about them? • What exactly do they do (range of products/ services)? • Geographical coverage • How big are they, what capacity do they have? • Who are their main customers? • What others say about them, eg customer reviews • Where are they heading – what new things are they working on and what will their future business be about?	• Supplier's website • Company information websites (eg hoovers. com, avention.com, skyminder.com) • Other internet research • Supplier's literature • Industry publications • Send a questionnaire or Request for Information (RFI) • Ask those who know them • Visit them or ask them in person
How can we determine if they are suitable? *(deep research about specific suppliers)*	• Quality Accreditations (eg ISO9001), awards, certifications • Financial information • References from other key customers	• Send a questionnaire or Request for Information (RFI) • Ask those who know them • Check company registration and ownership details • Visit them or ask them in person • Industry publications and experts • Financial analysis experts (eg Dunn & Bradstreet) • Customer reviews and references

Tool 8 – market assessment

Purpose – to understand the marketplace we will source from, what is happening in it (today and anticipated), our unique position within this market and how we might maximize our position.

How to use it – conduct the market assessment once there is clarity regarding what we are going to buy and the supply base we anticipate using; logically do this at this point in the power buying process, although in practice we may end up doing some or all of this assessment at any time prior to this. Don't rely on old knowledge or thinking; ensure the understanding is fresh.

When needed – it is essential in every buying scenario to have at least a basic understanding of the marketplace.

A marketplace is the arena of commercial dealings. *Webster's Dictionary* describes it as the 'economic system through which different companies compete with each other to sell their products'. Our entire global economic system operates through, and depends upon, a complex array of different marketplaces. Huge energy is directed at attempting to understand them; stock markets and financial institutions all over the world make money and manage our pension funds by understanding and modelling how markets are behaving and therefore the anticipated success of those companies that exist within and make up the marketplace.

If we can understand the market we are buying from we can buy more effectively, maximize our outcomes and protect ourselves from risk or making bad mistakes. Being equipped with a good understanding of what is happening in the market is also an essential component of negotiation and helps us know how badly or otherwise the other party might want a deal. A market assessment is therefore about attempting to answer four key questions:

1 What is the market?
2 What is happening in the market now (and what is anticipated to happen in the future)?
3 What is our unique position in the market?
4 What can we do to maximize our power position in this market?

Understanding what the market is

To understand the market we must first be clear: 'What is the market?' This might sound odd as it is easy to assume we know this already. In fact, we may not and taking the time to understand what the market is can open new possibilities for us. This goes hand in hand with supplier fact find where we attempt to answer the question:'Who are the suppliers who could do this?' Together, these questions help us begin to understand the market, the suppliers that make it up, how big it is and therefore what opportunities might be unlocked if it were possible to consider a wider or bigger marketplace.

A marketplace is defined by the number of suppliers that it contains. Markets therefore have boundaries, sometimes natural boundaries and sometimes artificial. Market boundaries take many forms and all markets are bound in one or more ways. For example, taxi firms exist the world over, but despite what Uber might tell you, it is not a global market, it is a natural collection of small markets, each bound by practicality, licences to operate, the limited demand for long haul taxi services, and, ultimately, the simple fact that most drivers want to be able to get home for their tea. Markets might be defined by natural geographical boundaries, eg the London taxi marketplace. Markets may have specific locations or physical boundaries. The traditional village square market could only ever be as big as the number of stalls that the space could accommodate. Today the walls of a shopping mall provide the same physical boundary. Other markets might be bound by size, available capacity, or how much is spent (for example the size of the US fast food market is estimated at \$120bn per annum). If half the world's population stopped buying fast food, the market would soon half in size. Imposed market restrictions or regulations create boundaries; for example, US import trade tariffs for food protects US producers by restricting the size of the available market. Another factor that can define the boundaries of a market is what we are buying and the available providers who can supply this. For example, if we are buying specialist aluminum castings then the market is defined by the number of companies who can make castings. Geographical boundaries might also apply here if it is only economic to ship heavy castings so far.

The wider the market boundaries, the wider our choice, and therefore the greater our opportunity to buy more effectively. As we saw in tool 7, this must also be tempered by pre-qualification so we are not overwhelmed by a mass of suppliers to consider. Figure 7.2 illustrates the effects of market boundaries on market opportunity with the number of potential suppliers of a given product or service varying according to the different market boundaries that we might determine.

Figure 7.2 Effects of market boundaries on market opportunity

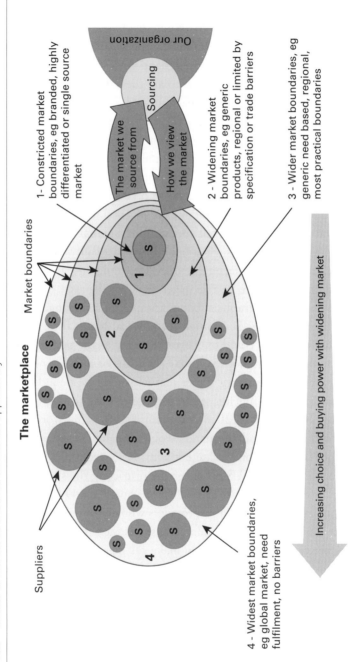

The marketplace

Market boundaries

Suppliers

Our organization

Sourcing

The market we source from

How we view the market

1 - Constricted market boundaries, eg branded, highly differentiated or single source market

2 - Widening market boundaries, eg generic products, regional or limited by specification or trade barriers

3 - Wider market boundaries, eg generic need based, regional, most practical boundaries

4 - Widest market boundaries, eg global market, need fulfilment, no barriers

Increasing choice and buying power with widening market

It is in the supplier's interest to limit market boundaries and restrict our choice. We can identify this happening using the *Power Check* tool to determine when a supplier is attempting to get us into *Proprietary,* ie where the marketplace contains just one supplier. Hence challenging where possible can be beneficial. In *Tailored* and *Generic* determining choice, and therefore our power, is often about perspective and how we view the market. If our buying choices limit us to a specific branded item, then we have instantly limited our market, but if we could consider alternatives then we open up our market and the possibilities of getting a better deal from the resulting competition. We may be able to widen this choice and possibility further by considering an even bigger market, say looking beyond local suppliers to wider regional or even global sources where practical and possible.

Understanding what is happening in the market

If we can understand the market we will source from, then we can understand the risk and opportunities it presents today and tomorrow, and so we are better informed to decide where, when and how to buy and, in particular, what buying or negotiation tactics we might use, in order to get the best deal. Understanding a marketplace might sound like a challenging activity, and indeed it can be an entire science all of its own, but it is also something that we do every day, perhaps without thinking about it too much. We are in fact all experts at understanding what is happening in marketplaces. If a manufacturer announces they are bringing out a new version of an established product, chances are we can grab a bargain if we buy one of the last of the current version, if this meets our requirements and we don't need the latest thing then we can buy well. If we learn that global oil production is being cut, then we know that the price of oil will rise and we will pay more for our gas tomorrow than we did today and so filling our tank today becomes worthwhile.

Marketplaces are complex systems, often operating in chaos, driven and influenced by an ever-changing variety of world, environmental, institutional and people factors. Depending upon our buying scenario we must decide if we need to undertake a major research project or if is enough to do a quick check. Perhaps we already know or have a feel for it – generally those involved in a buying activity tend to get a feel for the marketplace they are sourcing from. That said, the health warning given earlier about not assuming we know everything to be known about our position still applies here!

Where a rigorous market assessment would be beneficial, then we can do this by considering the various factors that influence how a market behaves (given in Figure 7.3) and by using the established models that can help us here. These include PESTLE analysis, Porter's Five Forces (adapted for buyers), understanding supply vs demand, and also considering any factors unique to us that are relevant. Collectively, all these factors provide help us determine a good market assessment and our relative position, which in turn helps us determine how best to buy. Therefore, the template for tool 8 provides for working through each component of the overall assessment using the key models and I shall explore each one in turn.

External factors that influence a market

The PESTLE tool (or other variants of this tool) can help us see the issues, trends, risks, changes and forces of change that are shaping the market and determining its future direction. PESTLE stands for *Political, Economic, Sociological, Technological, Legal* and *Environmental* and for each of these we consider what might be happening or the forces or drivers that might be shaping the market. Thinking about what might be happening under each of these headings helps to determine any key factors that could mean a marketplace is for or against us now or in the future and what risks or opportunities we might want to consider. Figure 7.4 explains the headings of the PESTLE tool.

Using Porter's Five Forces to help understand the market

Porter's Five Forces (Porter, 1979) is a classic marketing tool, developed by Michael E Porter. The tool is used by companies to help determine corporate strategy to cope with competition and successfully sell into a given marketplace. As a marketing tool it works by the company looking into the market it is seeking to trade within and assessing the five individual forces that determine the relative position of the company. As buyers, we can use Porter's Five Forces to help understand the market we want to source from, except that here we must use the tool slightly differently and use an adapted variant (Figure 7.5). In this version, Porter's original 'threat of new entrants' and 'threat of substitutes' (both things that would concern us if we are selling into a market) become 'scope for' instead, as these can help improve our buying power. Also, our position and perspective changes;

Figure 7.3 Factors that influence how a marketplace behaves

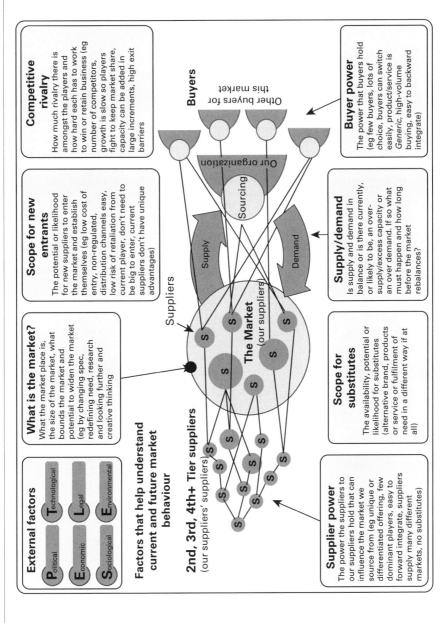

External factors

Political **T**echnological

Economic **L**egal

Sociological **E**nvironmental

Factors that help understand current and future market behaviour

2nd, 3rd, 4th+ Tier suppliers
(our suppliers' suppliers)

What is the market?
What the market place is, the size of the market, what bounds the market and potential to widen the market (eg by changing spec, redefining need, research and looking further and creative thinking

Scope for new entrants
The potential or likelihood for new suppliers to enter the market and establish themselves (eg low cost of entry, non-regulated, distribution channels easy, low risk of retaliation from current player, don't need to be big to enter, current suppliers don't have unique advantages)

Competitive rivalry
How much rivalry there is amongst the players and how hard each has to work to win or retain business (eg number of competitors, growth is slow so players fight to keep market share, capacity can be added in large increments, high exit barriers

Suppliers

The Market
(our suppliers)

Supply

Demand

Sourcing

Our organization

Other buyers for this market

Buyers

Supplier power
The power the suppliers to our suppliers hold that can influence the market we source from (eg unique or differentiated offering, few dominant players, easy to forward integrate, suppliers supply many different markets, no substitutes)

Scope for substitutes
The availability, potential or likelihood for substitutes (alternative brand, products or service or fulfilment of need in a different way if at all)

Supply/demand
Is supply and demand in balance or is there currently, or likely to be, an over-supply/excess capacity or an over demand. If so what must happen and how long before the market rebalances?

Buyer power
The power that buyers hold (eg few buyers, lots of choice, buyers can switch easily, product/service is *Generic*, high-volume buying, easy to backward integrate)

Figure 7.4 The PESTLE tool explained

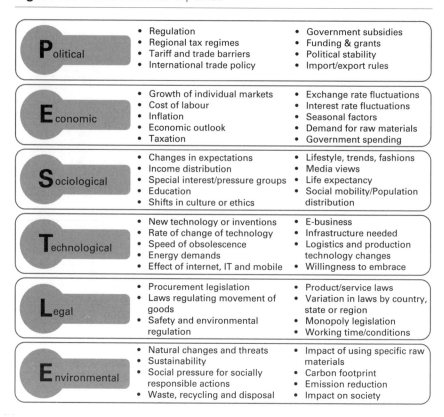

- **P**olitical
  - Regulation
  - Regional tax regimes
  - Tariff and trade barriers
  - International trade policy
  - Government subsidies
  - Funding & grants
  - Political stability
  - Import/export rules

- **E**conomic
  - Growth of individual markets
  - Cost of labour
  - Inflation
  - Economic outlook
  - Taxation
  - Exchange rate fluctuations
  - Interest rate fluctuations
  - Seasonal factors
  - Demand for raw materials
  - Government spending

- **S**ociological
  - Changes in expectations
  - Income distribution
  - Special interest/pressure groups
  - Education
  - Shifts in culture or ethics
  - Lifestyle, trends, fashions
  - Media views
  - Life expectancy
  - Social mobility/Population distribution

- **T**echnological
  - New technology or inventions
  - Rate of change of technology
  - Speed of obsolescence
  - Energy demands
  - Effect of internet, IT and mobile
  - E-business
  - Infrastructure needed
  - Logistics and production technology changes
  - Willingness to embrace

- **L**egal
  - Procurement legislation
  - Laws regulating movement of goods
  - Safety and environmental regulation
  - Product/service laws
  - Variation in laws by country, state or region
  - Monopoly legislation
  - Working time/conditions

- **E**nvironmental
  - Natural changes and threats
  - Sustainability
  - Social pressure for socially responsible actions
  - Waste, recycling and disposal
  - Impact of using specific raw materials
  - Carbon footprint
  - Emission reduction
  - Impact on society

instead of looking into the market, we become one of the buyers within it and therefore the 'power of buyers' force includes us along with all the other buyers from the market. Finally, the buyer's variant means that power of suppliers relates to the suppliers into the market, ie our supplier's suppliers or second tier suppliers, not those suppliers we are seeking to buy from. Using the buyer's variant of this tool is crucial to understanding the forces acting on a marketplace from which we are sourcing. You can read more about this tool and how to use it in *Category Management in Purchasing*, also by Kogan Page.

Porter's Five Forces, adapted for buyers, forms part of our market assessment within tool 8 in the appendix. Here we consider each of the five forces that are explained in Figure 7.5 and determine how potent each is. The summary net effect of these forces then helps us determine if we have power within a given marketplace, along with the factors that could change and alter the strength of our position, or which we would need to change to increase our power.

Figure 7.5 Porter's Five Forces adapted for buying

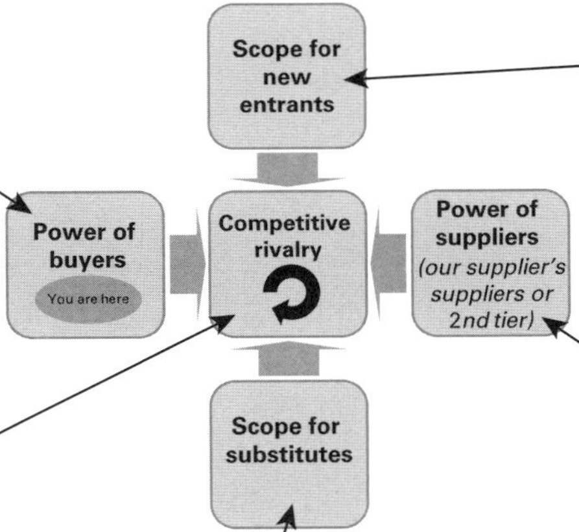

Power of buyers

How much power we and other buyers have in this market. High if:

- There are few buyers
- Buyers purchase in high volumes (relative to the size of a supplier)
- It is easy to switch
- Product or service is *Generic*
- Scope for backward integration
- Absence of control over distribution channels (therefore more choice)

Competitive rivalry

The degree of rivalry between the suppliers in the marketplace. High if:

- Many similar size competitors
- Players fight to keep market their share (eg if industry growth is slow)
- Players want to remain and ideally be dominant in the market
- Capacity has to be added in large increments (temporary oversupply)
- High exit barriers – suppliers hang in there and work harder to compete

Scope for substitutes

The availability or potential for substitutes. High if:

- Substitutes are emerging, available and being adopted already (could be generic, brand, product or need substitutes)
- Substitutes offer price/performance advantage making them compelling
- No or low cost of switching to a substitute

Scope for new entrants

The potential and likelihood for new suppliers to enter this market. High if:

- Low cost/barriers to entry
- No or minimal regulation
- Easy to gain access to existing distribution channels
- Little chance of retaliation by existing players
- Don't necessarily need size to enter
- Absence of advantages for incumbents (eg governmental incentives)

Power of suppliers

The power held by our supplier's suppliers (2nd tier). High if:

- Customers (our suppliers) are locked in
- They provide differentiated or unique products or services
- The market is concentrated (ie a few dominant players)
- Threat of forward integration
- No substitutes for what they do
- They don't rely on this marketplace (ie are active in many markets)

Adapted from Porter (1979)

Central diagram boxes:
- Scope for new entrants
- Power of suppliers (*our supplier's suppliers or 2nd tier*)
- Competitive rivalry
- Scope for substitutes
- Power of buyers (*You are here*)

The old law of supply and demand

Another component within our market assessment is a determination of the basic economic principles of supply and demand. We could go deep into this topic and entire textbooks have been written on this very subject. Economic theory on this subject can at first appear a little daunting, but supply vs demand is in fact something that explains how humans have learnt to trade and exchange value for centuries and this can help our market assessment.

If there is a need or desire then there is demand that, as buyers, we are ready to pay to satisfy. In a marketplace, the overall demand is how much or the quantity of a product or service that is desired by buyers. The quantity demanded depends upon how many buyers are willing to buy at a certain price. Where there is demand there is usually supply; since the time when we started walking upright the human entrepreneurial spirit has spotted demand or even found ways to create it so as to offer goods or services that would meet the buyer's needs and therefore be desired. Supply therefore represents how much the market can offer and this is what quantity of the product or service suppliers are willing to supply for the price they receive.

The market price is therefore a reflection of supply and demand. Assuming all other factors remain equal, the higher the price, the fewer people will demand the product or service and so the lower the demand. Obvious stuff, as if something is so expensive that it means we need to forgo other things we value we will avoid buying it. This is called the law of demand. Similarly, for suppliers, the higher the price the greater the quantity that will be supplied – suppliers will naturally want to supply more if they can realize greater revenues by doing so. This called the law of supply. These dynamics exist and work together so, in simplistic terms, if demand increases prices rise and if demand falls creating an oversupply, prices fall. For several years now, a world shortage of chocolate has been predicted to hit us by 2020 (Tam 2017). An apparent soar in demand for cocoa-based products from China, Indonesia, India and Brazil, coupled with a reduction in availability and poor crops or bad bean quality from the Ivory Coast has created a cocoa bean deficit and prices on world markets has started to soar in recent years. Bad news for chocolate lovers if those price hikes get passed on to consumers, but retailers also know such increases could impact sales so hold off as long as possible, squeezing suppliers for as long as they can – introducing a further dynamic to how supply and demand works.

The dynamics of supply and demand are such that they will naturally tend to drive towards the theoretical state of equilibrium where the level of demand in the market matches the level supplied. Yet markets are slow to respond – if a news story were to break, warning us that new research suggests eating chocolate makes your hair fall out, then some consumers might react to the follicle threat by stopping buying chocolate. Demand would fall instantly, although suppliers will still be producing chocolate at the same output and there will be a time lag before the drop in demand is understood and output is reduced accordingly. Add to this all the chocolate that will already be out there within the distribution channels and there will be a period of oversupply short term. During this time consumers still buying chocolate who are not phased by the risk of hair loss (or for whom that ship has sailed already) will be able to snap up a bargain as prices are cut to shift stock.

Traders and speculators around the world make money by spotting and taking advantage of these moments of temporary imbalance in marketplaces, which in fact never quite end and equilibrium never really exists as markets are constantly changing. Both supply and demand can fluctuate according to price, or price can fluctuate according to supply or demand. Therefore, while we can conclude that the price we pay is determined by what is happening in the marketplace this assumes the market is behaving as a pure market with no other intervention, which doesn't really happen in practice.

It is in the supplier's interest to avoid being at the mercy of market forces and suppliers will influence and even control a market if they can. This can happen in many different ways. If a supplier can create scarcity by reducing supply while demand remains strong, it can yield a higher price. This tactic is used by high-end luxury car manufacturers who will often make a limited production run with long waiting times to create exclusivity (a word marketeers use for creating scarcity), and we have all been at the mercy of global oil production being controlled to hold oil prices at certain levels. Yet such approaches only work in certain scenarios – where there is demand and a lack of alternatives. A Ferrari firmly resides in the *Proprietary* quadrant in our *Power Check* tool! For years OPEC set global oil prices, but increasing production from the Gulf of Mexico in recent years provides oil production capacity that sits outside the OPEC controls, reducing the ability to create scarcity. If a dentist decided to create scarcity by only offering appointments on a Tuesday, the ruse would be short-lived, as loyal customers would quickly find another dentist (unless there was some compelling reason to remain). Scarcity is such a powerful force that sometimes the illusion of scarcity is enough to drive consumer behaviour: online retailers typically include information about apparent current stock levels – warnings such as 'hurry only three left in stock' are commonplace and appear often enough to lead the consumer to hit the 'buy now' button.

So far we have talked about how price affects or is affected by supply and demand, but there are further dynamics of supply and demand that work independently of price. If the price remains fixed but demand suddenly increases, then supply would increase to satisfy demand at this same price. This is a common scenario, where producers see the price point as what the market can bear – in other words the supplier(s) will make more money by increasing production, whereas increasing price might damage market share or compel customers to switch away. If, going back to our chocolate example, a later news story overturned the hair loss story but instead suggested that eating chocolate helped with weight loss, demand for chocolate would undoubtedly rise, yet producers would be keen to keep their price points in order to remain competitive and keep market share, and so production and supply would increase as the overall market would increase. Take away the need to compete, or introduce some collusion amongst players, and then prices might rise also. Similarly, supply could decrease at the same price, say if the predicted cocoa bean shortage takes hold and there are simply not enough cocoa beans to satisfy production with, as unlikely as it might seem, suppliers seeking to hold pricing to remain competitive or because they believe the market won't bear a price increase.

Considering what might be driving supply and demand can help us understand a market. Sometimes the dynamics are easy to spot, and sometimes it may be quite difficult to establish anything meaningful due to complexities of a particular market or what is influencing them. The other components within our market assessment and prior tools can help here along the price model within the *Price Check tool*. In our chocolate example, cocoa beans would be *market pricing,* where the price is determined by pure supply and demand market forces. However, a product such as the Apple iPhone is *value pricing,* with the price of the latest model set by Apple, not apparently by any sort of market supply and demand force but rather based upon what consumers are prepared to pay for the value they perceive. Yet whilst big brands work very hard to create and sustain a *proprietary* position (*Power Check* tool), with great demand and firm global price setting policies, this is only sustainable as long as consumers continue to want to buy. If iPhones suddenly stopped selling because they were too expensive or because alternatives became more attractive at lesser price points, it is likely the pricing policy would quickly change; after all, the cost to produce a smartphone has little relationship to the retail price.

Effects of supply and demand can also be controlled to a degree, and governments around the world do this to protect economies or in response to sociological or environmental factors. For example, a hurricane warning quickly drives people to go and stock up with essential food, gas, other supplies and perhaps torches, batteries, a generator and so on. Such items can quickly become scarce and retailers are often quick to seize the opportunity to make more money by putting up prices of essential items (this becomes *greed pricing* in our *Price Check* tool). Without intervention, the market changes in the light of the hurricane warning. In the state of Florida where hurricane warnings are commonplace, the law prohibits extreme increases in the price of essential commodities, supplies and hotels. 'Price gouging' is taken very seriously and the public are encouraged to report any instances. This state intervention essentially places controls on the market that change how the market works to prevent it working against the consumer in a time of emergency.

We can conclude therefore that everything we buy is ultimately subject to the market forces of supply and demand; sometimes this is pure, immediate and obvious and sometimes it is controlled, delayed, and hidden by the power of governments, brands or uniqueness. As part of our market assessment it can help to consider supply and demand as part of our overall assessment and determine if there are any factors that might present an opportunity now or in the future, eg because of an oversupply or a risk that prices might rise due to increasing demand. This insight can therefore help with our buying decision and can help shape how we might buy, when we might buy or indeed if we might be better placed to fulfil the need in a different way.

Fetch the crystal ball

What is going to happen in the market in the future? If we could know this for certain we could perfectly time when we buy and take full advantage of changing market circumstances. However, the reality here is that this is very difficult to do and if we could do it we should be give up buying and pursue careers as global stock brokers as this tends to pay better by quite some margin. Looking at how a market will change is nothing more than pure speculation, but what we can do is make some informed judgements as to the sorts of things that are likely to happen.

The best predictor of future trends is often current trends. Our market assessment so far has looked at all the factors that help us understand the current position and these too can help us predict what might happen. Some things are more certain than others; for example, if our PESTLE analysis reveals that a change in legislation means what we buy will be subject to a new tax from a certain date, we know that the price we pay will rise then.

Other things are less certain but the work to consider the market will naturally lead us to understand what might happen in the future. This is exactly how professional people whose likelihood depends upon understanding how marketplaces work. There is no exact science here but immersing ourselves in as much as we can understand about the market gives us insight that can help see the future to some degree. With this information we can speculate on the fact that it would be better to fill our tank today rather than wait until tomorrow. What we don't know is by how much it will increase, or what we might have to pay next year, or how much longer we should consider oil-based products as a viable fuel, yet we know enough to help inform our buying decision and indeed how we might negotiate if we have scope to do so.

Understanding our unique position in the market

In addition to understanding how a market behaves, a full understanding of our position in a market requires us to also consider any factors that are unique to us that could advantage or disadvantage us. For example, if we are Microsoft, our size, global spend and the kudos of becoming a supplier to Microsoft carries a power that increases how attractive we are to any market. Yet if we are a small restaurateur buying ingredients we have little strength of position. Therefore, it is only possible to fully understand our position within a market if we also consider the strength of our position within it. This might sound similar to the *Power of Buyers* we explored earlier, but this relates to all buyers from a market, whereas here we are considering any factors unique to us, or a consequence of our internal buying decisions. This might include:

- how much we spend relative to the suppliers overall annual sales;
- how attractive are we to do business with; and
- the degree of choice we have and ability to switch supplier, especially if our choice is limited due to our buying decisions (eg creating a unique specification).

Considering these factors also helps us to find ways to increase our strength and attractiveness or to see new things we can do. Buyers often fail to appreciate how much value suppliers place in supplying to certain organizations. For example, a school buying new playground equipment may lack buying power, as despite some choice it is a relatively low spend for the supplier. Yet a school proposing to promote the supplier, perhaps with prominent signage such as 'Acme Playground Equipment proudly supporting St Mary's School' along with local newspaper articles suddenly becomes a more attractive proposition to the supplier, and one that could demand more attractive pricing. Buying often provides scope for creative thinking to increase attractiveness – most buyers miss this, but all it takes is a bit of brainpower.

CASE STUDY – Understanding the marketplace for commercial print

Once the market for commercial print was huge and strong. Today the situation is far from that. It is a market that has repeatedly reached saturation in recent years with too many suppliers competing to remain *(High Competitive Rivalry)* and falling demand. Markets usually tend to shrink when they become saturated or when the market size decreases or because the need can be fulfilled in another way, eg with a new technology or product. However, in the commercial print market, the shrinkage that would normally be expected through consolidation has not happened to any degree *(Oversupply)*, largely due to the legacy pension commitments *(PESTLE – 'L')* within long-term players.

Demand for print has steadily given way to online (falling *Demand, PESTLE 'S' and 'T', Scope for Substitutes)*, levels of saturation have eased temporarily as suppliers have gone bust, but then the rate of decline here continues to accelerate, meaning it is not long before the market once again becomes saturated. Despite the online revolution there is still demand for print, with the old-fashioned magazine, newspaper or publication still having its place, for the short term at least. This varies with geography. In France print is alive and well, with major retailers regularly bombarding households with printed flyers about the latest offers. In parts of the US such practices are not tolerated due to the environmental impact *(PESTLE – 'S and E')*

New printing technology has also changed this marketplace, helping those who could invest in it to find new competitive advantage by greater capacity at lower equipment price points along with new 'customer tailored' printing options *(PESTLE – 'T')*.

A further dynamic here is an odd one. All these factors should suggest that buyers hold power *(High Power of Buyers)* yet there have been poor buying decisions by publishing houses where buyers appear to have been spooked by risk of losing supply in the rapidly changing market and so have been quick to do long-term deals, thus further stimulating market saturation and oversupply in a declining market.

Finally, industrial commercial printing equipment requires high levels of investment, often funded by long-term borrowing from equity partners, meaning the suppliers in this market hold virtually no power *(Power of Second Tier Suppliers)*. All these things considered mean that the market for commercial print is in our favour and we hold good power here to leverage the market providing we ensure we keep our requirements *Generic*. We don't need to do a long-term deal, we just need to find the best deal now, and if there is a future need repeat the process once more.

Using the tool

The *Market Assessment Tool* – template 8 in the appendix – provides a means to work through each of the components that, when considered together, provide an understanding of the market. Use the tool by conducting as much of the assessment as possible and practice for what we are buying:

1 **PESTLE analysis** – think about what we are attempting to buy and consider any forces or drivers under each of the six headings, now or in the future, that impact this market and therefore could present risk or opportunity. Note anything significant.

2 **'What is the market'** – determine by considering who the suppliers are and what the market boundaries are, if these are set or if we could look wider and strengthen our position.

3 **Our strength in this market** – determine the unique factors that could give us (or deprive us of) strength such as spend, degree of choice or our overall attractiveness. Could we improve our strength by changing aspects of our buying decisions?

4 **Supply vs demand** – If possible, assess current supply vs demand within the marketplace. Try to find out if there is or likely to be a shift in either that could impact the marketplace.

5 **Porter's Five Forces** – Work through each of the five forces in turn. Make an assessment of how strong each force is and mark each on each gauge. Note the rationale for each.

6 **Summary market assessment** – Consider the combined effect of all parts of the assessment so far and decide, on balance, what is happening in the marketplace between being 'against us' or 'in our favour'. Mark this on the gauge and note the key insights gained. Also consider and note any factors that would help maximize our power position.

Tool 9 – power buying plan

Purpose – to develop a plan for how we will buy based upon the outputs and insights of all the tools so far.

How to use it – once tools 1–8 have been completed and we are sufficiently informed to determine how to buy.

When needed – every buying scenario needs a plan whether informal 'in the mind of the buyer', or a more detailed one as outlined in this section.

Tool 9 is the *Power Buying Plan* where we determine how to buy and fulfil the need we identified back at the start, by responding to all the preparation work, analysis and insight so far. For a very simple purchase or where we have no choice then our buying plan may be straightforward and we just need to get on and buy. For other scenarios then we need to match our total buying power, perhaps strengthened as a result of specific actions we have taken along the way, to a buying approach that will best suit our needs. Where our buying is anything other than straightforward then there is no surefire process to determine the best way to buy, instead we need some good old-fashioned brainpower to take all of the pieces of the jigsaw that represent the tools worked so far and use these to decide how to move forward. The template for tool 9 guides us through this process with four key activities that help determine a power buying plan and I shall explore each in turn.

Power buying readiness

How we buy must respond directly to the overall objective we are trying to satisfy, defined back in tool 1. However, we have come a long way since then. Perhaps our original objective (eg secure lowest price or best service, etc) remains appropriate or perhaps the journey to this point now suggests a reframing of our objective. For example, if the original objective was to buy what was specified by someone else in our organization, but we have been able to convince that individual that we could buy better by considering other suppliers, then our objective has changed. We must also check back to the needs and wants that we identified in step 1 to make sure these are fully formed and, most importantly, have been updated where relevant based upon our work thus far.

Ultimately however, no matter how great the opportunities we may have identified to buy better may be, we can only act upon these if there is scope for intervention to do something differently. If we do not have this, or cannot influence others to agree to do something differently, then we have no choice but to get on and buy what is specified. This is a common scenario, and one that buyers in organizations should not become disheartened by. Before we go any further we must therefore determine whether we have remit to influence how we buy, and, if we do, the next step is to consider what buying power we might hold.

Do we have buying power?

How we choose to buy depends upon how much buying power we hold. The tools in steps 2 and 3 each consider a different dimension of buying preparation and power. Individually they are useful to understand or position. Collectively they inform us as to what our overall power position is. Again, this requires some brainpower to consider the net position and so the gauge shown in Figure 7.6 (and also included in the tool 9 template) combines the outputs from our *Power Check* tool, *Price Check* and *Market Assessment*. We can use this to place an arrow on the dial according to where we judge our power position to be ranging from no power (eg in a *Proprietary* buying scenario with no ability influence this) to strong power (eg in *Generic* with the market strongly in our favour). The different states from all the tools are given on the gauge in power ascending order. Note that the relative

Figure 7.6   Summarizing our buying power

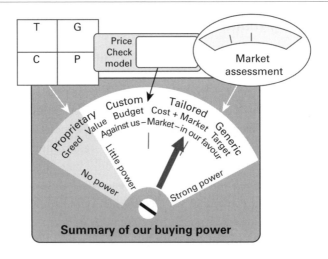

positioning of these doesn't necessarily signify a relationship between them but rather a guide to make an overall assessment that should err towards the lowest position any one of these tool outputs suggest. It should be remembered that this is not an exact science but a guide and means to reflect on what power we might hold.

Time to 'power up'

How can we improve our buying power? With our current power position determined, then assuming we have scope to influence how we buy, we can consider how we might 'power up'. We have in fact already begun this process back at tool 6 when we considered the different *Power Boosters* we could apply. We now return to these and with our overall buying objective (or any revised objective) in mind we can check again that we have the optimum mix of *Power Boosters*. Then, for each one we have selected, we can determine the specific courses of action we will go and take to use each booster. For example, if we have identified we can buy better by changing specification, then the action is simply to do just this and update our *Needs and Wants* accordingly ready to buy to our new requirements.

The power buying plan

The final part of our power buying plan is to determine how we will buy and the exact buying strategy we are going to move forward with. There are many different buying options open to us and which one(s) we select must be determined by all of our work so far. Certain *Power Boosters* naturally point to specific buying options including *Demand* or *Competition* and I'll expand on these below. The remaining ones are more general and tend to be complementary to a buying option rather than defining the option. The template for tool 9 guides us through the step of linking *Power Boosters* to buying options.

Demand buying options – make vs buy vs doing without

Buying options derived from the power booster *Demand* are:

- don't buy – buy less or do without; or
- don't buy – do it ourselves or satisfy the need in a different way.

Instead of a buying plan around how we will source, both of these options are around how we will not source. Good buying doesn't always mean we end up buying, it means we determine the best way to fulfil the need. Buying less or doing without could in fact be the most appropriate course of action for our organization. For example, if we want to reduce costs associated with business travel for employees, the biggest cost reduction may well come from introducing and enforcing new policies around permitted reasons for and forms of travel. Similarly we could do it ourselves. The 'make vs buy' decision is a fundamental strategic decision for any company and one that will shape how a company is set up and operates for many years. Such a decision is not always straightforward but there are many things to consider beyond the analysis of our costs versus what a supplier proposes to charge us. In the early days of outsourcing back in the 1980s, many of these initiatives failed spectacularly, creating higher costs and quality issues. Firms quickly learnt that they didn't really know their true costs of doing it internally or failed to adequately transfer knowledge. Outsourcing has come a long way since then.

If we end up choosing a buying option around managing demand, then this is not just a buying decision but a strategic direction that the full organization must sign up to. This is a classic example of how effective buying must be more than something any procurement or buying function does, but an organization-wide concern.

Competitive buying options

Buying options derived from the power booster *Competition* are:

- find the best deal in the market;
- get multiple proposals or quotations and pick the best; or
- run a competitive bid process to get quotations and pick the best.

Buying options for the power booster *Competition* are the courses of action we can take to take advantage of competition within a marketplace. Clearly such options are only relevant where there can be competition where there is more than one supplier we can consider in the market, eg we are in *Tailored or Generic* in the *Power Check Tool* and the buying decisions that define our *Needs and Wants* have not constrained the potential marketplace. There are different ways we can use competition to realize an effective buying outcome, all based around our overall objective along with our *Needs and Wants*. These include:

- *Find the best deal in the market* – this is often all we need to do to buy well and something we do every day as consumers, and we are probably all quite good at it. To do this we simply take *Needs and Wants* and find the best deal to deliver these from the potential suppliers in line with our overall objective. However, this simple buying approach is often impeded by organizational systems, custom and practice. For example, if office supplies can only be purchased with a purchase order or on account from the appointed supplier's catalogue, then the chances are that that organization is overpaying for office supplies and missing the benefits competition can bring. Instead a search on an online market-place such as Amazon armed with a company credit card will probably find a much better deal for the same items albeit a little less convenient.

- *Get multiple proposals or quotations* – we ask prospective suppliers to make a proposal or provide a firm quotation against our *Needs and Wants* (or extracting the relevant bits) for the goods or service we want to buy, we then select the best deal based upon our overall buying objective (which might not necessarily be the lowest cost option). This buying approach could be informal, eg based upon issuing a verbal request or part of a more formal process. Getting multiple quotations is a common procedural requirement placed on buyers, usually when the company doesn't understand how good buying works. Policies such as 'we must obtain three quotations for everything we buy and chose the lowest' are not always effective. Such measures are usually applied as a crude means to manage junior or inexperienced buyers while trying to prevent favour-itism or corruption. Obtaining multiple quotations has its place and can create a competitive tension between players to make the best proposal they can, but only where there are multiple suppliers available to us, who are keen to win our business (*Tailored* or *Generic*). When we choose this buying approach suppliers must understand they are bidding against others. This should naturally drive things towards the best price point in the market, making effective buying easy.

- *Run a competitive bid process* – this is a more formal means to obtain multiple proposals or quotations. This buying approach has many differ-ent names: bid, tender, invitation to tender (ITT), competitive process, request for proposal (RFP) or request for quotation (RFQ). No matter what the process is called, the purpose is the same and is a formal means for a number of suppliers to make proposals and/or provide quotations. The winning 'bid' is then selected based upon some pre-determined selection criteria. In olden times a competitive bids process was a cumbersome undertaking – extensive bid documents were sent to prospective suppliers outlining the requirements. Suppliers would confirm their interest and then provide a comprehensive bid document by a set deadline. Large packs would be delivered by hand just prior to the deadline (to remove the risk of a bid being opened early and pricing intelligence passed to a competitor) and would then be opened and pored over in smoke-filled basements. Today most competitive bid processes are run online using one of the many e-sourcing platforms available. This buying approach is at the centre of most significant public sector buying around the world, often with extensive rules around how the process must be run and managed to ensure the utmost transparency and fair decision making. A step on from this process, also run using an e-sourcing platform, is the eAuction where companies make bids online against competitors in real time to win the business. I shall return to this later. Table 7.2 gives the steps involved in running a competitive bid process.

Other buying options

Other buying options derived from various power boosters might include:

- continue with the same supplier and buy what we bought last time, or
- choose to source from a trusted supplier that we have a long-term relationship with.

There are buying options that align with buying based upon a relationship with a supplier or choosing to stick with something we know. It doesn't always follow that to buy well there must be some sort of competitive process. Sometimes the greatest opportunity comes by developing existing arrangements. This assumes that we have the ability to choose this buying option and we may need to be prepared to demonstrate why this decision is right for the organization. Policy and procedure may require a competitive process, especially in the public sector, so deciding to continue with an existing supplier may not always be an option that is open to us. Where it is, this option is relevant where there is clear benefit to continuing with a certain buying approach. For example, if we are in *Custom* in our *Power Check* tool, with a supplier who is co-developing something with us, clearly it would make sense to continue this assuming the relationship is working well. Here, running a competitive bid process would do little other than damage the relationship. Instead value is secured by figuring out ways to work more closely with the supplier to unlock mutual benefit.

Table 7.2 The steps in running a competitive bid process (aka tender, RFP or RFQ)

Sequence	Activity	Key considerations
1 Decide bid format	Determine how the bid process will run: • Fully online using an eSourcing platform • Online with downloadable documents • Via documents that are e-mailed or physically sent	• Design the bid process around the format to be used. • Consider any policies or procedures that must be complied with, eg public sector procurement rules. • Consider the ability for prospective suppliers to participate – if they are new to online they may need some support!
2 Define the requirements	Define the requirement along with the process suppliers must follow and how bids must be submitted	• Include background to the company, this specific requirement and the overall need. • If possible indicate the scale of what is needed (how much, by when, etc) and ideally this should be attractive to a supplier. • Define the specific requirements the supplier must meet based upon the needs and wants – set out the responses required from the supplier and in what format they are required for each. These could include a mix of descriptive responses (eg to questions such as 'describe how you will fulfil requirement X') and precise values (eg 'state your proposed fees for Y'). • Define the selection criteria that will be applied to select the supplier – Be clear whether suppliers will be selected based upon their bid or if there might be further selection and negotiation prior to making a decision. • Define the process and timeline for the bid activity. • Include provision for suppliers to raise questions – to ensure fairness all questions raised and the responses given should be shared with all other bidders. • Include a legal disclaimer asserting copyright over content, making a bid is at the supplier's cost and that nothing constitutes any sort commitment to buy.

(continued)

Table 7.2 (*Continued*)

Sequence	Activity	Key considerations
3 Execute the process and manage the bidders	Prepare bidders in advance, invite them to participate then send them the bid or tender requirements e-invite/ document, manage suppliers through the bid activity	• Are they interested? – warm them up in advance and check if they will participate. • Do bidders need help to participate or use any online platform? If so organize this. • Ensure a point of contact for any issues. • Invite questions by a predetermine date. Ensure any questions and responses are shared across all bidders. • It is good to check suppliers will be getting a response in ahead of the closing deadline.
4 Analyse responses	Analyse the responses, synthesize and summarize the detail provided evaluate against pre- determined selection criteria	• Review all responses – use the predetermined selection criteria to evaluate responses and develop a summary evaluation.
5 Select supplier/ solution	Select the supplier(s) or solution(s) that most meets our needs or determine how to move forward	• Determine the supplier(s) or solution(s) we want to proceed with. • Depending upon how we have set up the process, appoint them or proceed to further selection activity and/or negotiation.

Using the tool

The *Buying Plan* – template 9 in the appendix – provides a means to summarize the work so far and determine how we will buy. Use as follows:

1 **Power buying readiness check** – check we are ready to buy by verifying that our original objectives remain appropriate; if so, restate, and if not, redefine these. Check our *Needs and Wants* are fully defined and updated and finally determine if there is scope for intervention or to influence what we buy. If there is none then simply proceed to buy otherwise continue through these steps.

2 **Summary of our current power position** – review the outputs from the *Power Check* tool (4), the *Price Check* tool (5) and our *Market Assessment* (8) and determine our overall power position based upon the combined insights from these. Draw an indicator arrow on the gauge accordingly (select the least power position from the three insights).

3 **Power up plan** – review our selection of the *Power Boosters* (tool 6) based upon our power position and restate/revise these. For each one, determine the specific action we will take to make each power booster work.

4 **Power up plan** – based upon our *Power Boosters* selection determine how we will buy from the different buying options available to us.

Summary

The key learning points from this chapter:

1 Step 3 *Determine* contains three tools that lead us to a clear way forward for how we will buy.

2 This step involves good fact find around suppliers and the market and also synthesizes all of the outputs from the first three steps of our *Power Buying Process.*

3 Tool 7 – *Supplier Fact find* helps us determine the suppliers out there that could supply this, which ones might be suitable and then to find out everything we know about them.

4 Tool 8 – the *Market Assessment* tool provides a structured means to determine what the market is, what is happening in the market (if it is

in our favour or against us, now and predicted) our unique position in this market and therefore what we can do to maximize our power in this market.

5 A rigourous market assessment has a number of components including using key tools such as PESTLE analysis, the buyer's variant of Porter's Five Forces and considering supply vs demand in the market.

6 Tool 9 – the *Power Buying Plan* is a means to determine how we will buy and the buying strategy that we will use. It guides us to check our buying readiness, our net buying power (considering all the tools we have worked), how we will power ourselves using our selected *Power Boosters* and the buying options that these point to.

Step 4 – securing the best deal

This chapter explores the three tools associated with making the deal happen. We explore how to finally select our supplier (or solution), how to negotiate where we have scope to do so and how to contract for what we are going to buy.

Pathway questions addressed in this chapter

13 What supplier (or solution) should we choose and how do we decide?

14 Should we negotiate? If so how do we go about doing this?

15 What sort of contract do we need? What do we need to do to agree the contract?

Making our power buying plan happen

We have come a long way in our *Power Buying Process* and by now we have developed a plan for how we will buy, informed by consulting and engaging internally, researching and assessing the external suppliers and market and by working through some core tools to help develop a plan that respond directly to our situation and strength in this market. All we have to do now is realize our power buying plan. This might seem straightforward. Surely we just get on and buy? Perhaps, but depending on what our power buying plan is, how we make the deal happen is as important as our planning to get here.

Depending on what our plan defines, we may need some sort of selection step. Furthermore, depending upon our situation, there may or may not be scope to negotiate with the supplier. If there is, then what we do here can make all the difference to our buying outcome. Finally, the deal is only complete once we have contracted with the supplier for the goods and services. There are many ways we could end up doing this, and once again depending upon our situation, how we do this can make all the difference to how the need is fulfilled and the overall value we secure from the engagement with this supplier.

The three tools contained in this step are given in the most logical sequence, but in practice they work in concert to bring the deal to its optimum crescendo. Negotiation may be a component of how we select a supplier and specific aspects of the deal we agree might subsequently be incorporated into a contract, or our negotiation might include discussions around specific contractual terms. Step 4 *Deal* works by applying these three tools together (Figure 8.1). We will look at each in turn.

Tool 10 – select supplier (or solution)

Purpose – to select the suppliers we will buy from or, where our power buying plan suggests a non-supplier option, the solutions we will implement.

How to use it – apply by developing and implementing an appropriate selection approach.

When needed – when it is necessary to select a supplier or suppliers, eg to conclude a competitive bid process.

Supplier selection is, as the name suggests, an approach to select one or more suppliers with whom we want to engage. It is a tool that is only relevant where we need to select a supplier, eg where our buying plan has determined a *Competition* based option – if we have already decided who the supplier will be, perhaps because we are committed to a long-standing relationship or we lack choice, then this tool is not required. Furthermore, if we have decided our solution does not involve a new supplier, such as a *Demand* option around reducing or eliminating the need, or fulfilling the need in another way such as doing it ourselves (make rather than buy), then the

Figure 8.1   Step 4 – Deal

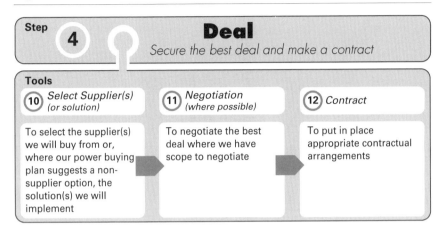

principles of this tool can still be relevant but to select a solution rather than a supplier. This tool 10 is placed at this point as this is the most logical place for the tool to sit, but in practice this runs throughout steps 3 and 4.

Selecting a supplier is like putting all the candidates into a funnel (see Figure 8.2) and running a series of selection and evaluation activities that progressively eliminate those who will not deliver our *Needs and Wants* whilst positively identifying the suppliers that offer the best solution from those that remain. The aim is to arrive at just one or a few with whom we wish to move forward. The selection process does not need to identify the final supplier but might be used to identify a very small shortlist with which we will negotiate and ultimately agree a contract. This selection process is typical within the commercial sector and things can easily change mid-process, for example requirements could change, we might identify the need for additional evaluation, discussions with suppliers might highlight new ideas we want to include, and so on. However, in the public sector this funnel might be quite different – it will need to comply with the provisions of the prevailing procurement legislation, which will usually demand that the selection process is clearly defined at the outset. Once initiated there is little scope to make changes. Furthermore, in the public sector there may be fewer steps, greater rigour and often less scope for negotiation refinement along the way with an underlying requirement that all suppliers are treated equally with transparency.

Figure 8.2 gives a representation of the overall supplier selection funnel process that runs across several tools with the four stages of the overall process: pre-qualification, the main supplier evaluation activity (which may

Figure 8.2 The supplier selection 'funnel' process

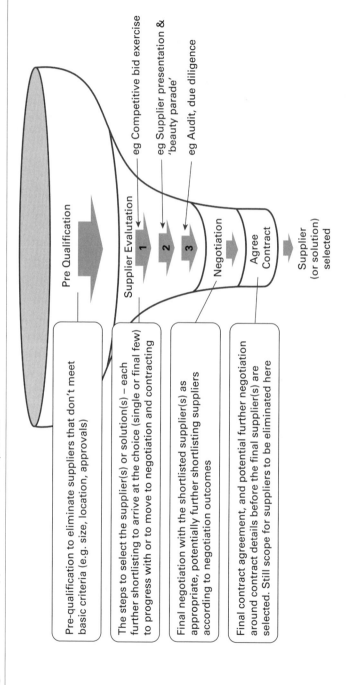

Pre Qualification

Supplier Evalutation

eg Competitive bid exercise

1

eg Supplier presentation & 'beauty parade'

2

eg Audit, due diligence

3

Negotiation

Agree Contract

Supplier (or solution) selected

Pre-qualification to eliminate suppliers that don't meet basic criteria (e.g. size, location, approvals)

The steps to select the supplier(s) or solution(s) – each further shortlisting to arrive at the choice (single or final few) to progress with or to move to negotiation and contracting

Final negotiation with the shortlisted supplier(s) as appropriate, potentially further shortlisting suppliers according to negotiation outcomes

Final contract agreement, and potential further negotiation around contract details before the final supplier(s) are selected. Still scope for suppliers to be eliminated here well involve several separate components), then negotiation (tool 11) and finally agreeing the contract (tool 12). Pre-qualification is the elimination of those suppliers who will not meet some fundamental requirements so as to not spend any more time considering them – by now we may have already done this back in tool 7 (*Supplier Fact Find*). Negotiation and agreeing the contract are covered later in this chapter.

Supplier evaluation could include several steps, each refining and further shortlisting the potential number of suppliers we are considering to arrive at the supplier(s) we will use, or select/further-shortlist during negotiation and contracting. Supplier evaluation could take many forms: for example we might simply review the potential suppliers and perhaps their quotations and decide who to use. Alternatively, we might conduct a more formal process, where suppliers are taken through a structured evaluation process, with each evaluation step defined in advance and the results of applying the process recorded to create a fully transparent process with accountability regarding the appointment of suppliers. In Western culture, transparency and accountability within professional procurement is regarded as essential good practice for most firms, with processes and procedures in this respect being common practice. In the public sector these processes are prescribed for buying entities and compliance is tightly managed.

Typical steps to evaluate a supplier as part of supplier selection might include the following sequential activities.

Supplier evaluation phase 1: select or shortlist based upon criteria

The first step towards selecting a supplier from those we have pre-qualified is to run some sort of evaluation and selection process. We explored this as part of tool 9 (*Buying Plan*). Here, for *Competition* scenarios, our way forward might be to 'find the best deal in the market', 'get multiple quotations and pick the best' or to run a 'full competitive bid process' (typically referred to as a tender, RFP or RFQ). Irrespective of our approach, we are still applying some sort of selection criteria to decide the supplier or shortlist of suppliers we want to proceed with. If we select a single supplier here, further comparative evaluations are not needed and we can skip straight to negotiation, if relevant. Table 7.2 in the previous chapter gives the steps involved in a competitive bid process.

Supplier evaluation 2: the beauty parade

Following a competitive bid process where suppliers have provided a written proposal and perhaps quotation to show how they propose to meet our needs, we might need some further evaluation to verify what they say, understand the proposal some more and make a final selection. For example, if we are buying consultancy services to support a project, the supplier's bid documents might be beautifully crafted, telling a compelling story of how the company can do great things; their fee proposal may also be favourable. However, until we meet the people who are going to do the work and talk with them about how they will tackle the assignment, it is not possible to fully evaluate the supplier's proposal. There are other factors also, and a typical competitive bid process only requires the supplier to answer our questions in a precise way. When we engage with the supplier in person, we open up the free-flow opportunity for the supplier to tell us what they can actually do, which may not have come across in the answers to our questions.

Furthermore, if we are going to work closely with the supplier, we need to be sure we can work with the people concerned. A written bid document will not tell us this, and the only way we can find out is by meeting them. This step might also be concerned with evaluating a product, a process, capability or approach to a programme of work.

A frequently used supplier selection activity is a supplier presentation, often called a 'beauty parade'. Just like hopeful beauty queens would parade in front of pageant judges, the same name has come to be used when short-listed suppliers give a final presentation regarding their proposals, one after another, to an assembled body of those who have an interest in what we are buying. A typical final presentation agenda (which should be set in advance) might include;

- summary of the requirements and the process by us;
- summary of the proposal from the supplier;
- how the supplier plans to implement new arrangements;
- how the supplier will look after our account;
- fee proposals, and;
- questions and answers (two-way).

The supplier presentation or beauty parade helps raise the competitive tension among the participants, as each knows that only the best will win.

Suppliers will therefore go to great lengths to project their offer and themselves in the best way, but they will also want to understand what it is we most want and how we will make our decision. This is good, as it is a sign of the suppliers matching their capabilities to our needs. Time should be given in the agenda to describe what we want and for any questions they have for us (ideally at the end of the session).

The supplier presentation is an excellent opportunity for supplier conditioning. It may, for example, be appropriate to ask the supplier to arrive with revised fee proposals or even to begin to attempt to negotiate their fees. Furthermore, a supplier who arrives and sees a competitor leaving from the previous session is likely to sense the need to raise the game. There is rarely any need to hide this, and even if we tried to, suppliers will attempt to find out the nature of the game by looking at the visitor book if there is one or by asking how many sessions are being run, whether the competition is national or global and so on.

The *Select Supplier* – template 10 in the appendix – provides a structure to conduct supplier evaluations for use by an individual or a team, for example the assembled group for the supplier presentations. Core to this is the identification of the selection criteria that we will use to evaluate the prospective suppliers, including the option of using weighted scoring. Criteria and weightings, should always be worked out in advance to avoid bias, and using an approach such as this to select suppliers provides a transparent and auditable basis for how we selected a supplier. For a team-based evaluation, a fully numeric assessment based upon the average of team members' individual scores can help dilute individual's preferences for a given supplier from gaining momentum and group discussion to debate and agree final scores helps ensure the final determination is robust and, more importantly, has the full support of the team. Furthermore, where a team has made a fact-based assessment leading to a structured determination it is difficult for others who might not support the choice of suppliers to challenge, oppose or resist the decision thereby helping to clear the way to realize our buying plan with our choice of suppliers. This is an important part of a team-based supplier selection process and crucially one that helps make the team accountable for the decision rather than the individual.

Supplier evaluation 3: due diligence

Sometimes it is necessary for a further evaluation phase to conduct checks or verifications of the supplier or what is being proposed. This step is often called due diligence and is about ensuring that the supplier really is who they say they are and really can do what they say they can do. It is about ensuring they have the necessary organizational capability, systems and arrangements in place. This step is like an employer offering us a job subject to taking up references, and here is where we check out the supplier's references. It might involve an audit of their facility, checking they have stated accreditations or certifications or financial checks or any other checks we might feel are necessary or are required to carry out.

Finalizing selection

Once our selection is made (either here or following negotiation and contracting) we must appoint the suppliers, let them know they have been successful and agree next steps. It is equally important to notify those suppliers who have been unsuccessful, something easily forgotten or neglected in the excitement of appointing the successful supplier, yet those who have been unsuccessful will most likely have spent considerable time and effort to get as far as they have. They may have incurred costs to support their sales process and attend meetings. Despite the fact that this is part of the game and of the cost of sales, it is good practice to provide feedback as to why their proposal fell short as well as keeping them 'on side' – we may need them in the future, especially if our selected supplier lets us down. Guard against unsuccessful suppliers trying to keep a 'foot in the door' or re-open discussions around a new improved offer that might change our mind (clearly raising the question why they didn't do that before). There is also the chance they may want to claim some sort of 'foul play' but this is unlikely as most suppliers will seek to keep future options open. However, if this happens:

- be clear that the decision is made and is final;
- keep the conversation around general point – don't get drawn into a debate;
- give balanced feedback – praise them for everything that was strong and outline the areas where the proposal fell short;
- if possible, offer hope for the future and outline opportunities the supplier might have to make new proposals, and;
- thank them for their efforts and hard work.

For *Demand* options where there is to be no supplier or no new supplier but rather we need to select a solution, a similar 'funnel' type evaluation can also be used, applying selection criteria to select a solution against our *Needs and Wants*. Other evaluation steps here might include internal surveys, testing, trials and consultation with those involved and so on.

Using the tool

The *Select Supplier* – template 10 in the appendix – provides a means to evaluate and select a supplier (or solution). Use as follows:

1 **Determine selection criteria** – extract relevant requirements from our *Needs and Wants*. All core *needs* require a simple 'go/no go' check. Include relevant *wants* and additional criteria for other relevant factors such as how easy it might be to switch suppliers, how the supplier might implement a new supply/service, future potential, etc.

2 **Determine weightings** – Weightings can be determined for each criteria according to their relative importance. Compliance with our *needs* should not be weighted but a 'go/no go' test with scoring for the rest. Agree how scoring will work - a simple 1–5 scale where 5 is high is recommended.

3 **List shortlisted suppliers**

4 **Brief the evaluation team** – for team evaluations, brief the team on the evaluation process, provide each with part-completed Supplier Selection template, agree how the team will score, eg what would constitute scoring a 5, etc, awarding scores relative to the other suppliers. Be clear if we are selecting a single supplier or a final shortlist during this activity.

5 **Score the supplier/proposal, note evaluations** – each reviewer should score each supplier against the criteria set, using the agreed scale and multiplying each score against the weightings and ensuring scoring is relative and note key observations.

6 **Calculate totals** – where a team is reviewing, calculate the average totals from across the team, discuss, debate, review why any unexpected results might have occurred, adjust scores where the team agree one or more individual scores are misaligned, but be careful not to backward engineer the scoring to arrive at a favoured outcome.

7 **Agree supplier(s)** – agree the supplier(s) we will select or who will proceed to negotiation. Note any qualifying factors such as 'we will use this supplier if we can negotiate the price down to X', etc.

8 **Appoint the successful and notify the unsuccessful**

Tool 11 – negotiation

Purpose – to negotiate the best deal where we have scope to negotiate.

How to use it – apply when there is scope to negotiate and then deploy the appropriate approach, negotiation style, tactics and techniques according to what power we have along with our value and relationship objectives.

When needed – Useful to maximize outcomes where there is scope to negotiate.

We have arrived at the *Negotiation* tool. If we have been considering multiple suppliers then, whilst our evaluations are complete, the supplier selection process may not be truly finished until we have concluded any negotiations and contracted with the suppliers. Suppliers we previously selected could still fail here; there could be points of dispute that our negotiation efforts fail to overcome or a contractual difference that can't be resolved. Worse still, the supplier might pull out at this final stage, which is a real possibility either as a tactic or if, for example, after reflection, they've decided their offer in their bid was too low and is unsustainable. We must be prepared for this possibility, perhaps keeping other shortlisted suppliers in reserve until we are certain we don't need them.

Negotiation is placed at this point in the *Power Buying Process* as this is where is most logically sits, however, negotiation runs throughout the entire process and every supplier interaction. This section provides an introduction to this big topic along with a highly effective negotiation planning tool (tool 11). Negotiation is a topic that fills an entire book and indeed my second book *Negotiation for Procurement Professionals* (also by Kogan Page) does just this and provides the Red Sheet® methodology for negotiation planning, and is recommended if you wish to develop further capability here.

A skill for life

Negotiation is a skill for life. It is something we do every day, something we have done all our lives and we are all probably quite good at it, even if we don't realize it. Despite this, when it comes to negotiating to buy something as an individual or professionally many people believe this requires special skills. In fact, it is more about building on our innate capability by learning how to use a structured process, understanding who we are (our personalities) and therefore how we might need to behave or act in a negotiation and, by building our own personal repertoire of negotiation tactics, techniques and things we can do to handle specific situations.

Negotiation is the process by which two or more parties confer or interact to reach a consensus or agreement. It is a means for parties to deal with differences or reach a resolution to a problem. We *confer* by the way we engage with our opponent(s). This may be face-to-face, and indeed in many cultures this remains the only way any sort of negotiation would be done, however increasingly we negotiate remotely, say by e-mail, phone, online eAuction, Skype or video conference and even by text. In fact, our daily text exchanges with family members are often mini-negotiations, although I doubt many of us view them in this way. Remote negotiation requires a slightly different skill set to those we do face-to-face and I'll explore that later. Reaching *agreement* is the aim of any negotiation and there are many things to consider here to do this well.

No magic fairy dust

Negotiation is not a magic fairy dust that can be sprinkled over any situation to unlock a magical outcome. Sometimes it is possible to achieve great results just by negotiating well, and sometimes, no matter what we might do, we cannot influence the outcome in any way. In any given buying scenario, there may or may not be scope to negotiate and so our first step is to determine what scope there is to negotiate, and even where there is scope the extent to which we might be able to wield good negotiation power. I often get approached by friends that know that I write about and teach negotiation who ask if I could help them with a particular high-cost purchase. Sometimes I can help or provide some pointers, sometimes though the best deal is the one on offer and there is simply no way it can be improved upon. Trying to negotiate for a leading brand product in a retail outlet is unlikely to get us very far. At best, we may be able to take advantage of a current promotion or a discount for a bulk purchase. Big brand companies will protect price points fiercely to preserve their brand value and will have strict policies for those selling their products so there is absolutely no scope to negotiate – the price offered is the price that will always be paid.

When buying a new car, if we research the market, time and pace our engagement, and push hard for all sorts of concessions we may be able to do a good deal, and perhaps one that is better than that the person before us got, but the deal will only be as good as the most the dealer or manufacturer is ever prepared to give away and then we must work hard to get it. Here our negotiation opponent will be preserving their margin through strict pricing policies effected by highly experienced sales staff who can take us through a stage-managed process. There is some limited scope for us to negotiate and then mainly around securing added value 'add-ons' rather than pure price reduction within the boundaries the sales person will be working with.

In contrast, walking into an artist's studio keen to buy a painting might present good scope to negotiate for the desired piece. Here the artist is the decision maker for a *Value Priced (Price Check* tool*)* item (ie price is based upon the perceived value not the cost of paint, canvas, time, etc).

The artist might be keen to preserve his value in the market or might spot the fact that the buyer likes the painting and has formed an emotional attachment, so is confident in holding firm in his position. Yet, if the same artist was struggling and desperately needed to sell a painting in order to pay his rent then here there might be an opportunity to negotiate hard and strike an incredible deal, way better than the same artist would otherwise be prepared to do. In this situation there is great scope to negotiate but the outcome depends upon the prevailing circumstances and of course our ability to negotiate.

There is only scope to negotiate if both parties might be willing or are able to make a deal and can reach a point of agreement. For example, if our artist is adamant that he would not sell any painting below £1,000, but the most we would ever be prepared to pay is £200, then no matter how hard we negotiate we will not reach an agreement. Yet if these were only starting positions and both parties were ready to move maybe a deal could be possible. We call this the Zone of Mutual Agreement (ZoMA) and a negotiation can only be successful if we believe there is most likely a ZoMA. Part of our planning and early engagement with a supplier is therefore about attempting to decide if a ZoMA exists. If we are certain it does not, then there is no scope to negotiate.

Scope to negotiate is not only about whether we can make a deal – there may be situations where it is inappropriate to negotiate. For example, where our relationship with the seller is of paramount importance, then attempting to negotiate might be damaging. This doesn't mean we should never negotiate in a long-term relationship, but our negotiation approach needs to match our relationship aims here (I'll return to this). There are times when it is OK to decide not to negotiate. This is something many of us do in life everyday with loved ones, by electing not to negotiate about something but accept it for the good of keeping the relationship strong.

Our scope for negotiation, which therefore determines how we proceed is one of four options:

- no scope to negotiate (eg there is no ZoMA or we can only buy this on the seller's terms) – Don't try! Either do the deal on the seller's terms or walk away;
- not appropriate to negotiate (eg the relationship is more important and negotiation could be damaging) – Avoid negotiating for now or for good depending upon the scenario;
- limited scope to negotiate – Here we can try to secure whatever we can such as some added value items/service; and
- there is scope to negotiate – In which case we should proceed to plan our negotiation.

We can determine scope to negotiate by reviewing the results of our *Power Check, Price Check* and *Market Assessment* tools. *Generic* or *Tailored,* in a market that is in our favour, could put is in a good position whereas *Proprietary* with *Greed Pricing* would suggest there is no scope.

Negotiation blindness

Where there is good scope to negotiate then the next question is what sort of results might be possible? There is a common misconception that experienced negotiators possess some sort of special technique to know what good looks like and the precise best point that could be reached in a negotiation. The reality is very different. I mentioned buying a car: imagine if we tried to negotiate a good deal for the car, if we could know the lowest price point the sales person could go to and all the different things he or she was authorized to include in the deal. Then our negotiation would be easy – we would simply need to keep going until we got everything. However, in reality it is unlikely we would know this.

In most negotiations, we are blind or, at best, have only some idea what the greatest possible outcome might be, and even then we may lack the power to get close to this. Clearly what the seller will want is to not give much away. Add to this the fact that the sales person may well be incentivized based upon how much they sell, and will most likely have received much more training in sales, negotiation and perhaps even psychological techniques, and we have our work cut out to make any real progress.

There are times when good research and tools such as cost breakdown analysis can equip us with precise intelligence about the best possible outcome for a negotiation. Usually this is when we are buying non-complex goods or services that we would find in the *Generic* or *Tailored* quadrant in our *Power Check* tool. For example, if we are buying cleaning services for a known number of cleaners, working a defined number of hours, we could determine the cost of labour, materials and reasonable management time, overheads and profit to figure out what a good price for the service would be. But this is not something that is possible when trying to buy a new car, and even if we could we are just a single consumer buying from a large organization so our power is limited.

Getting *Agreement* is part of both sales and negotiation and if we are mostly blind then we need some other way to gauge when we have reached the point that we can make this agreement and close on the deal. This is where we get to the heart of what negotiation is – a stage-managed display of interactions, tactics and human behaviour, sometimes informed by facts and data, sometimes not, where agreement is reached at the point parties *feel* like they have reached the best point. Crucially, it is often not what or where the agreement is that is important but how parties feel about it, and most of the things people do when negotiating are in fact designed to make the other feel a certain way. Imagine trying to buy the car and feeling like the seller was ripping us off and demanding more money than was reasonable, we would most likely walk away. If we didn't, it would leave a bitter taste and it would be unlikely for us to return, we would probably tell others not to go there also. Instead if we negotiate with the sales person and come to feel like we have secured a great deal, perhaps securing a good price reduction and some added extras along the way, then we will feel good and won't want to let such a good deal get away. Therefore, negotiation is more about selling, no matter what side we are on, and is how parties create the illusion of a great deal to compel the other to agree. In contrast if the seller was too eager to give discount and add-ons it would feel too easy and leave us thinking we did a bad deal because more could have been had. The creation of this illusion during negotiation is a complex process and those good at it have many tactics and techniques that help, so knowing this, and building up a repertoire of personal tactics can help (Figure 8.3 provides some common tactics). Generally, these fall into one of the following categories all based upon making us feel in a certain way:

- *You're already there* – the other party makes you feel like you have got them to the point where there is no more, for example, saying no or delaying. Their concessions become small and diminishing, all to make you feel like you've got to work to get something worthwhile.

- *Fair play* – the other party appeals to sense of fairness by suggesting if they give we must give or perhaps uses some sort of moral argument.

- *It hurts* – negotiators often make like they are suffering, whether a plumber screwing up his face and drawing a sharp intake of breath at the suggestion of discount or an account manager making a big display of how difficult it is to go any further.

- *Policy* – hiding behind rules, obstacles or policy set by others creates an apparent immovable constraint that is difficult to challenge.

- *Hoops to jump through* – creating many things that prevent making easy concessions.

- *Scarcity* – creating the sense that if you don't want it others will and it's running out fast.

There are many more. All of this means we are feeling our way in an environment where the supplier will make us work hard for any concessions.

The power to negotiate

To negotiate well we must understand what power we hold, if any. Here we turn back to the insights we have gained. *Power Check* and *Price Check* give us vital intelligence here and help understand how the supplier is determining price, and our *Market Assessment* reveals if there is current or future leverage available. Add to this our understanding of the supplier from the *Supplier Fact Find* as well as what we have learnt from our *Consult and Engage* activity and we have the ingredients we need to make a determination of our negotiation power.

Power in a negotiation is not an absolute value or level, but rather a balance of our power relative to theirs. There are five distinct components of power in a negotiation, so to determine our overall power we must consider each of these, and the power position they give when combined:

- *Degree of dependency* – how dependent one party is upon the other. For example, we are dependent upon them if we have no or few alternatives, they are dependent upon us if they need our business, losing it would hurt them or we are a significant proportion of their sale turnover.

- *Relationships* – the degree to which there are established relationships between parties that can influence outcomes or undermine our negotiation. For example, we are trying to negotiate hard but the supplier is an old friend of our CEO and uses this relationship to wield influence or we have helped this supplier build their business so there is a degree of obligation there.

Figure 8.3 Ten top tactics that can help in a negotiation

10 most common tactics

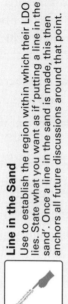

Salami Slicing

Use to secure an overall advantage by driving a series of apparently small individual agreements. However, all the little things add up to a much bigger shift in position.

Higher Authority

Use to make arguments irrelevant and create artificial boundaries. One party creates a constraint or reason why a certain action is necessary.

The Nibble

Use to secure a small concession from the other. One party asks for a small concession that is easy for the other party to give away and that the other party is unlikely to question.

The Decoy

Use to avoid giving too much away. One party creates a decoy by pretending to give great importance to an issue or requirement that is actually of little or no consequence.

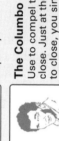

Hypothetically Speaking

Use to leverage movement. One party asks a hypothetical question to test if the other party might agree to something, eg "if i do X will you do Y?"

Line in the Sand

Use to establish the region within which their LDO lies. State what you want as if 'putting a line in the sand'. Once a line in the sand is made, this then anchors all future discussions around that point.

For a Deal Today…

Use to compel the other side to make a decision or close. One party creates some sort of deadline designed to compel the other into closing or making a decision.

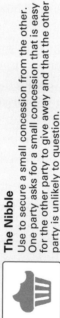

Split the Difference

Use to bring an end to a negotiation by driving an apparent mutual concession. Typically used when people are uncomfortable with negotiation.

Good Cop, Bad Cop

Use to win trust whilst wearing the other party down. The 'bad cop' is unpleasant and aggressive. The 'good cop' takes over, smiling and showing empathy.

The Columbo

Use to compel the other side to make a decision or close. Just at the point when the other party is ready to close, you simply say, 'Oh… just one more thing…'.

- *Market* – the degree to which the market is in our favour or their favour as determined in our *Market Assessment*.

- *Time* – whether one or the other party has time pressures and crucially whether the other knows this. For example, if we need to urgently agree a deal because the goods or service are required on a specific impending date or if the supplier has cash flow challenges and needs to secure some new business fast.

- *Future opportunity* – the degree to which one party is offering potential future opportunity to the other. For example, a suggestion we make to a supplier that there is likely to be lots of future business if the deal on the table can be improved a bit can help swing things in our favour. Similarly, the supplier can gain power by suggesting future advantage or benefit by choosing them it could tip the balance to doing the deal in their favour.

It helps to assess power by visualizing the balance using an indicator gauge and placing an arrow somewhere between us and them based upon our determination. Figure 8.4 gives an example and this gauge is part of the template for this tool included in the appendix. Here an indicator arrow has been drawn to represent our combined power balance assessment based upon our research into the all the different factors. However, as the adage goes, knowledge is power, and for either us or our opponent to understand our true power position we must know about all the factors that influence it. For example, if we are entirely dependent upon the other party, this only affords them power if they know about this. Therefore, in any negotiation situation we, or our opponent, might go to great lengths to keep certain aspects of the actual position hidden from the other and only selectively reveal information. A good poker player would never give any sign or suggestion that he had just been dealt a poor hand but instead works to keep game mates guessing, perhaps even wearing dark glasses and a hat to hide any telltale body language signs. It is the same for negotiation, so parties might work to create the illusion of power. We call this projecting power, and in using our gauge assessment we have the option to add one or more additional indicators to show a projected power position that one party might be trying to create. The difference between the projected power and the actual power based upon our research helps inform us how to structure our negotiation approach. Suppliers will certainly seek to project power and it is for this reason that doing our homework and prior research to gather as

Figure 8.4 An example of using the 'negotiation power gauge' to assess our position

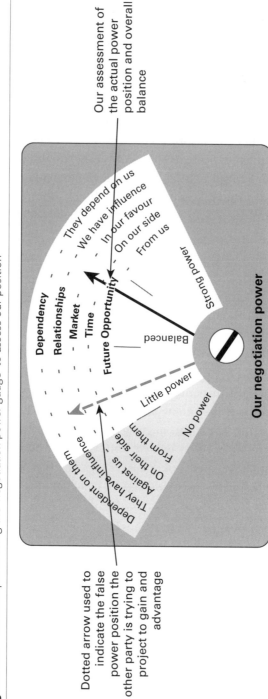

much intelligence as we can in advance in order to understand our true position can make a dramatic difference to how we negotiate and the outcome we can secure.

I see what you're thinking and I hear what you really mean

In some cultures, the only way to negotiate would be face-to-face. In Western culture, this approach is still favoured by many, especially sellers because if you can see and hear your opponent, and you know what to look and listen for, it is possible to get behind the words being used. A supplier telling us he is not authorized to apply further discount but accompanied by some inadvertent movement like touching his face or there being something different in his voice, might mean he is lying – vital intelligence in any negotiation. It might also not mean anything. I have witnessed or been part of many hundreds of negotiations and in most cases it is body language, the choice of words used or the way the words are spoken (tone, inflection, speed, nervousness) that gives away a position or reveals the true emotion of the other. Worse, those who are inadvertently revealing their position often have no idea they are doing it, and, if the opponent is familiar with what to watch and listen for, then they have a very strong advantage – like a secret hotline into the mind of the opponent.

The problem here is our subconscious is constantly looking out for us, and in a stress situation such as a negotiation it can do all sorts of things to try and protect us. An involuntary eye movement, a shift in our seats because we're telling a lie (or bluffing), pupils dilating because we're excited about the deal on offer, embellishing our sentences with extra words to hide something we are uncomfortable with saying (eg 'I was *just* checking the cakes in the tin were still OK'). To negotiate well we need to have a grasp of body language and spoken language. This is not as simplistic as learning what certain things mean – contrary to popular belief it doesn't follow that if someone's eyes go up to the right they are lying or if they fold their arms they are closed. It all depends: on the person, the situation and their degree of self-awareness of their actions, and how they speak. Experienced negotiators therefore don't just look or listen for such cues, but rather clusters of cues, and they may well calibrate us before we start – the small talk before we begin may be more than them just being interested.

The phrase 'poker face' comes from the idea of being able to be fully in control of one's own body language so as to not give anything away.

Good negotiation demands a similar poker face and even poker body from us, coupled with the ability to see and hear telltale signs in the other. It is possible to learn how to do this, we all possess the ability to read body language and hear hidden meaning in the words people say, it is part of how we have evolved to survive and trust others. Most likely we already do this but just don't realize it – perhaps you kind of know when someone is not being completely honest with you, but you just don't know how you now this. Applying this to negotiation is about tuning into what we already do here and learning a few basic principles. Body language and spoken language is an entire topic all of its own and further reading is recommended. My book *Negotiation for Procurement Professionals,* also published by Kogan Page, provides two full chapters on these topics.

Negotiating remotely

Anderson and Thompson (2004) suggest that in face-to-face negotiations powerful negotiators use positive affect (a positive outward demeanour, empathy and friendliness) to the other party, to invoke similar states in the other party, leading to increased trust, cooperation and better outcomes. Remote negotiations can therefore work to our advantage as it reduces the influence of the experienced salesperson's 'nice manner'.

Increasingly negotiations, or parts of a negotiation, are being conducted remotely, without a physical face-to-face engagement by phone, e-mail, text, web-conference, video conference or via an intermediary. Whilst the principles of negotiation remain the same, the approach needed to secure the right result varies and we need to be adept at applying negotiation principles no matter how we are engaging. Table 8.1 provides some tips on how to be successful for each of these.

Depending upon the technology deployed, the difficulty with the interaction is the absence or reduction in body language and spoken language cues to help understand what lies behind the words being said. This can make it very difficult to read the other party in the way many experienced negotiators prefer to do, but is also means they can't read us and so heightening the reliance upon the words spoken or written.

A bigger piece of pie or a bigger pie?

Not all negotiations are the same. A one-off negotiation to buy a car from someone we don't know is very different to the ongoing daily negotiations

Table 8.1   Remote negotiation

Type of remote negotiation	Tips for success
Written word *E-mail, SMS text message, social networking, web messaging, traditional written letter*	• Remember the written word is asynchronous; there will always be a gap between sending and receiving – use this to your advantage to consider your response carefully before sending. • There is increased scope for misunderstanding, so if you don't understand a communication or it annoys or makes you angry then seek clarification. • Never respond when angry. Instead sleep on it and consider your response carefully in the morning. • Allow time for the negotiation to progress. • Summarize regularly but be careful not to inadvertently signal acceptance unless this is your intent. • Consider wording carefully.
Audio *Phone, teleconference web phone*	• More effective if there has been a prior meeting. • Prepare thoroughly so you can concentrate on listening during the negotiation. • Listen actively to everything they say and how they say it. • Recognize key points. • It is easy to get carried away with the immediacy of the call as if it were a normal phone call. • Use silence, taking breaks, summarizing.
Video *Video-conference, web-conference, Skype or similar, FaceTime, etc*	• There is some body language visible, so approach as if face-to-face. • More effective if there has been a prior meeting. • Prepare thoroughly so you can concentrate on listening during the negotiation. • Listen actively to everything they say and how they say it watching for as many signals as possible. • Recognize key points. • Take breaks and summarize regularly.

(continued)

Table 8.1   *(Continued)*

Type of remote negotiation	Tips for success
Intermediary *Negotiation by proxy*	• Know you intermediary; if they are new then follow up references and check their track record. • If possible, incentivize them to maximize your outcome so they have something to win by pushing hard. • Recognize the risk that they may have relationships with the other party that could act against you. Ask them about this beforehand and watch for signs but assume the worst and manage them closely. • Actively involve them in the planning process and ensure they contribute to the development of an agreed concession strategy using their knowledge and experience to shape this. • Avoid giving them a free hand, but require them to follow the agreed concession strategy and to check in with you at certain points to seek your agreement to move further. • Agree the tactics they will use. • Depending upon the circumstances, it is sometimes advisable not to reveal your full LDO to the intermediary but leave yourself a margin that you can give later if needed. This can compel them to push harder.

with our family and children, where our primary objective is to maintain the right relationship with them for the long term. Therefore, the way we approach the negotiation and the tactics and techniques we use are very different. It is misguided to say that negotiation is always about seeking a win/win outcome; sometimes this is the case, say for negotiations where the long-term relationship is important, but more often than not, parties seek a WIN/win (big win, little win), and, as we have already seen, will work to make the other party feel like they are getting the big win even when this is not the case. If we are to negotiate effectively then we must be clear on the outcome we want here and this starts prior to our negotiation when we decide on our objectives for the negotiation. There are two dimensions to this – our value objective and our relationship objective.

The value objective is the most appropriate way to secure value out of the negotiation informed by our understanding of the situation and the insights from the tools we have worked so far. Here, there are two types of negotiation and therefore two approaches we can adopt to secure value and we must decide which one we will go and do (Figure 8.5):

- *Value claiming* – where parties seek to claim as much value from the negotiation, maximizing their share of the potential benefit, like dividing a pie of fixed size. What one party wins, the other gives up. Here we might use many and varied tactics, perhaps some hard, delivered by tough negotiators with the sole aim of maximizing our position.

- *Value creating* – here parties seek to work together to create more mutual benefit. Here the pie is expanded so how it is divided becomes less important – both get a slice of a much bigger pie. Value creating is about parties working to build outcomes with the interests of both parties in mind with the relationship being more important than the immediate. Tactics will be more open and negotiators need to be skilled at maintaining relationships.

The relationship objective is concerned with determining what sort of relationship we might want or need with our opponent during and beyond this negotiation, if any. Despite what the seller might suggest or how friendly they might appear, it is down to us to decide what relationship we want or need. For a one-off, value claiming purchase pursuing a WIN/win outcome in our favour, then we probably don't need any ongoing relationship. For a regular purchase with supplier we are going to use regularly in *Generic* or *Tailored* (*Power Check* tool), or where we will need to interact with

Figure 8.5 Value claiming or value creating

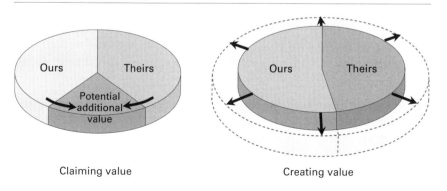

Claiming value   Creating value

them day-to-day, say to enable them to provide a service, then we might need some sort of relationship, if only to manage the supplier effectively. However, if we were working together with a small technology supplier to jointly develop a new product, then a good result might depend upon us sharing in the success.

The type of relationship varies according to the buying scenario and by considering our relationship objective we can determine the right negotiation approach that will resonate with this.

Planning for success

Where there is scope to negotiate, an understanding of our power position and clear objectives for the negotiation, we can move on to creating a plan for how we will attempt to conduct the negotiation event. Planning is frequently neglected, perhaps because it is easy to assume that when we get into the negotiation we can figure things out, indeed many negotiation text books place the emphasis upon things you can do during the negotiation event itself rather than the planning, yet it is the planning that makes the biggest difference to the negotiation outcome. Poor planning can be a surefire way to get a less than optimum result.

When we negotiate, we cannot completely control how the discussions might go, after all we are facing off against our opponent who will have their own ideas and objectives. Negotiating is like trying to sail a small boat across a large expanse of water. We might set out knowing where we are trying to head for, but no matter how much we might want to we cannot just go straight there, instead we must tack from side to side to catch the wind, constantly changing our course to do so, and then the conditions might become difficult or we could get blown off course. Planning a negotiation plan is like plotting a course that we aim and hope to achieve, perhaps with some waypoints on route, but with the knowledge that the weather and choppy negotiation waters might pull us off course. With a plan we will be able to have something we can bring discussions back to and regain our heading. Our negotiation journey may not be a single event but there may be multiple events and interactions along the way and this should also be part of our plan.

Planning begins by listing our negotiables. Negotiations are rarely just about price, but rather the various different things that are important to us. We can determine this from our *Needs and Wants* tool. We don't need the entire list; after all, if a fundamental *Must Have* is to buy from a supplier who can comply with a certain legal standard, this is not something we should negotiate, but part of the *Supplier Selection* pre-qualification process already outlined. Therefore, we extract from our *Needs and Wants* those aspects that we need to negotiate. This might include things like price, payment terms, timing (eg lead-time, delivery, time to provide service), service levels, etc. The things we have determined to be *Must haves* are those that must be secured, whilst the *Nice to haves* are things to aimed for, but also represent areas of potential compromise and trade-off.

For each negotiable we must determine what we ideally want and how far we are prepared to compromise for each. Picture a negotiation around a specific negotiable such as price as two people standing some distance apart. Both want to agree but to do this they must walk towards each other, taking a series of steps (concessions) until they are together at a place both one happy with (agreement). One takes a step, the other reciprocates and this keeps going until agreement is reached. Picturing this negotiation 'dance of two parties' can help us plan our approach. Essentially we need to know for certain in advance how far we are prepared to move towards the other. Once parties can see where the other is standing (our opening positions) then each will decide where they think the point of agreement is. Often this happens without conscious thought, and frequently will end up being midway between both positions, especially if inexperienced, driven by a sense of fair play and reciprocity (I give, you give, equally). Sometimes this is just fine, but effective negotiation is about deciding exactly where the right point of agreement should be, not necessarily the fair and equal point, ie making them walk further towards us. Furthermore, our opponent may choose to begin standing deliberately further away to create the illusion there is a greater distance between us and make us come further in their direction. This is a common tactic where the supplier starts with a deliberately inflated price for example for us to work to claim the reductions they were always planning to give, but in the process causing us to feel like we have claimed territory and ended up doing a great deal. This is called anchoring, and is part of the 'line in the sand' tactic – once a position has been given, discussions will centre around this 'anchor,' so creating a false anchor can give advantage.

Our negotiation plan is therefore about managing how we take steps (or trade concessions) in a negotiation, and about managing our position and understanding their true position (with any false anchoring detected and countered by good homework on our part). We do this by determining our MDO (Most Desirable Outcome) and the LDO (Least Desirable Outcome) for each negotiable and then attempting to figure out what the supplier's MDOs and LDOs might be. We also need to be confident there is a likely overlap or ZoMA between each LDO positions. Figure 8.6 illustrates this.

Figure 8.6   The LDO, MDO and ZoMA

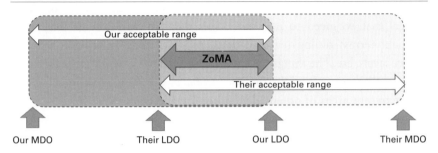

It is easy to know our MDO. The LDO represents the point that we are not prepared to go below. It is important to define this up front, and many people fail to do this, which leads to doing a bad deal. The difference between the MDO and the LDO represents the areas of compromise or trades that can be made within the process. However, it is also important to aim high and focus as much as possible early in the negotiation on the MDO, since a good negotiator on the other side of the table will soon smoke out our LDO. Tactics might include creating a 'false LDO,' much closer to our MDO than the real LDO in our minds and working to this, giving away only small concessions, or being slow to make movement and demanding something for something in each case can help. Getting the supplier to reveal their MDO is straightforward as they will usually be keen to offer a starting point that we can know either in advance or early on in the discussions – again, beware of this being deliberately inflated to create a skewed negotiation landscape. Suppliers will of course be very reluctant to reveal their LDO, so – as we have already seen – we will be blind. This is where the negotiation begins and the sequence of discussions, tactics and engagement we embark upon is all in the pursuit of working near to, reaching, and if possible even getting beyond, their LDO for each negotiable.

Managing through the four stages of negotiation

Negotiations have four distinct stages to navigate through – *Open*, *Explore*, *Bargain* and *Deal*. Recognizing each stage puts us in control so we can lead and manage discussions through them.

Open

The negotiation event is opened, typically by one party opening it to get discussions going. If parties have come together in a meeting room, then one side may give an opening statement that might thank the other for coming and set the scene, perhaps conditioning the other about expected outcomes. Making an opening statement is an assertion of power and claims territory, so make a point to give one. If they open first, then counter this with your own opening statement. Then it is a question of getting the negotiation moving, perhaps by discussing an easy concession, asking the other what they are looking to achieve (attempting to get them to reveal their MDO), or perhaps by revealing some or even all of our position.

Explore

Parties explore positions and attempt to find out exactly what the other wants, their motivation, the potential obstacles and where things might be able to move to. Here we want to understand the MDOs, but more importantly begin to gain a feel for where their LDOs might lie. They will be doing the same to us as well. Remember, we are blind here, so we must rely on tactics that get them to reveal where things can move to or by being able to spot where there is more to be had. The ability to read body language and spot hidden meaning in their spoken language helps here. Remember our struggling artist that needed to pay the rent? If we were negotiating with him to buy a painting and his words were asserting a position of never discounting his work, yet something in his demeanour was suggesting a certain desperateness to get a sale, this might tell us we could push further and get a better deal. Questioning is a key component of exploring positions and typical open questions here might include:

- Position testing – 'Is there room for manoeuvre here?'
- Getting a line in the sand – 'What is your proposal here?'
- Hypothetical – 'If I were to offer X, could you go to Y?' This creates an easy question to answer as it is not a real commitment, only a hypothetical test.
- Building reciprocity – 'I'm prepared to negotiate on X but will you give on Y?'
- Obstacle finding – 'What would it take to get you to improve your offer here?'
- Motivation testing – 'What matters the most to you here?'

Bargain

In the *bargain* stage we build on what we have learnt and understood during *Explore* by secure points of agreement and lining up the deal. Here we continue to use similar questioning to those above but we are attempting to conclude each point of negotiation. For example *Bargain* might include using a hypothetical question such as: 'If I agree to X will you agree to Y?' Here there is a slight shift in language to seek real agreement. Once we have an individual point of agreement then we are nudging closer to an overall agreement. So *Bargain* is about both striking the individual points of agreement that collectively build up the deal as well as building up a picture of where their LDO might lie and what they might agree to. Be careful here though because once agreement is given, it is hard to go back as this can make us feel like we are being unethical and 'going back on our word'. A common negotiation tactic is 'salami slicing', where the other party secures agreement to a series of small concessions from us, each small and of little consequence, but collectively become sizeable, and then seeks bigger concessions to make a deal – causing us to give away too much. Where we agree, the 'something for something' principle should be born in mind, so if we give, then we expect them to give. It is good to avoid making a firm agreement or making it conditional, eg 'I could potentially agree to that, let's first conclude our discussions on X.'

Deal

Here we look to conclude the deal and conclude the negotiations. Timing here is key as there is a point in any negotiation (and in any sales process) where the opponent is ready to make a final agreement (even if that might involve a bit of coaxing). Recognizing this point is key, as keeping going past it can work against us, as the other party might begin to lose confidence whilst the more we negotiate the more we might have to give up. Many negotiators make the mistake of waiting for the other party to take the lead on closing, as if we are offering our position for them to make a decision on. This is taking the subservient position, which dilutes how the other might see our power position. Instead, by taking the lead we affirm and reinforce our power position. A smart salesperson, and therefore a smart negotiator, will know just when to close, sometimes this is clear by visual or spoken cues (eg the person buying the car being visibly excited about the vehicle, showing a clear emotional attachment) or by having lined up all the individual points of agreement during the *Bargain* stage. Closing the deal might need something to compel the other into action and questions such as 'We've done our homework and this is our best position so can we agree this', or 'If we can agree to this today then I will agree to X... so shall we do this then?' and so on.

Getting good and always having an alternative

There is one primary source of power for any negotiation and that is the power of alternatives. Here we need a BATNA (Best Alternative To a Negotiated Agreement) – never leave home without one! If we have got to get a result, all our negotiation efforts will give away the fact that we need to close or reach an outcome. If we have a plan B or an alternative we can accept, then our entire negotiation approach will take the stance of 'I don't need this, I'm going to hold out.' If you've ever been in a situation where you had two job offers at once, perhaps you'll remember how much more confident you felt in pushing hard for a better package than if you had just one offer which you really needed to accept. Always have a BATNA: it works wonders in negotiations, and if you don't have one, find one – there are always alternatives.

There also are many things we can do to have power during the event itself across the less tangible aspects of negotiation such as demeanour, behaviour and the tactics and techniques we use. Such things are less easy to describe as they represent how an individual brings together a different series of learnt responses for specific situations – it would be like trying to describe how to ride a bicycle. Instead getting good at negotiation is about building on our knowledge of how to plan by understanding and managing our personal style and behaviour as well as building up a repertoire of things we can do in certain situations. *Negotiation for Procurement Professionals* (Kogan Page, 2016) includes 100 winning tactics and techniques along with chapters on understanding our negotiation personality and so further reading here is recommended.

Using the tool

The *Negotiation* – template 11 in the appendix – provides a means to evaluate and select a supplier (or solution). Use as follows:

1 **Determine scope to negotiate** – based upon the insights gained so far and our understanding of the buying scenario. Proceed only if there is scope to negotiate.

2 **Determine our negotiation power** – consider the five sources of power in a negotiation and use *Power Check* and *Market Assessment* insights to make a determination of the overall balance of power by drawing an arrow on the gauge. Add additional 'projected power' arrows if required.

3 **Determine how we will negotiate** – tick the appropriate box(es) and base all negotiation planning upon this selection.

4 **Determine objectives for the negotiation** – determine the value and relationship objectives. Determine what we are negotiating, who we are negotiating with and why we are negotiating. List what we know about our opponent and the overarching objectives for the negotiation/primary outcomes we need to secure.

5 **Determine a negotiation plan** – list the negotiables (extracted from the *Needs and Wants*) and determine our MDO and LDO for each. Determine our BATNA(s) and attempt to anticipate what their BATNA(s) might be. Plan the negotiation through the four stages. Determine the individual sequence of topics of discussion and any specific tactics or techniques we plan to use.

Tool 12 – contract

Purpose – to put in place appropriate contractual arrangements.

How to use it – use to conclude the arrangements with the supplier once we have completed negotiation.

When needed – essential, as every buying transaction has a contract of some description: here we determine the degree to which we might need to define the contract or aspects of it.

In any personal or commercial transaction, there is always a contract of some form between the buyer and supplier. Whether a big document written in legalese that both sides pour over before agreeing, us buying on the supplier's terms or simply an informal agreement established through the actions parties take with each other, the contract may take many different forms. Tool 12 is concerned with considering the degree to which we can influence and shape the contract, if at all, and how to go about ensuring the right contractual arrangements are in place that support effective buying.

What constitutes a contract and the nature of contract law vary around the world. Furthermore, if we are sourcing from different countries there may be subtle differences in legal approach or indeed the value or lack of value some cultures place on the contract itself (with relationships being more important than any contract in some cultures). In this section we can only begin to consider the intricacies of contracts, so some further reading or advice on the matter is recommended. As buyers, possessing a good understanding of how contracts work, 'knowing our way around a contract' and being able to ensure the right contractual arrangements are put in place is an important skill. Acquiring this by reading and practice is relatively straightforward, but it is also important to recognize that in most cases we, as buyers, are not lawyers and so it is equally important to know when to seek the support and involvement of legal experts. I will attempt to lay out some basics here.

Contract basics

A contract is an agreement, enforceable by law, between two or more persons to do, or abstain from doing, some act or acts. Contract law is based upon the latin phrase '*pacta sunt servanda*' which means promises must be kept. A breach of contract is recognized by law around the world and as such there is action we can choose to take should a breach occur.

When we talk of a contract, it is easy to think of it as a dull, lengthy document written in legal language. In fact, the contract itself is what exists when all the required components that constitute a contract are in place. Under English law (and there are differences around the world), four components are necessary for a contract to be formed. To explain these, consider the example of buying a jacket from a shop:

1 *Offer* – the offer is when we have visited the shop, viewed the range of jackets, perhaps tried some on and decided which one we want to buy and therefore we make an offer to buy the jacket from the seller at a stated price. Note that the advertisement by the seller of the jacket in the store with its price tag is not an offer under English law. It is called an 'invitation to treat'.

2 *Acceptance* – this is acceptance of the offer, for example the seller agrees to sell the jacket. Acceptance can be signalled in a variety of ways. It doesn't necessarily require someone to say, 'Yes, I accept your offer.' That a store allows the buyer to pick up something, take it to the checkout and have the checkout attendant initiate the transaction with a credit card, is a form of acceptance by action. For a complex commercial purchase this acceptance might be the signature of a contractual document by one or both parties. It is important to appreciate what constitutes acceptance so to avoid inadvertently giving it.

3 *Consideration* – there must be an exchange of something of value between the parties, such as paying the stated sum of money in return for the jacket. When a failing company with no or negative asset value is given away for rescue by another company, it is never actually 'given away'. Instead it will be sold for one pound or one dollar or some small token amount so that a contract can exist between the buyer and seller.

4 *Intent* – this is the intent by both parties to enter into, and be capable of entering into, a legally binding agreement and be bound by that agreement. This tends to be clear in a shop-based transaction.

A documented contract could be any means that supports how these components come together. In many countries a document is not required for a contract to be made and the governing law recognizes a verbal or oral contract as legally binding. However, such contracts are open to wide interpretation from the parties involved, and without witnesses there is scope for the parties to change their stories. That said, verbal or oral contracts can form part of everyday buying, for example, a property owner agreeing a piece of maintenance work, or instructing a garage to undertake some repair work on a car. Such contracts have their place, generally where there is good trust and the risk is low, but if we end up in a dispute it can be our word against theirs. A contract can also be formed by custom and practice, for example if a supplier regularly provides, and is paid for, the same goods or service over a long period of time; then a contract could be deemed to have been formed in some countries. In this case a window cleaner who has been engaged to provide regular services over several years could have good cause to claim a breach of contract if his services were suddenly terminated without good notice. For most professional buying situations, it makes sense to formalize all aspects of the agreement within a written contract, and in some instances, such as buying property, this is the only way the contract can be made. Table 8.2 lists and explains some of the different forms a contract might take when buying.

Why contracts are important

Contract law, in its various forms provides that where what was agreed as part of contract formation is not met, ie there is a breach of contract, then there are legal remedies open to us. So, in theory, if the seams on the jacket we bought came apart the first time we wore it, then we could commence a law suit with the supplier for breach of contract. This might seem an extreme remedy and not something an average consumer would

Table 8.2 Some of the different forms a contract might take when buying

Type of contract	Definition	How terms are defined
Oral (verbal) contract	Parties make a verbal agreement to a course of action. Discussion and negotiation might precede getting to a point where parties signal they agree, perhaps with some gesture like a handshake or giving a verbal instruction. A gardener might say his hourly rate, the customer might offer to employ him to do three hours work each week for the next six weeks, the gardener might then agree to this and accept the offer thus forming a contract.	Specific terms or requirements would be communicated verbally as part of, prior to or at the point of verbal agreement. For example, the customer says the gardener must not park his truck in the road but pull it onto the drive.
General buying (online, in-store or to a catalogue)	General everyday buying process. Typically represents most corporate transactional spend. Supplier is offering goods or service for sale (invitation to treat): contract established when customer offers to buy (eg by taking goods to a till or completing an online order and check out process) and the offer is accepted when the store or company processes the order and takes payment (consideration). Assumes both parties are capable or and intended to enter into such a legal arrangement and be bound by it.	It is common to find terms undefined other than statutory provision, for example small shop owners rarely require customers to accept their terms before agreeing a sale. Where terms are defined they are usually defined by the seller, are blanket terms covering all transactions, not readily negotiable, and agreement may be implied or require explicit acceptance (eg online check-outs requiring 'I accept terms box to be checked').

(continued)

Table 8.2   (Continued)

Type of contract	Definition	How terms are defined
Purchase order	Customer places an order, either written or verbal for the supply of specific good or services to specific requirements or terms and perhaps stating an agreed price. Purchase order (PO) constitutes an offer, which is accepted upon the supplier processing the order for the agreed consideration.	Terms either defined in the PO, or separate terms referred to and invoked. Where terms are undefined or if the supplier acknowledges the PO but then asserts different terms, risk of uncertainty as to whose terms prevail.
Master or framework agreement	An overarching document that defines how the relationship and an area of supply will work. Not usually contractual (but can become so if it makes minimum commitments or resembles a contract too closely) and defines the agreed terms and arrangements that will apply for each PO placed. Contract is established when a PO in accordance with the agreement is offered and accepted.	Terms defined within the agreement and written so as to take primacy over any individual PO terms. Requires PO to specifically be in accordance with the agreed terms of the master or framework agreement.
Full written contract	Supply arrangement is defined in a single written contract, or multiple written contracts, that define all aspects of what will be provided, the terms, key deliverables, what will happen should things change, agreed price or fees and timing. Acceptance when executed and signed by both parties.	Terms defined within the body of the contract. May define specific aspects of the supply arrangement in a schedule or statement of work.

contemplate or know how to go about doing. Thankfully, in practice, there is legislation that regulates how contract law is realized so it works day-to-day and provides more practical remedies. In the UK, the Sale of Goods Act 1979 consolidated the original act from 1893 and has since been amended many times; in its latest form it remains core legislation for commercial contracts between businesses. For consumer purchases in the UK, this act is now consumed into the Consumer Rights Act 2015. Other similar legislation exists around the world. Legislation such as these acts that regulate contract law sets out our rights here and the obligations of the seller, so that taking the jacket that is not of satisfactory quality back to the store for a refund or replacement becomes straightforward and something that most sellers would willingly cooperate with and would recognize the consumer had a certain time period within which to do this.

Contract terms

When things get a bit more complex and there are other things that need to be considered in what we are buying then the contract we agree must provide for this as well. For example, if we purchase and download some software from Microsoft, at some point prior to finalizing the transaction, and prior to being able to use the software, we will be required to agree to their terms and conditions. Here we will find a written definition of the basis upon which the contract is being formed and the associated provisions within this; for example, if we read the terms we will find we are not buying the software itself, and we won't assume any rights to Microsoft's code, we are buying a licence to use the software, for certain limited applications and for a specific period of time. We are agreeing we won't modify their software and that they can update it and perhaps access data around how their product is used and so on. Microsoft's standard terms and conditions for software are applied the world over (with some regional variations) and will align with legislative obligations, but they are very much Microsoft's terms. If we don't like them or would like to change something it is unlikely they will be interested. It is a simple choice: if we want to access the software we must accept their terms. These terms, and indeed those for most online purchases, are rarely read, let alone understood, by consumers and those in business, trusting that the company is being fair and that it must be OK because everyone else does the same. There are many buying scenarios like this, but as an individual and in business, where we simply do not have any ability to influence the terms of the contract, all we can do is decide if these are acceptable or not and if we are prepared to buy or walk away. Such instances tend to be where we are in the *Proprietary* quadrant (*Power Check* tool) and, in the case where we have low power and/or we are buying from a large company, in *Generic* also.

Therefore, most contracts will include terms and conditions so as to fully define the contract. A contractual term is any provision that forms part of a contract and as such gives rise to a contractual obligation. When we buy and where there are terms needed to determine all the provisions then these must become part of how we define and agree the contract. A contract cannot be said to be complete if the terms and conditions are not fully laid out, and not legally binding if they are vague or ambiguous.

The terms and conditions don't always have to be set by the supplier. There are other buying situations where we can and should influence the contract terms in part, extensively, or perhaps even determine them in the first place. Where we have influence, then ensuring the right and appropriate contract and terms are in place is an essential part of the buying process and one that can improve our buying outcome if done well. It should not be viewed as a decoupled activity, perhaps the domain of separate legal experts, nor should we simply blindly accept a supplier's contract terms; instead we should be actively involved in making sure it is right. Nothing focuses a supplier to deliver like a contract, and a good, well-structured contract will provide:

- a formal definition of what has been agreed by each party;
- a definition of what happens when things change or go wrong;
- a formal definition of the detail of what is to be provided, how our *Needs and Wants* will be met, and the way in which this will happen;
- potentially a definition of how the relationship will work;
- a basis to monitor and measure the supplier's performance; and
- the way parties can exit the contract, if at all should things change.

The terms and conditions for any contract will vary according to what we are buying, other background factors and what is necessary. This applies even in the simplest of contracts: consider, for example, an oral contract where a tradesman is engaged to do some painting – the contract sum could be agreed on a handshake, subject to the tradesman supplying his own paint and having the job completed by next Thursday, assuming no unforeseen issues arise (both terms that accompany the agreement).

As we have already seen, it generally makes sense to formalize the contract in a written form, and so here we must consider the written terms and conditions that will make part of the contract and how they will be presented. When we buy, and we have influence, then agreeing the written contract is as important as the purchase itself. Written contracts take many different forms (Table 8.2). No matter which form is being used then the process of reaching agreement can happen in one of three ways:

- The supplier presents the contract with their terms and conditions for us to accept/review/reject or request and agree amendments. Note, suppliers rarely invite review or amendments and will usually hope their terms might just get accepted but will usually expect or be prepared for some discussion.

- We draw up the contract with our terms and conditions and offer to the supplier, again with the hope they will be accepted but recognizing the supplier might want to review and agree changes.

- The contract is jointly developed – typical of joint collaborative projects with a supplier.

How the above happens is not always obvious. In a written contract designed for the buying scenario then the process of agreement would seem straightforward. But what about when we issue a purchase order (PO) to a supplier? Many companies seek to establish a standard set of terms and conditions that form part of the PO, incorporated within, e-mailed with the order or, if in hard copy, printed on the reverse. Similarly, many suppliers will accept an order and issue an acknowledgement of the order on the basis that it is, as per the supplier's terms and conditions, supplied in a similar fashion. So, whose terms apply? This practice is called the 'battle for the forms' and is something courts tend to take a dim view of when dealing with alleged breaches of contract. As buyers, we must work to either be comfortable with the prevailing terms or work with the supplier to establish clear agreement and definition of the terms that both parties agree and are working to.

Examining a written contract for the first time can appear quite daunting, but in fact it is quite straightforward and whilst there might be many paragraphs of legal text, contracts are generally a collection of individual sections and clauses, each serving a particular purpose to define some aspect of the agreement, placed together in a way so sections don't conflict but work together to form the overall agreement. Agreement or acceptance might happen by both parties signing the document (called executing the contract) or by action such as a supplier accepting a purchase order with its terms and conditions and proceeding to supply the goods. To begin to understand a contract it helps to get familiar with what all the different sections do, how they work and why they are there. Table 8.3 lists some typical contract terms and sections that may or may not apply depending upon the scenario, however, there are some key elements that all contracts would have which include:

- *Parties to the agreement* – who the agreement is between, including names, addresses and perhaps company details.

- *Obligations of parties* – what both parties are agreeing to and their obligations in this respect. Here is how what constitutes the contract is defined, how offer and acceptance happens and exactly what is being agreed. This might be something like: 'This document in its entirety constitutes an offer and is deemed to be accepted when both parties sign the declaration.'

- *Contract duration* – where the contract is to run for a set period, otherwise when the contract will be deemed to have been fulfilled.

- *What will be provided* – the agreed goods or services that will be provided and any associated specification. If multiple items then these will be listed somewhere.

- *Time and place* – when and where goods/services are to be provided.

- *Price or fees* – agreed price of the goods or fees for the services, including any formula where these are to be determined by other factors, any agreed mechanism for variation, currency and reference to what the fees include or exclude, for example in business contracts it is usual practice for fees to be stated exclusive of sales tax or VAT.

- *Payment terms* – when and how payment is due, any stage payments, penalties for late payment, etc. This is an important clause for a buyer to consider and might form part of negotiations with the supplier – the longer the payment terms, the longer we hold onto our cash vs the supplier's perspective of wanting to get paid as quickly as possible. Increasingly, in business buying around the world, payment terms have become more extended. Table 8.4 gives some typical payment terms.

- *Terms and conditions* – the related terms and conditions for the contract will be specified, either in the body of the contract, especially if bespoke to the contract, or separately, and if so will be referenced accordingly. Statements such as 'In accordance with our standard terms and conditions available at...' might typically be found say on a purchase order or within a seller's sales documentation. Typical terms are given in Table 8.3.

Table 8.3   Some typical contract terms and what they mean

Clause	Purpose
Recitals	A clause that precedes the main text of a contract and provides an outline of what the contract is about, perhaps the reason for the contract, the parties involved and why they are signing a contract.
Representations and warranties	Statements of the basic matters or facts being presented in the contract to clearly state things that would otherwise be assumptions. Representations are statements of current or past facts, allegations or arguments, for example that the supplier has the right to sell the goods and the goods are what is specified. Warranties tend to be more focused towards the future and state what parties promise, for example 'Supplier warrants that the goods are free of defects' or 'Goods have a lifetime warranty against manufacturing defects.' Where no specific warranty is expressed then there would usually be an implied fitness for particular purpose.
Liabilities and limitation of liability	This relates to the liability of each party to the other on breach or for other occurrence such as negligence, infringement of intellectual property, failing to comply with statutory duties or other significant issue (that would typically be defined in the contract). How liabilities are set is typically a point of negotiation with a supplier. Parties would naturally want the other to be bound to unlimited liabilities or at least very high levels of liability that would provide the ultimate security in the contract. Similarly, parties will naturally seek to limit the liability that they must accept. Whilst there are situations where unlimited liability is necessary, eg in situations where a breach results in death or serious harm, generally they tend to be agreed based upon what is appropriate by considering what might go wrong, the likelihood of this happening, the severity of impact should it happen, what insurance provision the other holds, or would need to hold should things go wrong (there is little point having a high liability obligation if other party's insurance doesn't match it) and ultimately what parties are prepared to accept. It is not uncommon for a supplier's liability to be limited to the value of the goods or service they are providing.

(continued)

Table 8.3   *(Continued)*

Clause	Purpose
Indemnification	Also called a 'hold harmless' agreement – this is the promise by one party to assume liability of behalf of someone else. For example, if the supplier is providing software to us that originates from a third party, that subsequently the third party claims our supplier does not have the right to and so issues a lawsuit against us for use of their software. With an indemnification clause set up, if the supplier is negligent they must indemnify (or reimburse) our costs from any lawsuit from a third party then we would have legal protection and have minimised our risk. As for liabilities, commitments to indemnification should align with levels of insurance provision.
Termination	This defines how the contract will terminate (ie in the case of a fixed-term contract), or can be terminated. The right to terminate should something go wrong is normally expected, eg in the event of a breach or insolvency of the other party, and such terms will usually be mutual and may provide discretion to the other. Termination for other reasons depend upon what the contract needs to do and what parties want - so this might be another area to negotiate. For example, we might want a simple low-risk contract with a gardener with a clause that says either party has the right to terminate for whatever reason by giving one month's notice. In contrast, a contract with a construction company for a new build is not something we would want them to be able to walk away from midway. As buyers, it is therefore important to consider the scenario and how we or a supplier might want or need to terminate and what would be appropriate. It is also important to check the mechanism for termination. Some, less reputable, suppliers try to include clauses that make termination difficult such as requiring written notice by a specific means to be provided to a specific address on just one defined day in any year, otherwise the contract rolls on. Such contractual clauses should usually be rejected.
Confidentiality	Also referred to as a non-disclosure clause, this defines the obligations of parties to protect and preserve confidentiality of certain specified information, know-how, materials and so on that the other receives or accumulates as part of the contract, and perhaps even the fact that parties have entered into a contract together.

(continued)

Table 8.3   *(Continued)*

Clause	Purpose
Dispute and jurisdiction	Defines the process that will be followed should a dispute arise from the contract. This might include a single option or various escalating provision such as initial referral to nominated individuals within the parties' organizations, referring to arbitration (in which case the arbitration body would typically be named) or resolution through specified courts deemed to have jurisdiction for the contract.
Governing law	Different countries have different laws and the content and effect of those can vary significantly. Furthermore, international contracts might involve activities in various counties. This clause therefore states which laws govern the contract and therefore how to interpret the contract and what was agreed should things go wrong.
Modification of agreement	Defines how the contract may or may not be modified. For complex, long-term contracts it is normal for things to change and for parties to agree changes to certain provisions. Clearly a contract that can be modified by one party at a whim would be somewhat self-defeating; therefore, such a clause might typically state modification is only by mutual agreement if at all. Structuring contacts so any elements likely to vary are included in a separate, referenced schedule can help to make agreement of modifications to contracts more straightforward and perhaps not necessarily require legal support as the body of terms will remain unchanged. Check this is sufficiently mutual.
Severability	This is the provision for if part of the contract was found to be illegal or otherwise unenforceable and in which case defines what then happens to the agreement. Typically, severability clauses state that should this happen the remainder of the contract would still apply as well as what parties agree will happen to the unenforceable parts – perhaps the option to modify them or simply delete them.
Procedure for renewal	Defines how the contract may be renewed at expiry or end. This could provide for automatic renewal, mutual agreement, the option of requesting a renewal or simply that the contract ends.
Insurance	Insurance clauses define obligations of one or more parties to hold specified insurance cover to a defined level, and perhaps obligations to furnish the other with evidence of such.

(continued)

Table 8.3 *(Continued)*

Clause	Purpose
Intellectual Property	Intellectual Property (IP) clauses provide for who owns what as part of the contract. These are highly important clauses when buying and care should be taken to ensure the right clause is in place. Contracts typically provide an exhaustive list or definition of what constitutes IP within the context of the agreement. This might include documents, know-how, designs, patents, copyright, trade secrets, trademarks, etc. Clearly, if we engage a supplier to work for us we would not usually want them to acquire rights to our IP. Similarly, the supplier probably won't want us to acquire rights to their IP. However, if we have engaged the supplier to create something for us, such as a design agency creating a new logo, then we would want to own the rights to the logo once supplied. IP clauses can get quite complicated and might need to deal with IP we or the supplier already own and retain ownership of but are used to support contract fulfilment (usually called background IP), what happens to new IP or custom components created during the contract as well as any rights to use the knowledge gained from the contract elsewhere. Furthermore, where an agreed clause clear asserts ownership of IP then there may need to be some sort of licence agreement in place for the other to use the IP as part of the contract.

- *Execution (authorization, agreement, signatures and date)* – the tangible evidence and record that party or parties have agreed the contract. In a written contract this would most usually be via a signature panel, often at the end of the contract. Those authorized to do so on each side signal their agreement by physically signing copies of the contract and each party retains a copy signed by all parties. Today there are modern online electronic signature authorization systems so parties can sign remotely. For other contracts there will be some sort of authorization or agreement. Purchase orders will usually be authorized and signed by a duly appointed individual within the company, and when we buy online we tick a box to signal our acceptance of the seller's terms and conditions.
- *Schedules, appendices, addendums, short particulars* – it is common, and useful, to separate out the body of the contractual terms, the elements

Table 8.4 Some typical payment terms

Term	Explanation
CBS	Cash before shipment
CIA	Cash in advance
CND	Cash next delivery
COD	Cash on delivery
Contra	Payment for goods or service from the supplier is offset against goods/services the supplier has purchased from us
CWO	Cash with order
EOM	End of month – payment due at the end of the month. Variations include xEOM and xEOMy where x = number of days and y = date in the following month, for example: • 60EOM – Payment due at the end of the month after 60 days from date of invoice. In practice 60EOM15 means payment due on the 15th of the month after the end of month that is 60 days from date of invoice. In practice this means that actual time ranges between 75 days and 105 days
Net x (eg Net 30, Net 60, Net 90)	Payment is due the specified days after the invoice date
yMFI (eg 28MFI)	Payment is due on the specified date of the month following the invoice date etc. 28 MFI means payment due on 28th of following month
2% 10 Net 45 (or variation)	Payment is due 45 days from date of invoice but a 2% discount is available if payment is received within 10 days

that might typically be developed with legal support, from the specific components unique to what we are buying or those elements that might need to change or get updated. Therefore, schedules are used, appendices referenced in the main body of the contract so they become part of the contract, but separate to help make the contract more practical. Typical separate schedules might include:

– agreed SLAs (Service Level Agreement) where the agreed performance level is specified;

– statement of work – defining the detail of exactly what will be done, when and where, scheduled activities etc;

- how parties agree they will work together, perhaps with obligations for regular review meetings;

- additional policies or reference to other documents that are to be followed/observed/taken account of; and

- lists of individuals with nominated responsibilities as part of the contract.

Developing contract skills

The best way to learn how contracts work is simply to start reading them and developing an understanding of what is being said whilst seeking out answers and help for that which is not understood. With understanding comes that ability to start amending or agreeing changes. That is in fact how most buyers I know who are adept at understanding and working on contracts have learnt this skill. Remember also that contracts must be clear and free from ambiguity and must not be vague in any way in order to be binding. As such they tend to be written in a very precise language, free from grammatical error and therefore have much less punctuation than in normal writing and statements that don't leave room for misinterpretation. Even a single comma can change the meaning of a contract, so if you are someone who would normally start correcting written word that doesn't meet your grammatical expectations, this is something to avoid doing when working with contracts. With all that in mind, if you don't understand what is being said then it should be questioned. Once upon a time contracts could be a single huge body of text capable of hiding all sorts of things from the untrained eye. Today, good contract practice means that most contracts will be structured with sections, headings that explain what each section does, clause numbers and standard definitions – so if there is something that needs to be explained, or where clarity regarding what is meant by a word or phrase would be important to avoid ambiguity, then it is given a definition, typically at the start of the terms and conditions and then whenever this word or phrase is used throughout the document it will be capitalized. Parties to the agreement would also be given standard definitions. For example 'This contract is made between the ABC company whose address is DEF (the 'Contractor') and the UVW company whose address is XYZ ('Customer').' The contract then only needs to refer to Contractor and Customer throughout the body of the text. Such an approach allows the use of standard boilerplate or model forms of contract with simple substitutions.

When things go wrong

A contract can end in one of four ways;

1 by performance – the contract has been fulfilled with all agreed obligations met by all parties;

2 by agreement – parties agree to end the contract or one releases the other(s) from the agreement;

3 by frustration – something has happened that has made completion of the contract impossible and/or the obligations of the contract cannot be met; and

4 by breach – where one party does not fulfil one or more of the agreed obligations or specified terms and conditions, where the goods or services are defective or not of satisfactory quality or where a party fails to provide, or makes the other aware it will not be providing, the agreed goods or services.

A breach of contract is enforceable by law, with legal remedies open to us including the potential to secure damages for losses from the breach, but actually pursuing legal action can be very difficult and ideally should be unnecessary.

It is here where we meet the difference between the *legalities* and the *practicalities*. Whilst we may be entitled to take the supplier to court if there has been a breach, actually doing this is a different matter. Across all the procurement teams I've worked with around the world that have ended up in some sort of serious dispute with a supplier and have ended up having to pursue legal action, I have only seen one get what they would call a successful outcome in court. Most others talk of years of high-cost lawyers' bills, huge stress, loss of goodwill, damage to reputation and either walking away, compromising or settling out of court. Even if we win a legal action with a supplier we may be no further forward as we either still need to work with the supplier or find another supplier. Generally ending up in litigation with a supplier is something that should be avoided at all costs as it rarely ends well, no matter what the outcome is. There will be situations where legal action is the only option, but it is something that should always be avoided. However, in general, and assuming we have chosen our supplier well, things don't tend to go wrong because suppliers decide not to fulfil their part of the agreement, but because of other factors such as:

- misunderstanding between parties of what was actually agreed;
- something changes and parties hadn't thought about or agreed how things might work in the new situation;

- relationships between those involved breakdown;

- lack of communication, eg where a contractor providing maintenance services depends upon the customer adequately communicating daily maintenance schedules; and

- there are unforeseen issues or, despite good intent, one party struggles to fulfil their obligations in practice.

Across all of the above factors, the majority of these are avoidable, therefore we can minimize the likelihood of dispute, and indeed provide for how we handle it should it happen, by working to ensure a good, well-thought-through contract in place. Furthermore, a good contract holds the potential to reduce or minimize our risk exposure, allow us to hold on to our cash for longer, secure greater performance from the supplier and so on. It's all a matter of ensuring we negotiate and agree all the relevant aspects so that contract becomes a natural definition and output to what we agree rather than a separate, detached legal document. If we can influence the contract, lead or be actively involved in its creation, then some specific considerations that help here include (these are all included in the *Contract* template in the appendix):

- *Clear definition of what will be provided* – developed from the relevant extracts of our *Needs and Wants*.

- *Risk* – ensuring we are comfortable with the risk we will be exposed to, and also the risk the supplier will be exposed to (and their ability to handle it) through careful checking/use of right limit of liability, indemnification and termination clauses.

- *Maximizing our financial position* – minimizing risk of price or fee surprises by tight definition and agreeing certainty of price/fees and any mechanisms for variation and optimizing cash flow/cash retention by ensuring the right payment terms are in place.

- *Relationship* – perhaps defining aspects of how the relationship will work, roles, responsibilities, how/when parties will review the relationship.

- *Providing for things going wrong* – well-thought-through dispute clauses that seek to remedy the situation between parties before escalation.

- *Providing for exit* – ensuring clarity regarding how parties can exit and the prevailing circumstances, but also obligations of each should this happen. Providing for exit also means having a clear plan not shared with the supplier for what we would do if we found ourselves needing to exit or if the supplier exited so we can be ready.

- *Appropriate contract duration* – suppliers will usually seek to secure a long-term contract as it provides them with certainty. However, this is not always in our best interests. Here we should refer back to the *Power Check* tool. If we are in *Generic* or *Tailored* then in theory there are alternatives and so a long-term contract would not necessarily be right for us and could limit our buying power. Instead we might consider short-term contracts with the option of re-evaluating our options in the market regularly. Whereas in *Custom* the chances are we might need a good, strong and collaborative relationship with the supplier, so here a long-term contract that works for both parties would be more appropriate.

- *How the contract will be managed* – where there is a need for ongoing management of a supplier (we'll cover this in the next chapter) then the contract should ideally be central to this and so should be set up in a way to enable this. This might include a SLA or defined performance to be met etc.

Using the tool

The *Contract* – template 12 in the appendix – provides, where possible and we have influence, a means to help guide and determine the right contractual arrangement. Use as follows:

1 **Determine scope to influence** – if none then we have a simple choice to either accept or walk away, or otherwise decide how much influence we have to either review and negotiate changes to an existing contract or develop a new contract.

2 **Determine how we will agree the contract** – if we are using a simple means such as oral, conduct or simple written instructions, then decide if this must be accompanied by any terms or conditions we wish to make part of the agreement, define these and incorporate them, eg if an oral contract ensures our agreement is based upon the additional conditions communicated to them.

3 **Determine or ensure the right contract and contract terms** – review or draft the contract as appropriate. Check that the contract is suitable, appropriate, and does what we need to ensure we realize the best outcome at the least possible risk. Negotiate with the supplier where needed and then execute or agree the final contract.

Summary

The key learning points from this chapter:

1 Step 3 – *Deal* – is about securing the best deal and making it happen. It contains three tools that lead us to a clear way forward to finalize our buying arrangements.

2 Tool 10 – *Select Supplier* – is a means to finally decide which supplier (or solution) to use. Where our *Power Buying Plan* has determined *Competition* options then this tool is most relevant. It works by adopting a 'funnel' evaluation technique to progressively eliminate suppliers (or solutions) that are unsuitable to arrive at the chosen supplier or suppliers. Evaluation typically includes many tests including the degree to which the *Needs and Wants* will be met and other factors such as the degree to which we can work with a supplier.

3 Tool 11 – the *Negotiation* tool – provides a simple structured means to plan and execute simple negotiations. Here we determine what scope we have to negotiate, and if so we then determine how we will negotiate, or objectives and the specific points of negotiation. For each we determine most and least desirable outcomes along with alternatives and plan the sequence of our discussions.

4 Tool 12 – the *Contract* tool – is a means to determine what scope we have to influence the contract, and if so to determine the best contracting approach. The tool also guides us to check that the contract is right and appropriate to maximize our buying outcomes and minimize our risk as best as we can, negotiating with the supplier where needed prior to agreement.

Step 5 – delivery: 09 ensuring we get what we agreed

This chapter explores the final three tools within the *Power Buying Process* that help us ensure we get what we agreed. We examine how we ensure the new buying arrangements are fully implemented, what, if any, intervention is needed to manage the supplier and how we check performance and deal with any problems.

Pathway questions addressed in this chapter:

16 How do we ensure the buying arrangements we have agreed happen in practice?

17 Do we need to manage the supplier? If so how?

18 Do I need to check that the supplier performs as agreed? If so how?

19 What do I do when things go wrong or if I need to drive improvement with a supplier?

It's not over until...

...we have got what we agreed! It is easy to assume that once we have made the agreement with the supplier that our work is done and everything will simply happen as intended. Sometimes it does, and sometimes, and no matter how well we have handled the buying process, there is more we need to do to be successful. The final three tools within the *Power Buying Process* (Figure 9.1) are concerned with ensuring our new buying arrangements are well implemented and that we get what we expect and agreed.

Figure 9.1   The final three tools within the *Power Buying Process* that comprise step 5 – *Deliver*

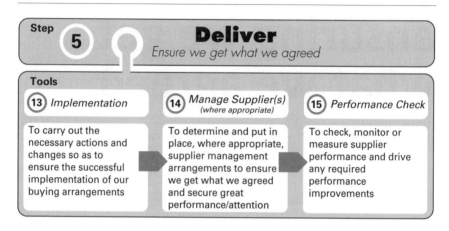

Tool 13 – implementation

Purpose – to ensure the successful implementation of our buying arrangements.

How to use it – use as appropriate to help implement our buying arrangements.

When needed – limited need for simple purchases and essential for complex purchases, where others will be impacted or will need to do something different for the new buying arrangements.

If we have bought something from a shop, or online, and we have received the item which is exactly as we expected, or if the garage has serviced our car and fixed the problem we had, then our purchase is complete. Assuming nothing goes wrong that would necessitate us returning to the supplier, then we can conclude that we are satisfied and there is nothing more we need to do. Sometimes buying is this simple, but sometimes less so and things can go wrong – the supplier could fail to deliver, be late, fall short of the agreed specification or requirements, provide something that is not fit for purpose or of sub-standard quality, or any other factor that might cause us to be dissatisfied. If the supplier fails to perform, we can take action, and tools 14 and 15 (described later) can help here, but there is a much greater factor that can prevent successful buying or cause us to fail at this final step and this has nothing to do with the supplier but rather how we plan for and implement any changes needed for the new buying arrangements.

Effective buying requires certain arrangements with the supplier, but it can also require deliberate, planned and sometimes extensive activities in our organization. Surely our part is straightforward? It might seem so but in fact when organizations buy, the failure to transition to a new buying arrangement is a common reason for failure, particularly for new buying arrangements where people need to change what they know or do in some way. If we identified a breakthrough change to the way we should buy something the organization will continue to use in high volumes, and we have negotiated an exceptionally good deal which is now defined in a new contract, our efforts become pointless if the rest of the organization fails or refuses to adopt the new buying arrangements.

Buying is an organization-wide concern; therefore any change to the way we buy is also an organization-wide concern. Ignore this and our buying project could stop dead; planning for it and taking the rest of the organization with us – even inspiring them to our cause – can guarantee great success.

CASE STUDY – Feeling the heat

A buyer working for a large firm of heating contractors identified a significant cost reduction opportunity was possible by changing the way the pipe fittings and consumables were purchased. A deal was done with a new supplier and the changes were rolled across the firm – instead of the heating system fitters travelling to local outlets to buy the parts they needed for each job 'on account', all parts would now be sourced from the new supplier who could provide 95 per cent of all fittings. Staff were issued with a new app-based ordering tool and parts would then be delivered to a central location, direct to site or to the tradesman's vans. Staff would only need to travel to local outlets in emergency situations or to obtain a specialist part.

This change meant considerable savings would be achieved with standardization (previously fitters each favoured certain brands which caused several difficulties when a different team had to carry out a repair) and better planning. The biggest gain was greater efficiency – eliminating the need for costly fitting staff to travel to collect materials.

Arrangements and instructions were communicated to all staff but despite this the change failed initially. Staff resented not being able to travel to get their own supplies. Those who previously favoured other manufacturers' brands of fittings found all sorts of reasons why the new brand was not suitable, deliberately causing failures in some instances. Creative ways to circumvent the new buying arrangements sprung up everywhere with secret stockholdings of old suppliers' products and a proliferation of emergency situations that demanded a visit to a local outlet.

Eventually, following firm intervention by a senior individual, the situation was brought under control and staff got on board and adopted the new arrangements. Weeks later, things worked just fine and the new fittings were mainstream, but the journey to get there was very difficult.

Planning the change

When we buy, implementation of any new buying arrangement demands good planning and management of the actions and changes required. If we are buying a single item that we've not bought before then the actions required here will be minimal (eg we buy the item, it arrives, we check it's OK, we use it). However, consider more complex buying scenarios such as a university changing its provider for security patrols, a manufacturer switching to a new supplier for packaging or a healthcare provider changing the brand of surgical gloves it buys for all its hospitals. In these cases, and others like these, successful buying becomes more about managing the change than simply buying the new goods/services. The things we should consider here are shaped by the nature of what we are buying, the buying approach we identified in our *Power Buying Plan* and the degree to which others within our organization might be involved or impacted. Specific things we might need to plan for include:

- getting the new supplier familiar with our organization and our people and how they can take over, eg the university security patrols will need to figure out their routes;

- making the changes needed, eg if we switch packaging suppliers then we may need adaptations to our manufacturing processes;

- new ordering procedures;

- how to get help or report problems, eg who should people call if there is a problem;

- replacing stockholdings, winding down or removing old stockholdings;

- getting to know and work with the new supplier – new people that our people need to interface and engage with day to day; and

- ensuring compliance – making sure the new arrangements stick and users are satisfied or making the change well (see below).

This step within our *Power Buying Process* is therefore concerned with planning and managing all the actions we must take in order to ensure our new buying arrangements are successfully implemented, and that we realize our intended outcomes. We can do this using a simple action planning tool (included in tool 13 in the appendix). For more complex buying implementations, more sophisticated planning tools or means to identify activities over time such as a Gantt chart can be used.

The reference point for developing a plan is what we are trying to achieve and the need we want to satisfy. Here we return to our *Needs and Wants*, specifically how the final buying arrangements must work and therefore what actions are required in support of this. We may need to involve those affected in developing the plan and so the *Consult and Engage* tool can help here.

There are different types of action planning throughout the buying process, including actions needed to help make our buying decision (eg managing trials, checking how it will impact customers etc), once we have decided how to buy but before we go ahead (eg changing stockholding), or once the new buying arrangement has begun (eg check compliance with users, solicit feedback). In all cases failure to plan for how we buy, how things will be done or what people will do is one of the most common reasons why buying can fail at the final stage, yet there is a greater reason why new buying arrangements frequently fail and that is people, and specifically how people resist change.

Overcoming resistance to change

Surely to buy well all we need to do to is tell people what they need to do? Sometimes this is true – an instruction from someone in authority might be enough, for example in a military situation where authority is respected and unquestioned an order might be complied with unreservedly. Furthermore, sometimes companies have complete control over all their purchasing and can simply 'switch off' suppliers that are not longer to be used and force full compliance to a new supplier. In most cases however, effort is needed to make a change happen. Across all the procurement projects I've been involved in that required people to make some sort of change, only a very tiny number could be driven in an authoritative or compliance controlled manner. For the remainder, much more was required. I've witnessed first-hand many creative ways to resist the change and find ways to not change.

Resistance to change is the biggest single reason why buying projects fail and therefore something we must be alert to and plan for. Resistance to change is a natural human trait that can manifest itself in many and varied ways, often without conscious thought. It is a powerful force that can stop good buying dead if not well managed. At the heart of resistance is fear – fear of the unknown, of the new, of failing, of loss, etc. People resist in all sorts of ways – emotional outburst, 'difficult behaviour' or simply making things fail are some of the more obvious signs of resistance. However, responses can be more sophisticated and might include people saying things like 'if it isn't broken why fix it', 'this was tried before and it didn't work so why waste your time', 'I'm a bit busy now, perhaps next week' and so on.

We are up against human nature here – if the people impacted are not on board or are unsupportive then chances are they will not be enthusiastic and less inclined to help make the change happen. Some may even feel inclined to impede the change, perhaps finding reasons why it is not a good idea or being slow to help support it. Some will even actively resist and sabotage the new arrangements. Crazy? No. The reality of human behaviour in organizations is such that the greater the perceived personal loss, threat to personal autonomy or impact to that which makes people comfortable, the greater the potential resistance.

Resistance can be minimized and sometimes eliminated, but to do this, those involved must feel part of the change and ideally have participated in determining the change somehow. Our original *Consult and Engage* provides the starting point for involvement supported by good communication with visible senior support and mandate. I'll expand on both of these.

Communicating the changes

Communication of new buying arrangements is one of the most important enablers of success including what, how and to whom we communicate details of the change and what we want people to do. Fail to communicate what the change is and the change won't happen. Communicate poorly and people won't do what we need them to do.

There is one even more crucial role for communication and that is to explain 'why'. If people believe in the change they are much more likely to support it; therefore, if we can create a 'felt need' within those involved so that they understand why the change is necessary and how it will help, it can make a big difference. Fail to create the 'felt need' and interest will be low, do it well and people will go to all sorts of extraordinary lengths to help ensure success.

Communication of new buying arrangements is more than explaining the changes, it is about winning support to a cause. To do this well we must grab attention with compelling communications. Here we can learn from all the daily examples of great communication that surround us and pick out the things that get our attention and avoiding those that turn us off such as the long rambling e-mails or 'death by PowerPoint' presentations. There are three steps to follow (these are included within template 13 in the appendix and Figure 9.2 gives an example of the communications plan to support implementation).

1 *Develop the central message* – decide 'what' we need to communicate and how to get the message across so it is short, succinct and includes the fundamental thing we need people to know. A good central message should communicate the nature of the change, what is expected and why it is important. It should also be something that can be easily remembered and quickly articulated, say when bumping into a colleague at the water cooler.

2 *Determine how to communicate* – decide on the best approach and media to reach those who need to know or will be affected, either individually or collectively. Be creative, find ways to get noticed and choose the best channel that suits the individual(s) or message, such as face-to-face, meeting, briefings, presentations, e-mail, posters, printed matter and so on. Whatever you choose make it work well, get someone who is good at communication to help if possible – a long e-mail that few read could doom your buying implementation to failure!

3 *Determine who to communicate to* – use the *Consult and Engage* list as a starting point and decide if this is sufficient and/or identify additional individuals we need to communicate to.

Figure 9.2   An example communications plan to transition to new buying
arrangements.

What do we need to communicate (key or central messages)?

We are making these changes because we must reduce our costs if
we are to compete and survive. We are overpaying for fittings (by
about 25%) + time travelling to collect fittings and all the different
manufacturers products used place a cost burden on us.

From 1st Mar we will move to the PlasTech fittings across the entire
business. Other manufacturers' products will only be used in
exceptional circumstances. Fitters will order via an app and supplies
will be delivered to central stores, site or a van. Using alternative
products or travelling to collect fittings will now require approval.

How will we communicate this (media or approaches we will use)?

- Brief staff at Monday morning meetings weekly before and after
- Publish a summary document explaining the change and providing
  instructions
- Supervisors to give training in using the App

Who will we communicate this to? ☐ **Consult and Engage list +**

All engineers	Stores personnel
Finance team	Current suppliers
Operational planning team	

Success factors for change management

New buying arrangements can also fail if there is no clear mandate for
the change. Changes to buying arrangements must have clear and visible
support and backing, ideally from a senior, respected individual if people are
to take it seriously. Furthermore, a lack of enforcement of the new arrangements (eg bad policy, process, poor control, no compliance) can also cause
things to go wrong.

If we are to implement new buying arrangements well then we must
manage the transition to the new buying arrangements. In practice this
means having a clear action plan and monitoring progress going forward
to ensure actions are delivered and that the plan is realized, working closely
with those involved to ensure people make the change and any problems are
dealt with quickly.

To summarize where we have got to, there are six key success factors we must provide for to manage change of new buying arrangements that involve or depend upon others:

1 **Planning** – ensuring all aspects of the change are considered and planned for.

2 **Participation** – ensuring all involved feel they have been part of designing the change.

3 **Creating a felt need** – so people believe in the change.

4 **Communication** – about the change, what, when, how and, most importantly of all, 'why' (to create the felt need).

5 **Senior support** – so there is a clear mandate.

6 **Managing the change** – actively managing the actions that make the change happen through to timely completion.

Using the tool

The *Implementation* template – 13 in the appendix – supports implementation of new buying arrangements. Use as follows:

1 **Determine key or central message** – consider carefully what we need to communicate so that we can transition to the new buying arrangements. Determine the key or central messages – succinct summaries of what people need to know designed to help create a felt need.

2 **Determine how we will communicate** – determine the media and how we will communicate. Be creative and find the best way to get the message across.

3 **Determine who to communicate to** – the list we identified as part of the *Consult and Engage* list and/or additional individuals as appropriate.

4 **Determine actions** – identify all the individual actions required to implement the new buying arrangement and specific communications actions. Assign and agree an owner for each and a date by which it must be completed. Use the same approach for all actions before we decide, before we buy or once we have bought.

5 **Manage action delivery** – don't assume that because someone has accepted an action that it will happen. Monitor progress closely, push for completion on time and chase up and action any overruns promptly.

6 **Manage the communications** – ensure we do what we set out to do.

Tool 14 – manage supplier(s)

Purpose – to determine and put in place, where appropriate, supplier management arrangements to ensure that we get what we agreed and secure great performance and attention from them.

How to use it – determine intervention required, if any, and action.

When needed – when supplier management intervention is necessary or desirable to ensure we get what we agreed (eg to secure or improve outcomes, reduce risk, etc).

Supplier management is sometimes necessary to ensure we get what we agreed and is concerned with the day-to-day management of the supplier and any interventions needed with them to do this. It is a core activity within SRM (Supplier Relationship Management) and an approach companies all over the world use to ensure they get the most from their supply base and reduce risk exposure. It is a topic all of its own and one I expand in full in *Supplier Relationship Management* (Kogan Page, 2014).

Not all suppliers need to be managed. If we are buying a single thing one time and we are confident it will be delivered as ordered then we don't need to manage the supplier. If we stop our car to buy gas we don't usually need to agree who our point of contact at the gas station is or consider what the long-term vision for our relationship with the gas station might be. All we need is a good transaction – gas for money. In most buying scenarios there is no need to manage the supplier, all we need is fulfilment of the transaction and to get what we agreed. In other buying situations, whilst we may not need any intervention with the supplier, we may want to perform some sort of basic check on what the supplier has provided to ensure we get what we agreed. It is typical for large manufacturing companies to have some sort of goods inwards inspection department. Here, despite parts having been ordered from reputable sources, goods get checked to ensure what has been supplied is correct to order, meets the specification, was received on time and in full, is not damaged and so on. Sophisticated routines are commonplace in manufacturing companies with the level of inspection determined based upon past history or how important a supplier/part is, perhaps involving sampling each delivery (where sample sizes have a mathematical relationship to the probability of detecting a wider problem and acceptable quality levels). Where we don't need such advanced inspection regimes then basic checks might be good practice to help manage a supplier. We probably already do this without thinking about it. If a parcel gets delivered and its clearly damaged chances are we would check if the contents are OK, or if a tradesman had done some painting for us, chances are we would want to check his work before we paid the bill. Basic checks are about verifying the goods have been received or service has been fulfilled OTIF ('On-Time, In Full') or OTIFIS ('...In Specification'), or otherwise as agreed.

For some suppliers, a basic check may not be enough and it might be necessary to check performance one time or ongoing. Performance checks of the supplier or what they are providing are appropriate where it matters that a certain level of performance is achieved and/or we don't have the confidence the performance will be achieved if we don't check. I will expand this in more detail below as part of tool 15 *Performance Check*.

When to manage suppliers

Some buying situations, where the supplier is important (eg because of what we are buying, chances of things going wrong, greater potential available, etc) we need to do more than check fulfilment or performance checks. Here we need deliberate intervention to manage the important supplier – what we do and how we do it should be determined according to what makes them important in the first place. There is no precise way to determine which suppliers are important enough to require management intervention. Companies spend a lot of time and effort figuring this out and many get this very wrong, wasting resources with those who don't need it or failing to spend enough time with the suppliers who can make a difference. Deciding which suppliers are important enough to require some sort of management intervention is a judgement based upon a range of factors including:

- how much we spend;
- current contractual commitments and how important it is that they are realized;
- how much they know our business and the degree to which this knowledge helps the supplier;

- strength of relationships;
- risk to us (see the five supply side risks below);
- our dependency on them (ie our inability to use another supplier, complexity of what we buy or in the *Proprietary* quadrant in the *Power Check* tool); and
- how they can help us in the future and how aligned they are with where we are heading.

Companies often develop complex systems to assess suppliers against criteria such as the above, perhaps involving algorithms that determine a score for each criterion which are then summarized to give an importance rating. Such systems tend to be flawed as 'highest score' can overlook suppliers we should treat as important but would score low, for example a small technology partner with whom we are currently spending little and present no threat to us, but hold potential to help us be great. Instead supplier importance should be determined by considering and making a judgement based on all the different factors and the *Help, Hurt and Heroes* method provides a simple to use approach here.

Help, hurt and heroes

Help, Hurt and Heroes is a simple method to assessment supplier importance and then decide what, if anything, we should do to manage them. We do this for any given supplier by asking 'Could this supplier hurt us?' ie there is significant risk, 'Could this supplier help us?' ie if we can work more closely with them then will the outcome most likely be more in our favour, and 'Is this supplier a Hero?', ie if we can work together with them could they really help us to realize new competitive advantage, achieve a new goal or eliminate a very significant risk? This simple method is one that everyone gets and understands straightaway. It can help put things in perspective and determine who we need to do more with, keeping in mind the fact that, for the vast majority of suppliers, no management other than to ensure fulfilment is needed.

For suppliers we determined we should manage, we must then decide how we will do this based upon what makes them important in the first place – one size does not fit all! If we decide a supplier is important because there is a strong possibility they will fail to deliver on time and lateness would hurt us, then our intervention might be along the lines of frequent progress checks and staying on top of them, whereas we might want to work more closely and develop a relationship with a supplier to whom we our outsourcing our manufacturing.

Supplier importance is typically represented as a pyramid where the supply base is classified into tiers according to importance (Figure 9.3). The base tier represents the vast majority of suppliers with whom we don't need any supplier management intervention. As we move up the pyramid we progress up through tiers of increasing supplier importance, and therefore heightened levels of supplier management intervention, and the number of suppliers reduces. Companies that are advanced in this area manage suppliers based upon some sort of classification like this; the tiers, names and types of intervention might vary but the principle is always the same. This is called 'supplier segmentation' and *Help, Hurt and Heroes* is a simple means to do this.

Figure 9.3 provides four levels of supplier importance linked to the different degrees of intervention with the supplier, each including and further building on the previous level as follows:

1 Non-important suppliers (vast majority) – no or minimal relationship, perhaps basic checks or performance checks and perhaps intervention by exception.

2 Important short term – management of the relationship and interface, and short-term interaction with the supplier to support fulfilment. (Most typical for suppliers who could *Hurt* us.)

3 Important ongoing (eg repeat business relationship) – regular intervention to ensure the agreed contract is being fulfilled ongoing, to monitor and manage risk and to conduct regular progress reviews (typical for suppliers who could *Help* or *Hurt*).

4 Strategic – long-term, joint collaborative relationships (eg for the *Heroes*). Build a relationship where parties work together to realize a mutually beneficial goal. Agree the long-term vision for the relationship, the specific key joint objectives and how parties will work together and collaborate day-to-day.

Figure 9.4 gives a simple *help, hurt and heroes* supplier importance and intervention flow chart; this, together with the *Supplier Management* tool – 14 in the appendix – provides a simple means to help determine where we need to manage a supplier. I shall explore the three levels of supplier management in turn.

Figure 9.3   The supplier importance pyramid and how we typically manage a supplier at each level

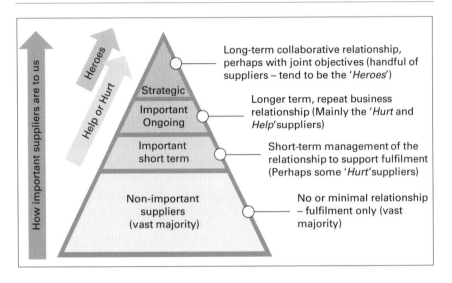

Managing the relationship

Good supplier management for important suppliers cannot be done in isolation, instead it should cover the entire relationship between the supplier and all parts of our organization that connect with this supplier in some way. It should also encompass more than just a single purchase but rather everything this supplier provides to us, both today and what is likely in the future. Remember that the suppliers to an organization are there to enable the organization, they are the organization's suppliers, they do not belong to the buying or procurement function, but rather are an extension of the business, and so supplier management is an organization-wide concern and one that involves everyone.

No matter what the buying scenario, companies don't have relationships with companies, but rather it is the people in those companies that have relationships with people in the other companies. If we are buying non-complex goods then there may not be much cause for individuals on each side to get to know one another. However, with more complex goods goods and services, higher spend, greater dependency and risk then more interaction tends to be required. There are also some supply situations where strong interaction is essential for good performance. For example, if we hire a training company to deliver a specific learning and development programme, customized for us, then individuals on both sides will need to work together to agree content, logistics, feedback and so on. Therefore, when we manage important

Figure 9.4 The help, hurt, heroes flow chart to determine supplier importance and intervention required

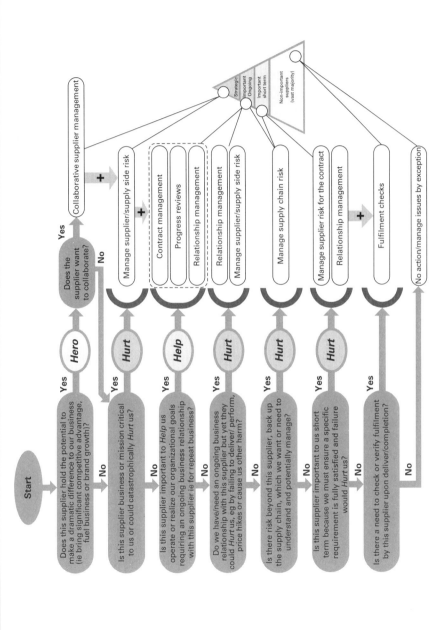

suppliers we need to stage manage the relationships between individuals. Fail to do this and either the right relationships won't happen or will be ad hoc, uncoordinated, perhaps driven by the suppliers', or individuals' agendas, potentially compromising our buying efforts and not securing everything we agreed or expect.

Managing the relationship between individuals is also necessary to ensure alignment on our side. It is commonplace to find those outside of a procurement or buying function holding the firm belief that they own the relationship with suppliers, perhaps in support of technical or operational aspects of what is being bought. This can create tension, especially if those same people don't appreciate the value possible to the entire organization if we buy well. Furthermore, whilst we may have a good idea of how to manage a supplier effectively, others in the organization may not and could undermine the strength of our position. Those in other functions rarely receive any training in effective buying and this, compounded with situations where suppliers seek to build multiple relationships across the organization (effectively seeking to 'divide and conquer') to get information, create dependency and gain an advantage can serve to give the supplier a power position over us. Effective buying for important suppliers therefore also means we need to create a unified approach across our organization with respect to how we interface and work with the supplier. By doing this we not only inhibit the supplier from gaining an undue advantage, but we also increase the likelihood of getting everything we agreed and not being exposed to unforeseen risks as we will be working more closely with the supplier. This level of supplier management is about doing just this and there are five things to decide and plan for;

1 *our people* – deciding and agreeing who in our organization needs to interface with the supplier in some way and for what reason;

2 *their people* – deciding with the supplier who will be the points of contact and interface on their side;

3 *how we will 'face off' to each other* – agreeing a mini 'face-off' map for key individuals: who will interface with whom on each side and the respective agreed roles within the relationship;

4 *ways of working* – agreeing how parties will work together, perhaps with some specific rules of engagement, eg the nominated person who looks after the relationship to be copied in on all e-mails between parties; and

5 *alignment* – secure agreement on the relationship management arrangements from the wider organization and also secure agreement from the supplier's team.

The crucial element within this is to create this mini 'face-off' map. Both parties need to discuss and agree internally how the relationship will work and who will do what on each side. The face-off map is simply the output of this valuable discussion, which then provides the basis to manage the relationship in this way. Figure 9.5 gives an example of a face-off map for a construction project to build an extension to a school. Here we have agreed roles and named points of contact on each side for project management, site management and senior points of escalation. We might also agree rules such as all communication between parties must be channelled through these individuals.

We may have made some provision within our contract for how the relationship should work, and if so this is our starting point. Otherwise, agreeing who will face off against whom and roles to support the relationship begins with our *Consult and Engage* tool, either as originally worked or worked again here in support of this activity. Once we have identified all the individuals then it is a case of agreeing internally how we will work and who will take what role. We can then engage with the supplier to agree people and roles on their side. It is crucial to secure internal agreement and alignment to the ways of working, as any rogue or maverick behaviour in our organization might undermine our efforts. This can be achieved by ensuring we involve and communicate to everyone concerned, secure the support of senior individuals and ensuring all concerned understand why a unified and aligned front is important. Here we may need to take time to educate and win over others for our cause. Organizations that do this well take the time to provide simple internal training on good buying practice to everyone who has any supplier contact. Another useful approach that can really help is to agree, organization wide, a simple set of dos and don'ts for supplier engagement, published and driven in as 'the way we buy' with as much senior backing as possible. You can create your own set, which can often secure greater buy in or use or adapt the following.

Top 10 dos and don'ts for engaging with suppliers

Do ...

1 *Keep it arm's length* – suppliers seek to build relationships which creates a sense of obligation. Keep it arm's-length and build a relationship on your terms.

2 **Have alternatives** – if a supplier believes you have no alternative you give them the power. Make sure they believe you always have an alternative.

3 **Avoid Proprietary** – differentiation, added value items or service, brand or bundled offerings give suppliers power so they become the only provider.

4 **Reveal with caution** – suppliers seek intelligence to determine their strength. Be careful what you reveal, especially about competitors, timings or future plans.

5 **Check them out** – find out their position: how busy are they, where are they heading, is there any risk, what is their overall position? All vital intelligence that can help you understand if you have power.

6 **Condition them** – set expectations about boundaries, limitations, constraints, challenges, or what you expect of them so as to apply a bit of pressure and keep things where you want them.

Don't ...

1 **Tell them your budget** – if you reveal your budget you are handing over power and control unless you have a way to verify subsequent price proposals. Get them to give a number first.

2 **Make an oral contract** – be careful what you say, if you make any sort of verbal commitment you could be entering into an oral contract.

3 **Let them condition you** – watch out for suppliers 'warming you up' for something they want such as an impending price risk or bad news. Challenge it and counter it early on.

4 **Take the first offer** – unless you are building a close relationship, always negotiate, challenge and push back and seek 'something in return for something' if you need to concede.

Finally, when we determine how we will manage the relationship with a supplier it is important to agree how we will deal with or escalate problems. Again, if we included some provision in our contract then we just need to restate this so everyone is aware. If not then it can help to agree internally and with the supplier exactly what we will do if things go wrong. This might be a process but could simply be nominated individuals on each side to whom we will escalate things should we need to.

Figure 9.5   A 'face-off' map for a construction project

Relationship management	List key roles in the relationship and the agreed points of contact for each side against each role		Any agreed relationship rules
Our team	**Relationship Role**	**Supplier's team**	Project Leads to be copied on all correspondence. All matters relating to be channelled through agreed points of contact
1 School Facilities Manager	Project Lead	Project Manager	
2 Admin and Finance Manager	Deputy Project Lead	Site supervisor	**How to deal with/escalate problems?**
3 Admin and Finance Manager	Invoicing and payment	Account Manager	Escalate any issues to agreed individuals
4 Headmaster	Escalation of issues or dispute	CEO	

Managing a supplier ongoing

For those important suppliers where there is an ongoing buying activity, say a supplier provides goods or services we regularly use for a significant area of supply, then we still need to manage the relationship with this supplier as above, but we will also need some additional intervention to ensure that we continue to get what we expect going forward. Once again, the precise nature of what we do depends upon what makes the supplier important to us but essentially, we will need to do one or more of these three things, which I will expand separately in turn, but in fact work in concert to deliver good supplier management:

1 contract management;

2 progress reviews; and

3 managing risk.

Contract management

Contract management is a phrase much used in the buying world and frequently misunderstood. It simply means two things:

1 managing the supplier to an agreed contract or contracts to ensure we get what we agreed and drive performance together with that which we need to do to manage each contract; and

2 organization-wide coordination and management of all the contracts across all suppliers, eg to ensure supply-base-wide compliance to strategic imperatives, risk management, planning for expiry, etc.

Here we consider the specific contract(s) with the supplier we are managing. As we saw in the last chapter, a contract with a supplier should not be viewed as simply a legal document that gets filed away, but rather a means to drive performance and reduce risk. Contract management is the act of seeing this through and is concerned with:

- understanding and managing all the contracts a supplier holds;

- understanding and planning, in good time, for the expiry of each contract so we are not taken by surprise and have sufficient time to consider and negotiate renewal or otherwise;

- monitoring and checking going forward that the supplier, and indeed we, are meeting all the contractual obligations we agreed in the contract, including any performance targets that need to be achieved;

- identifying and acting upon any issues or risks that might impede the supplier from meeting contractual obligations (I'll outline an approach here shortly); and

- dealing with, and managing the process of contract exit where appropriate.

In practical terms there are many systems that can help here, and a large organization would typically have some sort of contract database and performance measurement system. For the rest of us, contract management can be done more simply and is a case of making what was agreed in the contract something everyone lives and breathes. A system to prompt action ahead of contract expiry is useful, which could be as simple as a diarized reminder. Action here might be to renew the contract 'as is,' negotiate some new terms, extend, terminate or let the contract terminate due. In terms of ongoing performance to the contract and contract suitability then the *Performance Check* tool (outlined below) can help along with periodic checks that the contract continues to meet our *Needs and Wants*, perhaps as part of a progress review (up next).

Progress reviews

Progress reviews are periodic or regular reviews with the supplier to check on progress and overall performance in terms of meeting the agreed supply arrangements ongoing or in relation to agreed deliverables. It might sound obvious to suggest the notion of reviewing how things are going – surely this would happen naturally? Sometimes, but more often than not it doesn't. Time moves on and if everything seems to be working OK then the need to review progress with a supplier can become less of a priority. Yet progress reviews are an essential part of good supplier management for many important suppliers, especially for project delivery to provide an 'expectation tension' for milestones to be hit and to enable early action for delays or issues.

Progress reviews can be planned or reactive to an issue and are conducted together with the supplier; they may take place regularly, infrequently or on an ad hoc basis. There is no one single format or approach for a progress review but rather as needed to support a specific supplier relationship based upon what makes the supplier important along with whatever is happening at any given moment in time. Progress reviews should be two-way and would typically involve those nominated points of contact we identified within our 'face-off' map earlier. For an ongoing relationship, it may be appropriate to have different reviews involving different individuals, perhaps an annual review with key senior individuals on both sides, and more frequent reviews to discuss specific operational matters. In either case then the review should cover all the topics necessary to ensure we continue to get what we agreed and discussions should happen based upon prior planning and engagement with others as needed to prepare. Therefore the agenda should be set in advance and might look something like this:

Typical agenda for a supplier progress review

1 *Business updates* – from both parties.

2 *Review of performance* – this could be performance towards agreed goals or against agreed improvement objectives. For a project then this is performance to the plan and agreed deliverables. For ongoing supply then this might be how the supplier is performing. This could be around fulfilment (eg OTIF, etc) or specific ongoing measures of performance (see *Performance Check* below).

3 *Relationship review* – how parties are working together and if the 'face-off' arrangements and rules are being followed. Gain the views of others in our organization in advance to inform this discussion, perhaps even conduct a simple survey.

4 *The future* – discussion about the future on both sides including forecast or possible volumes of business, anticipated changes or factors for which parties need to plan. This could also include a discussion on new opportunities or innovation.

5 *Action planning* – agreed actions, owners and timescales arising from the meeting.

The above format can be adapted for most progress reviews. Reviews with suppliers can be hugely beneficial, unlock great potential and head off serious issues. However, if done badly they can work to the disadvantage of all. Watch out for reviews that 'look in the rear view mirror' too much. Whilst an element of reviewing performance with a supplier would naturally be concerned with examining what has happened and therefore if there are issues that need to be addressed, if the focus becomes about constantly berating a supplier and little else then it will drive defensive behaviour. If this supplier is important to us, and if we depend on them or even need them for the future, a more collaborative and supportive stance can be more productive, focusing on progress towards hitting targets as the primary focus.

Reviews also need to have teeth otherwise they can easily become pointless. If a supplier offers a really good idea that would be to our mutual benefit but all we do is record it in our notes but fail to progress it then we dampen the supplier's enthusiasm and they will be less likely to offer future ideas.

Finally, consider where the review happens. Getting the supplier to come to us seems logical, but there is benefit in going to them or alternating, especially if it would be worthwhile to us to see their facility or what they are doing for us firsthand.

Supplier risk management

Risk is something we each deal with in our daily lives and we will develop our own responses to deal with risk. Where we detect a risk we can't live with we will almost certainly do something to remove it or be ready for it. There can be all sorts of risk in our supply base. When things arrive a bit late or we need to send back the odd consignment, such occurrences are usually minor inconveniences – part of being in business. But if our end product depends on one specific ingredient or material that is single sourced, clearly there is risk. We might believe we understand this risk and perhaps have put in place a long-term agreement with the supplier, but what if a freak weather event suddenly wipes out the only production facility? What if our precious design and know-how suddenly finds its way into a competitor in the Far East who starts copying what we do and nobody seems interested in stopping it? What if the supplier simply fails to turn up when we need them?

Supply side risk management is part of good supplier management and appropriate or necessary for those suppliers who are important, especially if we have determined them to be important due to risk. There are five types of supply side risk (Figure 9.6) and these help us to consider the potential risks we face. Supply side risk management (and indeed any form of risk management) is about not leaving things to chance but rather adopting a more planned and systematic approach. It is about:

1 *Identifying possible risks* – considering all the things that might go wrong using the five risk areas as a starting point.

3 *Risk Likelihood (L)* – deciding how likely each risk is to happen.

4 *Risk Severity (S)* – deciding how severe the impact of each would be.

5 *Actions* – determining what actions, if any, we will take in response to each risk, how likely they are to happen and the severity should they happen. There are three possible responses here:

- *Live with it* – sometimes it is OK to make a deliberate and conscious decision to accept the risk, especially if L and S are low.

- *Mitigate it* – action to reduce or eliminate the risk from happening, eg if we are at risk because we have only one supplier, then finding a second supplier takes away the risk. Action here could also include progress reviews, keeping a close relationship and so on.

- *Contingencies* – accept that the risk might happen and cannot easily be mitigated, but make a Plan B for what we would do should it happen. This might include contingency plans, switching suppliers, reverting to back-up inventories and so on.

Whilst our focus might initially be risk for a specific supplier, sometimes it is necessary to look further and consider risks by suppliers to our supplier's supplier and so on back up the supply chain. If we have set a sustainability objective to buy in an ethically responsible way, and our brand is predicated on this fact, then it becomes necessary to look at risks beyond our immediate suppliers. In practical terms doing this is not easy and requires huge resource, but does follow the same basic approach to risk management. We may also want to look at risk across many suppliers and indeed the entire supply market. Here the results of our *Market assessment* back in stage 2, and in particular the PESTLE analysis, help inform as to when this would be appropriate.

If we were buying the services of a specialist company to remove radioactive waste our initial risk assessment would be a significant and specialist undertaking. However, for most buying scenarios where the supplier is important, a simple risk assessment is all that is needed. This can be done alone, or ideally brainstormed with others in the organization who have an interest. Severity and likelihood can be debated and given a simple high/medium/low rating.

Once we have assessed our risks then the actions we have identified become part of our supplier management effort and so it is good to agree clear owners and ensure any agreed actions are delivered.

The template for *Manage Supplier(s)* – tool 14 in the appendix – includes a simple condensed risk assessment form. Otherwise this same format can be extended and Figure 9.7 gives an example of a more comprehensive risk assessment for a supplier of data management.

Figure 9.6 The five areas of supply side risk

The five supply risk areas				
Failure or delay risk	**Brand reputation risk**	**Competitive advantage risk**	**Price and cost risk**	**Quality risks**
Risk of complete and possibly permanent supply or service failure or risk of delays in supplying goods or providing a specific service	Risks that, should they occur, can be disastrous for our brand either due to failure or practices in conflict with our principles and expectations of customers and stakeholders	Risks of competitive advantage being undermined and include theft of intellectual property, counterfeiting and goods sold on the grey market	The risk of outturn costs being higher than anticipated or planned for (with or without contractual protection)	Risk associated with quality failures, poor product or service quality and latent defects

Figure 9.7 Example of supplier risk management

Supplier risk assessment – For The Data Management Company Ltd						
Supply side risk	Likelihood of occurrence	Severity of Impact	Priority for action	Mitigation or contingency action in response to risk	Owner	By when
Supplier fails and goes bankrupt	L	H	Low	Ongoing monitoring of supplier and maintain close relationship	JH	Ongoing
Our data gets compromised	M	H	2	Audit supplier arrangements to ensure compliance to standards	MH	24 Mar
Major data corruption	M	H	3	Programme of ongoing mirrored back-up verification	MH	Ongoing
Catastrophe takes out data centre	L	H	4	Maintain second mirrored back-up in different location/country	MH	Ongoing
Catastrophe prevents access to data or ability to switch to mirrored back-up	L	H	1	Develop full disaster recovery plan with multiple access methods	MH	31 Mar
Supplier sells data operations to bigger company	H	M	5	Maintain close relationship with supplier to understand plans	JH	Ongoing
Supplier hosts data for other customers who are at odds with our ethics and values	M	L	Low	Audit of supplier, contract for disclosure	JH	31 Mar
Our data is accessed by US government for 'security purposes'	L	M	Low	Maintain 'safe harbour' rating	MH	Ongoing

One common reason for supplier-related problems is failing to really know the supplier and getting taken by surprise. When suppliers go bankrupt they don't usually give warnings to key customers in good time in advance but rather will do everything to hide the problem, attempting to keep confidence high and business rolling! Yet if we know a supplier and get close to them we are better placed to spot such problems before they happen. Good supplier management and managing risk involves staying close to a supplier that is important. Progress reviews provide the forum for discussions, but it is also important to keep close in other ways and take an interest in the supplier's business: follow their social media feeds, watch for them in the press, talk to them and ask lots of questions ongoing to as many people as you can.

Joint collaborative relationships

At the top of our pyramid of importance is the type of supplier we call 'strategic' – a much misused term by suppliers and buyers alike who want to believe they are part of a 'strategic relationship' when often they are not. Strategic suppliers are the very small handful of suppliers that we determine to be of strategic importance to the future of our organization. These are our *Heroes*. That means suppliers that:

- hold the potential to create competitive advantage, raise our share price make us better in our market etc, eg by providing some sort of technology, process, innovation or other unique contribution;
- have some sort of shared destiny and mutual dependency with us, eg we are working with them on new developments, innovation, improvements, etc;
- have a long-term agreement and commitment in place from both sides, eg an outsourced relationship; or
- are business or mission critical to us.

When a supplier is so important that we consider them to be strategic, we need a very different management approach to that which we would deploy for our other important suppliers. The elements of supplier management I have already outlined are still relevant and necessary, but these are part of a much greater effort to manage the supplier as part of a Strategic Collaborative Relationship (SCR).

SCRs are, by nature, long-term relationships where the familiar characteristics of arm's-length, supplier/buyer type relationships, usually on our terms, give way to real joint working, collaboration, cooperation, commitment by both to mutually agreed terms with individual on both sides working closely with one another day-to-day. At the heart of an SCR is almost always a mutually beneficial shared destiny, goal or outcome, with the relationship and those involved organized and aligned towards achieving this. Instead of policing, monitoring and checking a supplier is performing, in an SCR we jointly measure how far away we are from our goal – forward not backward facing. It is like climbing a mountain together, where each climber is willing and wants to reach the top and so helps the other and regularly checks progress toward the summit. Many buyers who have been taught their profession struggle to make the leap to managing an SCR. It is a completely different way of working and one that requires individuals who can build good relationships based upon trust, consistency and openness or sharing. It also requires the buyer and supplier organizations to work differently, orchestrating and coordinating how people from both sides work together and fostering strong communication and transparency.

SCRs are a topic all of their own and a fundamental part of SRM. Once again refer to *Supplier Relationship Management* (Kogan Page, 2014) for a more in-depth exposition. If I distill the topic of SCRs down to the fundamentals, we find there are three key enablers for a long-term, joint SCR and these are included within the template for tool 14, *Manage Suppliers*. They are:

1 *Long-term vision* – define and agree with the supplier the long-term vision for the relationship: what is the mountain we are climbing?

2 *Key joint objectives* – determine and agree with the supplier the joint objectives or targets to realize the vision, and when each will be completed by.

3 *How we will work* – agree the detail of how parties will work and collaborate going forward. The supplier management components above, including the face-off map, help here, but for this type of relationship more is needed including provision for how individual can work jointly.

Finally, as I said earlier, companies don't have relationships with companies, but rather individuals in those companies have relationships with individuals in the other companies. At the heart of a joint collaborative relationship with a strategic supplier are relationships between people. Therefore, success depends upon creating the environment for these to grow and bloom. When successful companies jointly develop something with another company, they don't issue a purchase order to the supplier and then wait for the supplier to deliver it, or try and do it by each working in isolation in their own organizations. Instead they have people work together, whether that be through regular visits, web conferences, secondments or putting everyone together in the same building. One common feature of joint collaborative relationships with suppliers is those involved form a high-performing team and will make time to have social events together. If you want to make a strategic collaborative relationship with a critical supplier really work, find a way for those involved to drink beer together, but share the cost to keep it truly fair and balanced!

Using the tool

Manage Supplier(s) – template 14 in the appendix – provides a structured approach to decide the sort of supplier management that is appropriate, if any, and then to plan the specific interventions and actions to make this happen. Use as follows:

1 **Determine how we will manage the suppliers** – decide how important this supplier is, based on all the tools we have worked so far. Tick the relevant box on the importance pyramid.

2 **For non-important suppliers** – determine only the actions, if any, we need to check or have confidence the purchase will be fulfilled as expected.

3 **For suppliers who are important short term** – complete the 'fulfilment check' section and the 'relationship management' section. Determine and agree across our business and with the supplier all the individuals on both sides who are the agreed points of contact and 'face off' in the relationship. Agree the roles to support the relationship in each case along with any rules for how the relationship will work and how any problems will be dealt with or escalated. Work to ensure all involved understand and agree to work as defined.

4 **For suppliers who are important ongoing** – in addition to 2 and 3 above, determine what ongoing management is appropriate for the supplier and tick all boxes that apply. For contract management, put in place any actions needed to support this. Where risk management is appropriate, conduct (ideally with others who have an interest) a simple assessment of risk, likelihood and severity and determine and follow through the actions identified. Where progress reviews are determined, decide on the topics to be discussed at each review and frequency or timing for reviews.

5 **For suppliers who are strategic** – in addition to all the above, determine together with the supplier the long-term vision for the relationship, key joint objectives and target dates to realize these and how we will work together. Work to make this happen.

Tool 15 – performance check

> **Purpose** – to check, monitor or measure supplier performance and manage supplier improvements.
>
> **How to use it** – optional tool. Apply where and when needed to manage performance and improvements.
>
> **When needed** – when there is a need to manage or measure a supplier's performance either for a single requirement or ongoing.

This final tool 15 is an optional tool that we can use where necessary to check, measure and manage the performance of a supplier, either for a single purchase or ongoing. It is a tool we use together with the rest of this step in the *Power Buying Process*. It also provides the means to manage specific aspects of how a supplier fulfils our requirements and so we might use this tool as a direct result of what we do within *Needs and Wants, Negotiation,* or *Contract* tools.

Supplier Performance Measurement, sometimes called Supplier Performance Management (to suggest action in response to measurement), but in either case known as SPM, is also an entire topic of its own but I will outline the key elements here along with a simple approach to bring about a supplier *Performance Check*.

Why check a supplier's performance?

For the vast majority of suppliers, we do not usually need to carry out any sort of check of performance on what they provide. If we experience or expect problems from a supplier then some sort of fulfilment check might be necessary to satisfy ourselves that the goods or services have been delivered/provided as agreed. We might do this by exception only when things go wrong, or by design if the supplier or what we are buying is sufficiently important to warrant it. For example, safety regulations at a water utility might demand that all deliveries of chemicals added to final drinking water undergo laboratory testing upon receipt before they are used. For some supply scenarios, we might need an ongoing regime of measurement and review, eg to check aspects such as quality or delivery performance and analyse the performance of the supplier over time to detect and take action for issues or worrying trends. This would be typical practice in sectors such as automotive manufacturing where the correctness and OTIF for parts received is critical if problems on the manufacturing line are to be avoided. Ongoing supplier performance checks may also help to see joint progress with a very important supplier. For example, a luxury goods brand might agree a project with a fragrance house to jointly develop a new range of perfumes. Here we might regularly measure, review and check performance towards an agreed launch and the success of a new range.

As with all supplier management and intervention, the nature of performance checks required depends upon how important the supplier is and what makes them important (and especially considering how important, critical or complex what they supply is). There are five degrees of *Performance Check* we can use and one size does not fit all!

- *Don't check* – appropriate for the vast majority of transactional suppliers.

- *Check by exception* – eg when things go wrong, to understand and fix the issue.

- *Fulfilment check (single purchase)* – checking one or more parameters to verify the supplier provided what was agreed, eg checking goods that are delivered or that the service has been fulfilled.

- *Ongoing performance monitoring (performance to date)* – using one or more measures of performance to agreed targets, measured and reviewed ongoing or at regular intervals, that provide a view of supplier performance against that which we agreed. Such monitoring tends to be backward looking, considering past performance, but ideally using this insight can also identify any trends that might demand our attention.

- *Ongoing performance monitoring (towards shared goal)* – it is also possible to design an approach that looks forward to what we hope to achieve rather than based upon what has happened. This is appropriate for those suppliers we identified as *Strategic* in our *Manage Supplier(s)* tool. Here we design targets and ongoing checks or measures based on the distance from, and the degree of progress towards, joint goals. Such an approach will still need to use measures of past performance but interpreted to create indicators of anticipated future performance.

Success factors for supplier performance checks

Key to using this tool is aiming for the right amount of checking or measurement, if any, and no more, and of the right things, used in a way that helps achieve the required outcomes. Buyers in organizations find all sorts of things to measure when it comes to suppliers. It seems there is a commonly held belief that part of being a buyer means measuring suppliers and measuring as many things as possible. Across the many companies I've worked with, I find that people like to proudly demonstrate their measurement system, perhaps boasting comprehensive supplier scorecards with as many as 20 or 30 measures or indicators on them. When I ask how all the analysis is adding value the answer is not always that clear. As the old adage goes – you are what you measure, suggesting that if we measure something then that will in some way drive outcomes. If a construction contractor signs up to a penalty term in a contract for late delivery or being over budget then they will orchestrate their entire efforts to achieve this first and foremost – nothing focuses a supplier like a contract! This is a good thing right? It certainly drives the required results and hits the target, but does it always achieve the right outcomes? Perhaps, but it is also likely to focus the supplier into finding ways to undermine the arrangement by watching for any sort of unplanned event or change in requirements that might allow them to suggest 'things have changed' and therefore transfer the blame for not hitting a target back to something the client did. Hitting targets and meeting contractual obligations can easily become the primary driver and motivator leaving little incentive for collaboration or maximizing mutual benefits.

Another key dimension in checking performance is what we do with the results. This starts with how analysis and insight gained by checking or measuring a supplier performance is presented and shared. Some companies have the luxury of state-of-the-art enterprise-wide information systems that can provide real-time, well-presented supplier performance at the push of a button. For most, supplier performance checks require more effort and brainpower to make it work – it is easy to collect data about an aspect of the supplier's performance but much harder to make it worthwhile. If great resource is consumed producing large reports that get circulated, ignored and whose only purpose is solely to fill a progress review agenda topic, then the value should be questioned. We only have a finite amount of resource, so we should direct this only at the supplier performance check activity that will have the greatest value and impact and help improve buying outcomes.

We must also remember that our suppliers are the organization's suppliers, so it follows that those involved throughout the organization might either need to be consulted about supplier performance (eg we should ask them if the supplier is meeting their expectations), and also that they might be interested in how they are performing.

Therefore, the design of any approach to check performance with a supplier must consider what is actually needed from a supplier (*Needs and Wants*). You are what you measure? Yes, and if you check or measure the wrong things, only things that are easy to measure or too many things with a supplier, then you will get what you measure. Even with the right checks and measures the intervention can be pointless if you fail to present, share or act on the findings in any meaningful way.

Monitoring supplier performance ongoing

Ongoing supplier performance monitoring is about setting up a system to measure and act upon the relevant aspects of performance for a supplier we use ongoing who we have deemed to be important enough to warrant this. It is all too easy to create supplier checking and monitoring systems that take on a life of their own, but the most effective approaches here tend to be the simplest ones that all understand and work with. Part of the problem here is that there is a raft of terminology around this topic and a buyer could be forgiven for thinking this is a specialist pursuit reserved for experts in this subject. This is not the case and setting up a good system to check, monitor or measure supplier performance ongoing is quite straightforward. Table 9.1 provides an explanation of the key terms and approaches found in the world of SPM.

The most common approach is using a supplier scorecard (and a simple scorecard is included in the template for this tool in the appendix). It is called a scorecard because, just as a scorecard is used in sport to keep tally of current performance, we use a scorecard for the supplier to keep tally of the areas of performance we wish to monitor. Figure 9.8 gives an example.

A supplier scorecard might be developed internally based upon what we want to monitor, but would most commonly be developed or at least agreed with the supplier. After all, if the supplier is to meet our expectations they will need to understand how they will be assessed. We must determine what aspects of performance we will measure and here is where it is easy to get carried away, but less is more! A supplier performance system should always be developed as if every different thing we measure or monitor is in some way scarce and costs a huge sum of money to do so. Such thinking compels us to consider carefully what is important. For example, a friend of mine owns a small restaurant and often if I am out with him he will call his staff to find out how things are going. There are many things he could ask – he could ask how much money they have taken, or if everyone turned up for work, or what problems have been encountered – but he asks none of these. Instead he simply asks; 'How many covers?' (ie the number of meals served).

This simple piece of performance information tells him everything he needs to know. From this he will have a rough idea of how much money was taken, how busy it has been, how many drinks were sold and so on.

With scarcity in mind we must decide the things we want to check or measure that will best help us understand how our supplier is performing ongoing. Every supplier scenario is different and so what we check will be different from one supplier to another. Just because we might monitor delivery performance with one supplier does not mean we should do it with all. We must also decide how we will monitor performance – how many things do we need to check? Do we need to measure an aspect of performance? Would an indicator based upon measurement interpretation be more useful? For example 'quantity received' is a measure of performance whilst 'average delivery performance over time' is a more useful indicator of performance and one that not only gives a backward-facing view of performance but can provide a future facing trend that might help us know if we need to take action. It is here where we get the term KPI (Key Performance Indicator), a much-used term in this area, which simply means an indicator (ie information about what is happening) around performance that is deemed to be key or highly important. The 'key' component is based around the concept of scarcity that I outlined above, but as I also said before, KPIs are commonly overused – too many will usually dilute the effectiveness of the performance checking regime.

The aim is to find just the right, small number of KPIs and perhaps simple measures that will tell us what we need about the supplier's performance ongoing. Once we have determined what these are then the following steps will complete the set up of our scorecard:

1 *Target* – determine the target or what must be achieved for each KPI or performance measure we will use.

2 *Data collection* – determine and put in place the arrangements to collect the information or data needed to check or measure each performance requirement. This may involve taking physical measurements (say of an aspect of quality), checking and recording other factors (say OTIF), extracting outputs from company systems and analysing the data to create our KPI result. For some KPIs this might be less about being able to measure something but more about gaining subjective feedback; for example, if our KPI was 'overall satisfaction of users' then there is no quantitative measure here, but rather we would have to convert several qualitative opinions into a summary number. This happens all the time

around us when we fill out a survey or give a five-star review for something we bought online. For our supplier performance check we might need a similar approach to determine our KPIs.

3 *Frequency* – decide how often the performance check against the KPIs or measures will happen (ad hoc when needed or at a set frequency, say quarterly).

4 *Implement* – agree the approach internally and with the supplier (unless there is a good reason to keep it internal) and also agree how results will be shared and reviewed.

Good supplier performance checks can help ensure we get what we agreed ongoing. However, it is worth remembering that sometimes the most important things cannot be measured. In my car I have a dashboard of measures and indicators, yet my decisions about driving are also, and more so, informed from other factors such as road conditions, weather, how the traffic is moving, perceived space from the car in front, risks, the feel of the car on the road and so on. These are more than responses to measures or indicators but a complex series of judgements I make without fully understanding or being conscious of how. Performance checks alone may not always be enough to truly understand a supplier's performance and where things are heading. Our scorecard might look strong, but if we have the sense things are going wrong with the supplier, say because key individuals are leaving or there are rumours of things changing, then there might be a deeper problem that our performance check won't detect, or at least won't detect fast enough. No matter how good our performance check arrangements are we should always work to stay tuned to all aspects of supplier performance overall.

Sometimes performance checks on the supplier alone may be enough, but for others where the ability to collaborate is key, understanding how we are performing within the relationship is equally important if the relationship is to be effective. There are scenarios where performance checks for a supplier relationship should be two-way. This might include arrangements to measure our performance for aspects such as communication and sharing, payment performance, relationships and so on. In practical terms this might mean having two scorecards or a joint scorecard.

If we put a system for ongoing performance checks in place then we must ensure that our approach continues to be effective and add value. What we need to check and measure might change over time according to circumstance, therefore our approach should always be dynamic with what, how and when we monitor should be reviewed periodically.

Table 9.1 Common terms used for supplier performance measurement

Term	Explanation
Measure	The value, degree of something that can be compared to a known reference point.
Indicator	Information about something, typically determined using one or more measures and some interpretation to provide something that is more useful than measures alone. Indicators can be lagging, ie information about what has happened, eg average delivery performance for the past year. They can also be leading – providing information about what is predicted to happen, usually based on what has happened, eg '30miles/km to empty' combines information about capacity of fuel remaining with indicators about past driving.
KPI	Key performance indicator – an indicator of performance that is determined to be key, more important in some way or essential and necessary ongoing to guide a business or function towards a stated goal or to provide an alert of a state that might prevent, or hinder reaching, the goal.
SLA	Service Level Agreement – often described as a measure or a measurement system but in fact is a means by which performance targets can be defined and formally agreed, say within a contract. An SLA might contain KPIs and targets for these.
Scorecard	A commonly used output mechanism and means to collate and display a range of different supplier performance measures or indicators and provides a representation of *performance over time* to a set goal or target. A supplier scorecard is typically used to support performance monitoring for an individual supplier so an organization might maintain multiple scorecards for all important suppliers.
Dashboard	An output mechanism and means to display a range of different supplier performance measures or indicators and display a representation of performance at a *specific point in time*. A dashboard could be used for performance measurement of a single supplier or, as is most common, to provide combined summary information across several or all suppliers about a range of key supplier performance metrics. Supplier dashboards are modern tools of executive teams, increasingly available, powered by modern data analysis and visualization tools either online or part of the latest ERP packages.

Figure 9.8 An example supplier performance scorecard

Supplier Score Card – For Entreprise Gadget Logiciel, France						
Lagging Measures or KPIs	**Result area and information source**	**Target**	**Q1**	**Q2**	**Q3**	**Q4**
Safety - Lost Time Injury Frequency Rate	Number of incidents or near misses at supplier, with product or during delivery	Zero	0	0	1	0
Assurance of supply - Delivery on time, in full, in specification (OTIFIS)	DOTIFIS report from ERP good receipt + Internal rejections	98%	98%	100%	99%	92%
Relationship performance - delivery of actions, support and communication	Stakeholder survey results, complaints from stakeholders	90% very satisfied	90%	100%	95%	82%
Leading Measures or KPIs	**Result area and information source**	**Target**	**Q1**	**Q2**	**Q3**	**Q4**
Growth and innovation - supplier contribution to business growth	Number new ideas delivered and total delivered value for both parties from them	2 ideas $50K/idea	0 ideas $0K/idea	3 ideas $78K/idea	2 ideas $10K/idea	2 ideas $60K/idea
Waste reduction - to meet corporate waste minimization goal	Production scrap rates, energy usage, packaging volumes and assessment	2%	5%	4.5%	4.2%	3.4%
Sustainability goals and compliance - Policy compliance within 2 years	Audit reports	100% in 2 years	78%	82%	82%	82%

When things go wrong – driving supplier improvements

Our performance check tells us how a supplier is performing against the agreed goals or targets and in terms of how we get what we agreed. What happens when things go wrong, when the supplier underperforms or simply fails completely? Clearly some sort of action will be needed to deal with the situation, perhaps having the supplier fix the problem or more, but always requiring some sort of intervention to drive improvement.

Deciding on the appropriate level of improvement required depends upon the need for improvement, what might be practically possible or worthwhile. If we order a product online from a supplier we don't know that costs £2.50 and gets shipped direct from China, and when it arrives we are disappointed, then perhaps we might try to return it, contact the provider or give appropriate feedback. Perhaps we might simply throw it straight in the bin and resolve not to buy anything more from that supplier. Perhaps the practicalities of getting the supplier to fix the problem are too great for the value of the item. Yet if a garage services our car but fails to fix the problem it went in with, chances are we would demand that they put things right – we would insist on some corrective action. Sometimes corrective action alone is not enough but instead we need the supplier to take additional steps to prevent it happening again. If we encounter several consignments of product from a supplier arriving damaged due to inadequate packaging, we would clearly want the supplier to replace the damaged items but also to take steps to change the packaging used for future consignments.

We might also want to help a supplier improve in situations where there is no problem but where there are benefits if we can work with the supplier to improve and develop some aspect of what they do. Imagine if there is something we are trying to source regularly, but there are issues with the reliability of current suppliers, and we approach one of our current, trusted suppliers who don't currently offer such a thing but have similar capabilities that we believe could be extended to supply this. If the supplier agrees, we would then work with them to develop them and their capability. Perhaps we might help fund the necessary investment, agree and guarantee a long-term supply arrangement and have someone work at their site and help them implement the changes – a different form of improvement and development.

Therefore, once again one size does not fit all and there are different possible responses according to the scenario:

- *No improvement* – accept the situation, tolerate what has gone wrong or switch suppliers if we can.

- *Reactive supplier improvement* – corrective action, corrective and preventative action and perhaps continuous improvement to:
  - fix a problem;
  - reduce or eliminate a known risk;
  - reduce cost;
  - improve process effectiveness or efficiency; or
  - improve poor performance.

- *Proactive supplier development* – working collaboratively with the supplier to advance towards an agreed goal to:
  - develop a new product or service;
  - create a new differentiator;
  - increase market penetration;
  - enter new markets or;
  - release new value that benefits both parties.

It doesn't follow that just because we want some form of improvement from a supplier that the supplier will respond. This depends upon the supplier's appetite, enthusiasm and ability to improve. It doesn't follow that if you tell a supplier how you want them to improve that they will do so. Maybe they will, maybe they don't want to, maybe they need help to change. If I buy something from a shop that turns out to be defective then if I take it back they will almost certainly fix the problem, perhaps with a refund or replacement. Why? Well, they have legal obligations here and would most likely want to make sure I am satisfied and so preserve their reputation and brand. I may also be a good customer and one they don't want to lose. However, if I ask the same shop owner to alter his range or make changes to the way things are stocked he may listen, may be interested or may simply politely thank me and do nothing. The supplier's appetite for certain forms of improvement can depend upon our relationship and how much buying power we have with them. If we are in *Propietary* in the *Power Check* tool then chances are the supplier might not be as interested as we want them to be. Yet in *Custom* they are likely to be receptive to our ideas and suggestions. Therefore, when we are keen for a supplier to make some form of improvement we need to understand the underlying position.

Furthermore, suppliers will rarely get enthusiastic about improvement if our approach with them is built solely around giving them a black mark every time they fall short. This is like berating a child for not getting the grades the parent expected. As many parents will testify, this can be counter-productive. A more productive approach is to attempt to understand what is preventing the child from performing or encouraging the child to do better, unless of course the child has decided simply not to perform in which case a different response becomes appropriate. Suppliers are no different – if we are poised ready to pounce at the first hint of failure the supplier will adopt a defensive and protectionist stance. Instead an approach based more around better understanding our supplier and what is causing any problems, and therefore how best to be intervene, can be more constructive.

Supplier improvement using STPDR

We can manage and drive supplier improvement using the STPDR process, a simple and straightforward approach for driving all types of supplier improvement (Figure 9.9). STPDR is a five-stage improvement process based upon best practice principles for business improvement and can be applied to a variety of situations. The five stages are *Study (the situation)*, *Target, Plan, Do* and *Review.*

The first step for any supplier improvement is to *Study* the situation to identify the precise nature of the problem we are attempting to fix or the area where we need improvement. This is a crucial but often missed step and it is easy to assume we understand the problem. If we are faced with a simple delivery issue then the problem may well be readily apparent, but not all supplier-related problems are that simple and it may not be until later that an issue surfaces. Imagine buying several tins of paint for a home improvement project which all appear to be identical, but once applied it turns out there is a slight variation in colour from one part of our painted wall to another. Here the problem only becomes apparent after use and we would then need to study the problem, to attempt to identify if it is a problem with the paint, the wall or the application, to check which tins are different, if they have batch numbers, and if so if there is a variation or anything that might tell us what has caused the problem. Only then could we begin to figure out what we need to do to remedy the problem.

Therefore supplier improvement begins by first defining the problem and then, if the cause is not obvious, to study the situation or problem in order to determine its root cause, eg is the problem the paint, the wall,

Figure 9.9 The five-stage STPDR Supplier Improvement Process

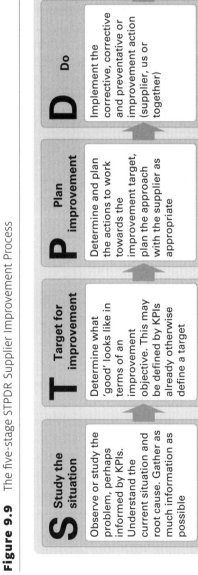

S Study the situation

Observe or study the problem, perhaps informed by KPIs. Understand the current situation and root cause. Gather as much information as possible

T Target for improvement

Determine what 'good' looks like in terms of an improvement objective. This may be defined by KPIs already otherwise define a target

P Plan improvement

Determine and plan the actions to work towards the improvement target, plan the approach with the supplier as appropriate

D Do

Implement the corrective, corrective and preventative or improvement action (supplier, us or together)

R Review

Check results and outcomes and if improvement has been a success (ie target met). Act if not met otherwise take action to ensure changes stick our application or something else? This may not be as straightforward as it might seem, largely because our biases can prevent us seeing other than what we want to see. Where there is no problem but we are developing a supplier then this shifts to studying what is holding us back.

With a good understanding of the situation, we can then determine what the improvement target is or the outcome we need. It is easy to skip over this with our natural human tendency to cut straight to a solution: 'The paint is the wrong colour' so 'I'll take it back and get some new paint'. An obvious response and we will automatically make similar responses every day without a second thought, but this is not a target, this is actually a proposal or plan of what we intend to do. Our brains have already processed the problem and decided on the course of action. In the case of our tin of paint this may be enough, but if we jump straight to solutions for more complex issues, we might lose sight of what we set out to achieve, or worse, those around us can't see or share our vision of our future direction and end up following aimlessly.

Our plan becomes the specific action to fix the problem or drive on the improvement in order to meet the target. This may be a simple one-off action (eg 'take the paint back and get new'), which would typically be expected for simple supplier problems, or could be a sequence of steps and activities of varying degrees of complexity.

The *Do* step is just what it says; it is about putting the supplier improvement plan into action. If we have completed the first three steps effectively then this step should be the easiest to get right. Success from *Do* comes through good project management in organizing, motivating and controlling resources and those involved to work towards the target.

The fifth *Review* step in supplier improvement is about two things: first, checking that the improvement has been made and we have reached our target, perhaps by studying the situation again, and secondly about instigating any new arrangements to ensure the improvement sticks, otherwise things may simply revert to the previous state. This might involve new arrangements, policies, procedures, training, etc.

Using the tool

The *Performance Check* – template 15 in the appendix – provides a means to check, monitor and measure suppliers and use the STPDR process when things go wrong. Use as follows:

1 **Determine performance check required** – decide if a performance check is required and if so to what degree.

2 For check of fulfilment only (single purchase) – check what the supplier has supplied/service provided and, if fulfilled, tick boxes as appropriate, note and action any issues as appropriate.

3 Where ongoing performance monitoring is required – determine one or more aspects of performance that we want to check ongoing (informed by *Needs and Wants*, *Negotiation* or *Contract* tools and other needs we determine). Work to keep the number of aspects of performance as few as possible, as if each is scarce. For each:

- decide the best way to get the performance information that will be most useful to us – select either direct measures of some aspect of performance, indicators or KPIs as appropriate;
- determine the target that must be met or we wish to work towards;
- determine the frequency to check or measure against each performance requirement, eg monthly, quarterly, etc, and;
- put in place the arrangements to collect and analyse the data to conduct the performance check.

Put the scorecard into practice and check or measure against each of the requirements regularly. Note each result, compare with any results for the previous period and note any trends or issues. Share with others internally and with the supplier. Action issues as appropriate.

4 Where there is a problem or an improvement is required – for a supplier-related issue or problem, decide on the level of response required and tick the appropriate box. From this, or in response to another reason for improvement, work through the STPDR process. Study the situation and note findings and any root cause. From here determine and note the target, plan, actions to implement the plan (*Do*) and then *Review*, verify the improvement is a success and identify actions to make any change stick.

Summary

The key learning points from this chapter:

1 Step 5 *Delivery* is about ensuring we get everything we agreed from our supplier and comprises three tools that work together to help is do this.

2 Tool 13 – *Implementation*– is concerned with realizing our *Power Buying Plan* and planning the specific actions and changes required to make it happen.

3 Successful implementation for a change to buying arrangements that impacts or involves others requires strong change management to avoid resistance to change and secure buy-in.

4 Tool 14 – *Manage Supplier* – provides a means to determine importance and how we will manage the suppliers in response to this. This might include managing the relationship, actions to manage supply side risk, instigating regular progress checks and, for those suppliers we deem to be strategic, actions to build a joint collaborative relationship and pursue a shared goal.

5 Where there is a need to check supplier performance, either to verify they meet our expectations and we get what we agreed for a single buying scenario, or ongoing, then tool 15 – *Performance Check* – provides a framework to do this. Checks and measures of supplier performance should be identified according to the buying scenario and what makes the supplier important. One size does not fit all and less is more – select only the essential checks, measures and indicators that tell us everything we need to know and use a simple scorecard system to check performance at regular intervals.

6 Where there is a need for supplier improvement, either in response to a supplier-related issue or problem or an improvement from an already good position would create a great result, the STPDR process provides a simple to use approach to ensure we manage the improvement and secure the right outcome.

Making power buying a success   10

In this final chapter we explore how to make the 5D Power Buying Process a success. We explore the role of procurement in today's global organizations, what sustainable buying is, the challenges involved and how to begin to practice it and we conclude with some final thoughts around how to continue the journey as a power buying professional.

Pathway question addressed in this chapter

20 How do I make *Power Buying* a success and continue the journey as a power buying professional?

Our journey through the *5D Power Buying Process* is now complete. The approach enables individuals or organizations to be highly effective at buying in all scenarios. Great buying outcomes are possible by working through each of the tools we have explored, and with practice, the approach, tools and concepts become familiar and second nature. With experience a good buyer can immediately understand the situation they face and the best approach to use. This experience comes with practice and begins with the things we face every day when we buy – which quadrant in the *Power Check* tool are we in? Which price model in *Price Check* is being used? What *Power Boosters* might help me, and so on? Making power buying a success is simply the case of becoming familiar with the tools and adept at applying them, consulting and engaging with others as appropriate.

The *5D Power Buying Process* alone is sufficient to navigate through the most complex or significant of buying situations. It is founded upon, and contains many elements of, modern best practice procurement and core strategic procurement tools. If you are keen to go further, extend your buying capability, or even pursue a profession in procurement, in this final chapter I will outline the main components of modern strategic procurement and its role to enable today's global organizations, how we can buy sustainably and how to continue the journey as a power buying professional.

Procurement in today's global organizations

Procurement (or purchasing, sourcing, supply chain management or however else it may be known) is a fundamental, strategic and enabling function in today's modern global organizations. As we saw back in Chapter 1, this has not always been the case, and rewind the clock 30 years or so and the function responsible for buying in organizations tended to be highly tactical and reactive. Today things still need to be purchased and orders need to be placed by organizations and so there is always a transactional component within buying. However, in leading modern companies this activity is distinct from the main procurement function, perhaps separated out either as its own function or a sub-function. Today the main role of an effective procurement function is strategic and informs and is informed by the overall strategic, aims and objectives of the organization. It seeks to ensure that the organization secures the greatest value and least risk from the supply base whilst unlocking the additional value that is possible by identifying and connecting supply chain possibilities with organizational needs and wants, and even end customer desires and aspirations. Core to realizing this is the concept of the supply base as an extended part of the organization and a source of value as part of an overall 'value chain' (Porter, 1985), which flow into the organization as products or services, pass through the organization and are transformed in some way by each function within the organization, directly or indirectly adding value in some way to create the new value in the form of final products or services which flow to the end customer. This is illustrated in the 3S model (sourcing, satisfying and strategy) as given in Figure 10.1 which defines how procurement must be positioned in a business if it is to add value beyond simple buying. Here procurement is responsible for 'sourcing' and the relationship with the supply base, with a solid connection through the value chain to the end customer, perhaps ultimately through functions such as sales and marketing, responsible for 'satisfying' the needs of the customer, and all informing and being informed by corporate 'strategy'.

Bringing the 3S concept to life in organizations is the key success factor in establishing a value adding strategic procurement function, which reinforces the comments in previous chapters around procurement being is an organization-wide concern. In practical terms this means that a modern procurement function must understand and connect with the entire business to ensure its needs are served and help coordinate new, better sourcing strategies. It is this cross-functional working that underpins the way all good procurement projects and activities happen.

Figure 10.1 The 3S model for effective procurement

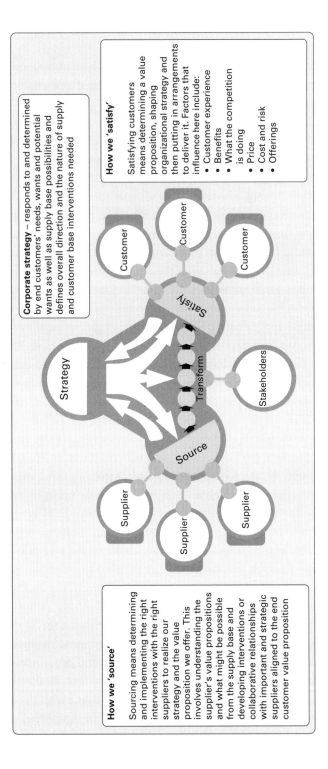

How we 'source'

Sourcing means determining and implementing the right interventions with the right suppliers to realize our strategy and the value proposition we offer. This involves understanding the supplier's value propositions and what might be possible from the supply base and developing interventions or collaborative relationships with important and strategic suppliers aligned to the end customer value proposition

Corporate strategy – responds to and determined by end customers' needs, wants and potential wants as well as supply base possibilities and defines overall direction and the nature of supply and customer base interventions needed

How we 'satisfy'

Satisfying customers means determining a value proposition, shaping organizational strategy and then putting in arrangements to deliver it. Factors that influence here include:
- Customer experience
- Benefits
- What the competition is doing
- Price
- Cost and risk
- Offerings

Customer

Customer

Customer

Satisfy

Strategy

Transform

Source

Stakeholders

Supplier

Supplier

Supplier

The modern strategic procurement function

There are a number of features that distinguish a modern high-value-adding strategic procurement function from one that just buys in any organization. These are that the function:

- understands where the organization spends money, how much and on what and why, today and future planned. It will understand the greatest opportunities and risks and lead or directly contribute to finding the best possible sourcing arrangements for the priority areas of spend so as to maximize value to the organization;

- knows which suppliers are most important to the business and will actively work to have the right sort of relationship with these, managing and working with them as appropriate;

- is supported by experienced practitioners who use modern best practice procurement methodologies such as Category Management and Supplier Relationship Management (more on these below), along with other best practice sourcing tools;

- does not work in isolation, but will actively engage with the wider business to understand the entire needs and wants of the organization, securing buy-in for new sourcing arrangements and helping the wider business understand and plays its role in an organization-wide strategic procurement approach;

- understands and responds to the ever-changing market places that supply the organization, seeking to match entire groups of spend on product or service against the right market and maximize potential/minimize risk;

- understands and takes steps to minimize or mitigate supply side risks;

- actively leads and manages strategic sourcing projects together with the wider organization to continually improve the value secured from the supply base or help realize organizational goals; and

- has board-level representation and the wider business understands and supports its role.

Whilst many reading the list above will recognize these features, there remain many companies out there that have huge spends but continue to buy tactically, missing the potential that is otherwise possible. Worse, there are organizations out there that believe they are doing great procurement, but despite the impressive titles and a fancy structure are still operating tactically. There are also organizations trying desperately to make good procurement happen but being hampered by maverick behaviour in the wider organization that undermines the procurement effort.

All this points to one single fact, one we have touched on throughout this book: if an organization is to buy effectively, and have a procurement function that adds value to and enables the organization to realize its goals, then the organization must embrace procurement as a strategic organization-wide philosophy, and one all understand and contribute to. Achieving this is possibly the single most difficult challenge for any organization.

Positioning procurement in the organization

The way procurement is positioned within an organization can make a difference to how effective it can be. There are three basic models here – centralized, decentralized or centre-led (Figure 10.2) – according to how procurement (including the transactional buying component) happens. In a centralized model a single function has responsibility for all buying and all relationships with suppliers and perhaps even responsibility for all buying transactions or at least approving them. Centralized procurement functions have complete control and so can drive in the most effective procurement arrangements based upon how it understands what the business needs. However, centralized procurement is increasingly rare, especially in large organizations, it is hard to establish retrospectively and whilst providing a means to control all buying the function can easily be disconnected with what the business needs or can hamper organization effectiveness. Decentralized procurement on the other hand is more commonplace and tends to be a product of how organizations have evolved – with local business units handling their own buying and relationships with suppliers in order to operate. Whilst decentralized procurement provides an agile approach to getting things done, it can also prevent the organization from operating strategically with local deals, multiple local relationships with suppliers and no joined-up approach. Organization-wide leverage possible by aggregation of spend is lost, along with the efficiencies of standardization, suppliers gain greater power and, depending upon the systems used for buying transactions, the organization can easily wind up having no or limited control or visibility of its buying. By contrast, in a centre-led model a single function takes responsibility for the most important areas of spend and supplier relationships and, based upon working with the wider organization, works to put in place single supply arrangements on behalf of the entire business. Local buying entities continue to enjoy some buying autonomy but work with and are led from or even report to the

Figure 10.2 The three models for positioning procurement in an organization

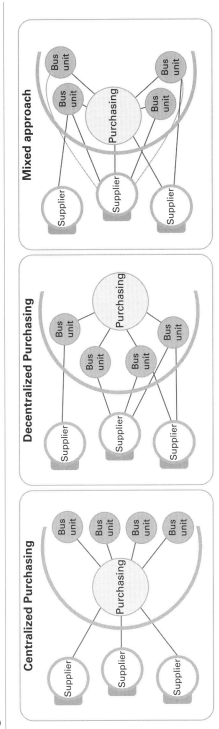

centre. Relationships with suppliers typically exist throughout the organization but are managed (using approaches such as the face-off map in the *Manage Supplier(s)* tool). Centre-led procurement seems to be the modern approach that allows business to regain control over its procurement effectiveness, perhaps transitioning away from decentralized procurement, to drive in strategic procurement approaches responding to the needs across the organization. Even where an organization mandates this approach, key to making this work is cooperation, selling the concept to all involved and, once again, everyone understanding and buying into the fact that procurement is an organization-wide philosophy.

The modern procurement function has many different elements it needs to manage and coordinate. Clearly the organization needs to buy things so there will be some sort of system for this, perhaps a Requisition to Pay or Purchase to Pay system (R2P/P2P) either stand-alone or part of a bigger Enterprise Resource Planning (ERP) system such as SAP or Oracle. Such systems will either sit within the procurement function or out in the wider business. Ideally such systems also help to support how the procurement function operates, providing important data and analysis to help prioritize effort. As we have seen already, the role of a modern procurement function is much more than buying but will be focused on maximizing the value the organization secures from the supply base. To do this, talented practitioners apply a variety of tools and approaches or lead or coordinate strategic sourcing projects together with the organization to identify and implement the most effective sourcing arrangements. There are many things I could include here, but I will finish this book by providing an outline introduction to what seem to be the most necessary enabling skills, tools and approaches for the modern strategic procurement function and professional. These are:

- the ability to buy globally;

- managing outsourcing;

- the effective deployment of the core strategic approaches of category management and SRM;

- seizing the benefits from modern sourcing tools such as eAuctions: and

- managing the supply base beyond or immediate suppliers, including driving in sustainable buying;

- maintaining personal ethics when buying.

I will expand each of these in turn and in each case outline how the *Power Buying Process* can be applied to support these.

Buying globally

Today we can buy from a global marketplace, and doing so can bring us advantage. Once upon a time buying was a local affair and sourcing from beyond our immediate situation would be the thing of specialists and for a unique reason. Today things are different and international buying is a core component of modern procurement in global corporations. Indeed, the skill set required here is pretty much essential for most procurement professionals. As individuals and consumers we now access sources of supply far beyond our home country, often without even being aware. Strawberries being picked in Spain today might be on our breakfast table in the UK tomorrow morning and an electronic gadget found on Amazon might be shipped direct from China to our door in just a couple of days. We may not even realize where the goods we buy originate from as the retailer has done all the hard work behind the scenes.

As buyers, globalization presents us with enhanced opportunities. Countries that were once only holiday destinations are now home to the next generation supply base, hungry for our business and ready to put in place the quality, health and safety, and environmental compliance systems Western customers might demand. The assumption that a supplier in a developing country can only achieve variable quality and uncertain delivery or that the workforce must be poorly treated is outdated. There are plenty of examples of poor practice to be found, but equally many examples of excellence, driven by Western companies working to develop their remote suppliers. I have visited suppliers in remote locations around the world that are better equipped and managed than most average European or US operations, and with full compliance to recognized quality, safety and environmental management systems.

The *Power Buying Process* enables us to access these opportunities from the global market with some key considerations:

- Understanding and qualifying potential suppliers might require some local knowledge and perhaps even visiting them.
- There are increased and different supply-side risks to understand and plan for.
- We must understand and plan for transportation, importing, duties, tariffs etc.
- There may be cultural differences we need to work with during *Negotiation*.
- *Contracting* might not work in the same way it does in the West with the contract itself regarded as less important than the relationship in some cultures.

Outsourcing

Outsourcing is when an entire function or activity within an organization is moved outside the organization to a supplier who will fulfil that function, often as if an extended part of the organization. Building on the value chain principle we mentioned earlier, part of the value chain gets moved outside the company to a supplier or suppliers. Outsourcing gained in popularity during the 1990s as progressive organizations recognized the value in focusing on their core competencies and moving non-core functions to suppliers where it was their core competency, who offered apparently cheaper options than the in-house cost. The global marketplace also offered new and exciting outsourcing opportunities with irresistible lower cost options and companies in their thousands downsized or restructured to embrace the outsourcing revolution. Indeed it is this outsourcing that has been a key factor behind the success of many of today's big companies and has fuelled the rapid growth of economies such as that of China in recent decades.

The outsourcing gold rush didn't completely live up to the dream it promised initially and there are many horror stories of costs actually increasing (often because the organization didn't really understand its true costs when the activity was in-house), quality falling short, customer experience being compromised or the organization winding up locked into a bad arrangement as the outsourced provider had amassed critical know-how, preventing easy switching of suppliers.

Today outsourcing remains a viable option for organizations and is part of the fundamental procurement 'make or buy' decision. Making outsourcing happen might seem daunting but it is in fact just another form of buying capability, except we don't use individual buying transactions, but rather establish a long-term supply arrangement. Making this work well is about ensuring the right arrangements are in place and once again the *Power Buying Process* can support this. Outsourcing is successful with a precise and well-developed set of *Needs and Wants*, a *Power Buying Plan* that seeks to secure value and *Manage Supplier* by building a joint, collaborative relationship, a *Contract* that provides for ongoing *Performance Checks* as well as the ability to exit or transition to new arrangements if things are not working.

Category Management

Category Management is possibly the most important component within a modern strategic procurement function. It is a strategic approach where an organization manages and drives value across its entire third-party spend by

Figure 10.3 Segmentation of categories of spend

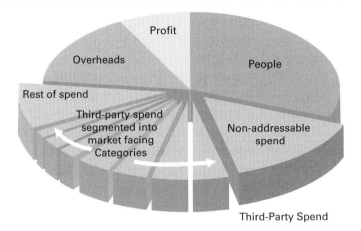

segmenting it into groups of products or services, or 'categories', that mirror how marketplaces are organized. Back in Chapter 2, Figure 2.1 illustrated where the money from sales goes and the significance of the amount of third-party spend within most organizations, and therefore the opportunity this presents us. Figure 10.3 shows the segmentation of as much of the third-party spend as is possible and practical. Individual categories can then be worked on to determine and implement the most effective buying approach for each that maximizes the value to the organization. Well deployed category management is a well-proven approach that can deliver dramatic step change benefits to the organization in terms of reduced cost, risk and increased value and innovation. This works, and is a very different approach to traditional organizational buying, because the category principle ensures individual sourcing approaches address the entirety of spend for all goods and services that come from the same marketplace, thus maximizing the organization's buying power overall.

Crucial to the success of category management is ensuring that the category segmentation is truly market facing, and many organizations get this wrong or segment based upon internal coding structures or how the goods/services are used. In essence, the right category is one where we can clearly identify the widest possible marketplace. The nature of the list of categories for any organization will vary, but might include indirect spend categories such as cleaning services, facilities maintenance, legal services, hotels, office furniture, IT hardware, mobile telecoms and so on. Direct categories according to what the organization does might include glass jars, labels, freight, wound care, valves, pipe, gearboxes, printed circuit boards and so on. Categories might be worked on in clusters to ensure the best overall approach, for example the umbrella category of travel might be worked on, but the actual market-facing categories where individual buying approaches are developed will be hotels, air travel, booking agency, rental cars, etc. Modern procurement organizations structure teams with nominated category managers, responsible for defined bundles of categories and will work with and even lead cross-functional teams to determine and implement new buying strategies for each category following a proven Category Management process.

Category Management is firmly established and standard practice for large organizations all over the world and is a well-proven approach that delivers real and sustainable benefit. The *Power Buying Process* is in fact a scaled down version of the Category Management process, incorporating many of the basic business improvement principles and includes many of the core tools and steps in a simplified and easy to apply form that can be used for any buying scenario outside of a category framework. Category Management represents the next step to take for any buyer wishing to progress further beyond than this book and is fully expanded in my book *Category Management in Purchasing* (Kogan Page, 2009).

SRM (Supplier Relationship Management)

SRM is also a core component within a modern strategic procurement function and is a sourcing methodology that is focused on suppliers rather than categories of spend. So which one should be used and when? And if it is both, then which order should they be deployed in? The answer is it depends. Both Category Management and SRM can add great value to an organization and despite different perspectives, many of the supporting tools and approaches are common. Category Management is spend- or category-centric whilst SRM is of course supplier-focused. Both have their place within a modern strategic purchasing function and each should be selected and deployed according to where the organization most needs to secure value.

The term SRM seems to carry different meaning depending who is using it. This is perhaps because for any given organization, different treatments across the vast range of suppliers are needed according to how important each supplier is to the firm. SRM seems to have become a term coined to describe each and every one of these approaches in one way or another. Clarity in understanding and defining SRM comes by considering it as the *overarching strategic philosophy and framework* under which different types of supplier intervention across the entire supply base exist. This might include interventions ranging from day-to-day management of suppliers who are important in some way through to the development of collaborative relationships with the critical few suppliers who can make a dramatic contribution to the organization. SRM is also an approach that prioritizes and targets interventions with suppliers according to overall organizational goals and available resources. It is about determining *what* the organization needs from its supply base to realize strategic goals, with *whom* we need a relationship or some sort of intervention to realize strategic goals and *how* we will deploy specific interventions with the supply base to achieve these goals.

A well-executed SRM approach can provide competitive advantage, fuel growth and brand development, reduce cost, improve efficiency and effectiveness and reduce supply side risk or at least help understand it so it can be mitigated. However SRM is not something that can simply be 'bolted on', and in a similar vein to that we have touched on many times, must be part of an organization-wide buying philosophy.

Within the umbrella concept of SRM, there are different types of supplier or supply base interventions that could be put in place, each serving a different purpose and relevance according to the degree and nature of supplier importance. There is a further concept that helps understand SRM and how it works together with category management and that is the way all the different components of SRM work together. The philosophy of SRM means it is not something that can follow a linear process or a defined series of steps (as we find in the *Power Buying Process* or category management). Indeed, across the plethora of what is written about SRM, it seems there is a common tendency to attempt to squeeze it into some sort of step-by-step approach, possibly explaining the apparent general lack of consistency or agreement as to what SRM is, and perhaps why programmes can fail to deliver the results needed. Such a step-by-step mindset works against us because every supplier is different, and those that are important are important for different reasons, each requiring a unique relationship or series of interventions according to our circumstances, theirs and what each party needs. One supplier may just need some compliance monitoring, whilst another might warrant a full strategic collaborative relationship. One may need intervention to minimize risk, another might hold latent value if we can work with them to unlock it, and so on.

SRM is in fact like an orchestra (Figure 10.4). Each of the sections of an orchestra play when needed according to the piece of music, all working in unison and taking their lead from a single conductor. In the orchestra of SRM, the areas of focus, the different approaches and interventions must play as and when needed according to what is appropriate for the circumstances, the current environment and the point in time, with the conductor providing a governance framework that guides how the

Figure 10.4 The Orchestra of SRM

various interventions come in or drop back. Each important supplier has its own piece of music and the melody changes constantly. The orchestra of SRM has five sections, these are:

- Supplier Management (SM);
- Supplier Performance Measurement (SPM);
- Supplier Improvement & Development (SI&D);
- Supply Chain Management (SCM); and
- Strategic Collaborative Relationships (SCR).

SPM, SI&D and SM focus on the direct contractual relationship with a discrete number of immediate important suppliers. SCM considers the entire supply chain beyond the immediate contractual relationship and perhaps even follows the chain further on towards the end customer. SI&D tends to focus on immediate suppliers but could also focus on entire supply chains and SCR is the most strategic component here and arguably the one that can potentially unlock the greatest value with a focus on a handful of immediate suppliers that are of strategic importance. These discrete approaches are not mutually exclusive – in other words, SRM doesn't mean we have to choose one or another, and it is possible and often necessary to adopt more than one type of intervention. For example, a supplier may require an SM approach but may also need SPM with some SI&D.

Core to effective SRM is segmentation, but this time segmentation of our supply base according to how important each supplier is and what makes them important. In our *Manage Suppliers* tool, a simple basis for segmentation is included with the output represented by the pyramid (Figure 9.2). My book *Supplier Relationship Management (*Kogan Page, 2014) expands this topic in full and provides the complete suite of methodologies, tools and techniques.

The role of eAuctions within the Power Buying Process

Auction rooms and eBay are familiar environments where we bid to buy things, and where the price normally starts at a given point and increases depending on the number of bidders, the desirability of the item and so on. In the world of buying, an eAuction is exactly the same, except it works in reverse. Initiated by the buyer, an eAuction is an internet-based event where invited suppliers can make bids for the price they are prepared to offer for a defined product or service, or a defined group of products and services (termed a *lot*). It happens in real time over a limited period and the buyer can often watch the action progress live online and see the bids from all the suppliers, but usually without being able to identify who they are. During the event, suppliers attempt to outbid each other by making bids and counter-bids, each bid lowering the price, so that at the end of the eAuction they are making their best offers. Price decreases during an eAuction, the reverse of eBay and similar auctions, and for this reason eAuctions are often referred to as reverse auctions or electronic reverse auctions (eRAs).

Figure 10.5 shows a screenshot of the last stages of a typical eAuction. The auction in question started with six suppliers (in this fictitious case, all identified) and involved multiple bids along the way.

There is no shortage of eAuction providers out there. Many offer added value solutions combining eAuction tools with other purchasing e-tools and even involve consultancy support. Solutions vary from a simple online portal where we can purchase a licence for unlimited use, to fully managed pay-per-event auctions.

The eAuction is a tool that we can use within the *Power Buying Process*, and is relevant and useful for certain buying scenarios where our *Power Buying Plan* identifies we need a *Competition* buying option and then becomes part of *Implementation* and replaces *Negotiation* (as the eAuction is simply another form of negotiation, except here it is not face-to-face, nor does it require any personal interaction or good negotiation to a position against a supplier).

Figure 10.5 Onscreen view of an eAuction

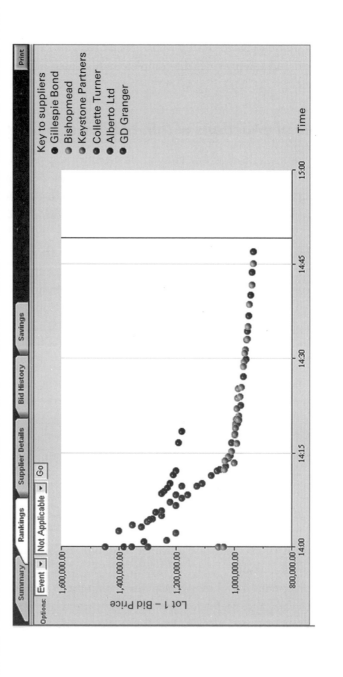

If well executed, the eAuction will push the price to the lowest level the market will stand. Furthermore, eAuctions shorten the time to decision and enable suppliers to bid regardless of location. Although suppliers were opposed to eAuctions in their early days, now they are viewed as part of the way the game is played. In fact, today suppliers typically view eAuctions positively as they serve to create a more level playing field, providing both buyer and supplier with a good level of transparency as well as reducing the supplier's sales costs and providing the supplier with intelligence regarding how their pricing compares to that of others in the market.

An eAuction is not, however, a miracle cure and will only work in certain situations where the supply market comprises a high number of capable suppliers providing standardized products or services that sit in *Generic* (*Power Check* tool) and perhaps *Tailored* according to how easy it can be for multiple suppliers to bid to supply the tailored solution. They will not work in *Proprietary* and are entirely inappropriate for *Custom* where success comes through a mutually beneficial relationship with one supplier. The suitability of eAuctions must be considered carefully, even in *Generic,* where products are heavily based on a commodity whose price is determined by market forces and where there is constant price volatility – an eAuction might leverage a good spot buying price, but could also yield a price increase instead if the market is not in our favour.

Key considerations in running an eAuction are:

- *Lotting strategy* – this is critical to success. 'Lotting' is the way the overall requirement is broken down into discrete packages of work in order for bids to be relevant and comparable to one another.

- *Specification* – closely associated with lotting, the buyer must clearly define and communicate the specification, derived from our *Needs and Wants* for each product or service that become each lot in the eAuction. Any ambiguity here could result in bids not being comparable.

- *Inviting the right suppliers* – use *Supplier Fact Find* to research and pre-qualify potential suppliers. There must be sufficient qualified suppliers to make the auction worthwhile, eg more than two, but ideally five to ten but fewer than 15.

- *Selection criteria* – use the *Select Suppliers* tool and determine the basis on which the supplier will be selected. Define and published this to participating suppliers in advance of the auction. Here we can choose to bind ourselves to 'lowest bid wins' or leave flexibility so that we do not need to choose the lowest option, but commit ourselves to validate closing bids before making a decision. This will help us if we subsequently have concerns over the lowest supplier's bid. It is also possible that the eAuction may not be the final decider and a further round of negotiation may be appropriate. This should only be the case where the auction itself was not a 'price-only' event. Again, those participating must understand how the process will work.

- *Training and communication* – don't just expect the suppliers to be capable of participating in an eAuction. Good communication is essential and the supplier may need training in using the system ahead of the event. It is also important to sell to the supplier the benefits of participating to maximize their interest and involvement.

- *Post auction* – using the *Select Suppliers* selection criteria, select the winning or shortlisted suppliers. All participants should be informed of the results. It is good practice to provide feedback to suppliers as well as to note any lessons learnt from the exercise.

Once the eAuction is complete and the decision made, the new supply arrangements must be put in to practice by executing the necessary actions and changes. We do this as part of the *Implementation* tool which might need us to ensure the wider business transitions to, and remains compliant with, the new arrangements or the dramatic benefits we realized during the eAuction could be lost through inaction.

Supply Chain Management

Our journey through the world of buying and modern strategic procurement would not be complete unless we touched on Supply Chain Management (SCM). SCM and Logistics is an entire topic all of its own with a wealth of publications, knowledge and education available out there so it is impossible to do justice to it here. Historically SCM has been regarded as separate to the practice of strategic purchasing. To the uninitiated, SCM may well be regarded as an approach to take care of transportation, logistics, warehousing – tactical, transactional and concerned with little more than the movement of goods. Today, however, effective SCM is much more than that and is also increasingly being recognized as a strategic contributor with new roles of Chief Supply Chain Officer now emerging, especially in organizations where the performance and security of the supply chain is critical. Yet, despite this, SCM and strategic purchasing remain quite different professions. The reason for this is perhaps historic; SCM has been around for millions of years and has been behind any requirement to get the right stuff to the right place in good condition exactly when needed, repeatedly and reliably. The principles around ensuring an effective flow of materials and information to satisfy a customer have altered little from the building of the pyramids to the relief of hunger in Africa (Christopher, 2011) whilst strategic procurement is the new kid on the block.

A distinction also remains in the educational space in these two areas. For example, in the UK I could sign up to do an MSc in Logistics and Supply Chain Management with one of the reputable universities specializing in this area or alternatively an MSc in Strategic Procurement Management. Each has modules to introduce the other, but they are two very separate specialisms taught by different experts, using different tools and approaches, with candidates making a choice to go into one profession or another. Furthermore, in the workplace this disparity continues with functional divides – the 'running' of supply chains is often something that sits separate from procurement, perhaps being the remit of a dedicated logistics function, operations, production or even a commercial function.

However, the situation is changing and organizations are finding that procurement and SCM can no longer operate as distinct functions if the organization is to buy effectively. This is driven by globalization, managing new global distribution supply arrangements, changing customer expectations and the imperative to ensure buying is sustainable, which demands understanding and active management of what happens back up the supply chain.

SCM naturally fits within an organization's overall SRM approach and has five components or pillars (Figure 10.6) that support a holistic intervention back up the entire supply chain, but also forward through the value chain and on to our ultimate end customer. The pillars of SCM (called 'pillars' as all need to exist together for the overall approach to work) are:

1 *Logistics* – managing the flow of materials downstream matched with demand.

2 *Demand* – understanding and managing demand through the entire value chain: understanding end customer needs and aspirations that might trigger future demand and how this is shared back up the supply chain.

3 *Information* – the nature of information, and the way it is transmitted throughout the supply chain.

4 *Risk* – understanding and proactively managing supplier and supply chain risk.

5 *Sustainable buying* – understanding the processes, practices and original sources in the supply chain and specific interventions to ensure a compliance with a specific policy (expanded in the next section).

Figure 10.6 The five pillars of SCM

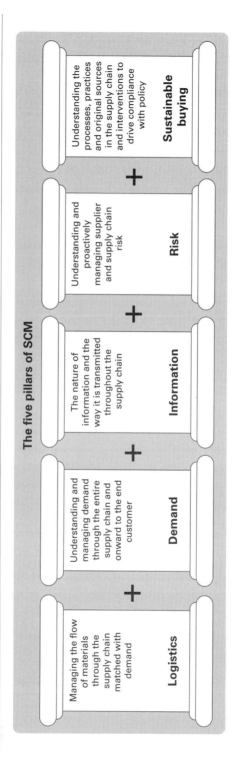

The five pillars of SCM

| Logistics | + | Demand | + | Information | + | Risk | + | Sustainable buying |

Managing the flow of materials through the supply chain matched with demand

Understanding and managing demand through the entire supply chain and onward to the end customer

The nature of information and the way it is transmitted throughout the supply chain

Understanding and proactively managing supplier and supply chain risk

Understanding the processes, practices and original sources in the supply chain and interventions to drive compliance with policy

Sustainable buying

Sustainable buying can mean a multitude of things, and indeed has many definitions including Corporate Responsibility, Corporate Social Responsibility (or CSR), ethical buying and so on. It is a considered approach to buying that seeks to ensure what we buy, and how we buy it is sustainable, not just for us but for the people and companies that supply it, for each step of the supply chain and for the environment and the world at large. This means being able to understand and take action where there are detrimental impacts such as child labour, forced labour, unsafe or poor working conditions, social impacts, inequality (gender, age, race, etc), environmental damage, pollution and obligations such as being a good neighbour and so on. There are many models that define all the potential impacts and provide standards or frameworks for improvement, published by the different institutions around the world that operate in this space. These include The United Nations Global Compact, ISO26000, The AA1000 standard, FTSE4Good index, Dow Jones Sustainability index and many more besides.

Surely someone should do something?

There are plenty of stories out there and it all began well over 30 years ago when good investigative journalism started exposing leading global brands for using sweatshops in countries such as Vietnam, China, the Philippines, Malaysia and India where poor working conditions and poor treatment of workers were standard practice in the manufacture of their products. Many of these original stories have not been forgotten – did it cause brand damage? Hard to tell, but what it did do was to change the game to compel some of those exposed to start leading a revolution to change the things that happen many contractual steps removed up a supply chain in an underdeveloped country.

Others followed suit and today there are many exemplar companies who put huge effort into ensuring their supply chains are good. Yet good investigative journalism still uncovers things that make good headlines at the expense of big companies, sometimes justified, sometimes less so. But if there was nothing to hide then there is nothing to report? The simple fact here is that despite the efforts of many in this space there are still plenty of examples of poor practice.

On 24 April 2013, the Rana Plaza in Sevar, Bangladesh collapsed, killing 1,129 people and injuring 2,515 people. The building was home to garment factories, manufacturing products destined for the racks of the leading brand name clothing outlets found on the streets and in the malls in Europe and the United States. More than half the victims were women, along with their children who were in nursery facilities within the building. In the weeks following the tragedy as the collapse was investigated it emerged that warnings that the building had become dangerous were ignored. The incident is considered the deadliest garment factory accident in history (BBC, May 2013). Politicians, advocacy groups and even the Pope spoke out, whilst protestors and consumers campaigned directly at retailers' outlets. The response from the fashion industry was mixed; some responded to provide help and some attempted to establish an accord on building safety in Bangladesh – in fact 38 companies had signed up to this as of May 2013 (IndustriALL, 2013). Yet 14 major North American retailers including Walmart refused to participate, claiming they had, for over two years already, been working on an agreement to improve safety in Bangladesh factories (Huffington Post, May 2013). Later that year these and other North American companies eventually announced plans to improve factory safety in Bangladesh, but these plans were criticized for failing to including any binding commitments to pay for improvements (*Greenhouse and Clifford*, July 2013).

This tragedy has passed by and is no longer headline news. Pressure groups continue to campaign and consumers continue to buy garments save a few who are serious about shopping basket activism and make choices accordingly. Overcrowded garment factories in Bangladesh and other parts of the world are not uncommon, and overcrowding and poor working conditions are just the start of practices that our Western eyes would judge to be unacceptable, yet can be found all over the world in the supply chains of many of the goods we buy without question. So surely someone should do something?

More than hugging trees

In fact, there are many things happening and the world has seen huge changes in recent times. Whereas 30 years ago 'sustainable buying' was unheard of, today it is increasingly part of what we do, as organizations and as individuals, yet the sustainable buying landscape can appear quite confused at first with widely varied levels of interest to embrace, or imperatives to act, to support the movement.

Until recently sustainably buying has remained largely a voluntary pursuit with companies rarely being held legally accountable for what happened in their supply chains. Yet this is changing as new legislation begins to emerge. The UK Modern Slavery Act 2015, designed to tackle slavery in the UK, makes it a requirement for companies with a turnover exceeding £36m per

Figure 10.7 The range of drivers for sustainable buying

annum to publish a statement confirming the steps taken to ensure no slavery or human trafficking is taking place in the business or in any supply chain. The California Transparency in Supply Chains Act 2010 serves a similar purpose.

There are different drivers for sustainable buying and indeed different business cases for action and these range from the imperative for compliance with current or emerging regulations up to corporate philanthropy (Figure 10.7).

Sustainable buying could be a concern of a company or an individual. It is something that has become more widely understood in recent times and indeed is considered, supported and even actively embraced by many individuals and companies. Once the idea of considering sustainability as part of buying was left to the sandal-wearing few who found solace in hugging trees. Today it is firmly part of many boardroom agendas for big companies around the world.

Why companies struggle to have sustainable supply chains

Buying sustainably is in fact one of the hardest things to do and for this reason many of the brands we love and trust genuinely want to achieve this and have discovered how hard it is. One of the main difficulties is knowing and managing what happens at the plantation or factory in a developing nation far away and many contractual steps removed. Even for closer to home supply chains there are challenges. Placing contractual obligations as part of our *Contract* step will only work for our immediate supplier but will not necessarily flow back up the supply chain. Increasingly organizations are working to understand their supply chains and, where appropriate, establishing direct relationships all the way back – it is the only way to do this. Understanding the supply chain helps the organization determine where change or action is required, and that is equally difficult. Change costs money and if the organization has no direct contractual relationship with the producer then creative ways must be found to invest in them. Furthermore, where changes are driven in, say, to manage working hours or eliminate child labour, then it is hard to know ongoing that such changes are in force. A physical audit is good, but things can easily change when the Western representatives walk away. A local presence can help too, but is easily bribed and despite all of this, those who stand to gain or lose will still find ways to hide poor practice. A cocoa farmer on the Ivory Coast whose living depends upon cheap or free labour will go to great lengths to hide what they do.

There are cultural differences too. In the West we regard child labour as wrong, but what if a family's ability to survive depends solely upon their 14-year-old daughter working to bring in an income. Is it still wrong?

All in all, sustainable buying for an organization is not easy but becoming increasingly necessary or desirable and companies around the world are finding ways to make it happen.

Tool 1 – *Define Objective* – includes the option to determine what our sustainability objective might be. If we want or need to buy sustainably, then there are different things we can do depending upon our size and buying power. Actions to purse sustainable buying by organizations and individuals include:

As a sizeable organization with good buying power

- Map the entire supply chain to understand what happens, where, by whom, etc and the potential detrimental impact 'hot spots' and determine priorities for improvement.

- Agree contractual obligations with immediate suppliers and work with them to agree with their suppliers and so on.

- Establish direct relationships where needed further up the supply chain, eg at the original plantation or factory and agreeing, and perhaps funding, improvements to meet required standards.

- Reduce the number of players in the supply chain and/or acquire the supply chain (called vertical integration) to gain more direct control over what happens.

- Direct auditing of suppliers or producers that present the most risk back up the supply chain.

- Establish local presence (with local knowledge and local respect), perhaps even with permanent presence on-site to monitor compliance.

As an individual or small organization with no or low buying power

- Stay informed of what is happening out there – read latest published articles and understand latest risks and thinking.

- Understand the areas of spend where there is the greatest risk and the nature of those risks, eg buying known problematic goods or commodities (such as cocoa beans, apparel, palm oil, timber/lumbar, etc) or from known problematic regions.

- Follow others who have already done the hard work here – either other companies who take this seriously or known good industry or consumer product or supplier marks such as FairTrade, GoodWeave RugMark (formerly). Marine Stewardship Council, EcoLabel and many others.

Finally, whilst I have outlined how sustainable buying is increasingly a concern of both individuals and organizations, it is a pursuit that comes at a cost. For many this may not matter or simply have become part of doing business but for others, or in certain areas, there is still a choice. Therefore, it is important to be clear about what we are trying to achieve and one of the reasons why this step is part of tool 1, *Define Objective*.

How to maintain personal ethics when buying

We will conclude this section with a word on personal ethics. Anyone in a buying role who has a dealing with suppliers is at risk of bribery and corruption and unless we understand and are prepared for this it might be easy to get caught out. In much of Northern Europe, North America, Australia and Japan, such practices are rare and regarded as unacceptable. (Transparency International, 2013). They may also be illegal. Elsewhere it can be how business is done, and may not even be considered as bribery but nothing more than building good business relationships.

Bribery is the offering, promising, giving, accepting or soliciting of an advantage as an inducement for action which is illegal or a breach of trust.

A bribe is an inducement or reward offered, promised or provided in order to gain any commercial, contractual, regulatory or personal advantage.

In the UK, the Bribery Act 2010 places a liability on organizations that fail to prevent people in the organization from bribing and is a significant anti-corruption standard alongside the US Foreign Corrupt Practices Act. Both the OECD (Organisation for Economic Cooperation) and the UN (United Nations) are working to ratify international conventions against bribery and corruption. Anti-corruption efforts are gaining momentum around the world (Greenaway, 2011). Anti-bribery policies, procedures and training have therefore become essential for many procurement functions and the management of a company now needs to be convinced that the company under its watch has the right arrangements in place.

Companies implement suitable arrangements here for those in buying roles or who interface with suppliers with policies translated into specific practice around supplier relationships, instilling the right culture and training for those involved. Bribes by suppliers can take many forms and might include:

- anything that could be regarded as illegal or improper or violates our or their policy;
- cash;
- gifts, either entirely or over a specified value. Companies may chose to specify a value here – if so this is usually low to only allow gifts of low intrinsic value to be permitted;
- hospitality, either entirely or above a certain specified value individually or in aggregate;
- anything where there is a suggestion that a return favour will be expected or implied; and
- anything where a public or governmental official is involved or a politician or political party.

There are always exceptions. There are instances where it is not appropriate to decline a gift, say when negotiating with a Chinese supplier who has travelled to meet with us. Furthermore, where we are doing business across cultural boundaries our norms around bribery could be very different to the supplier's and there could be good reasons to accommodate different approaches. It is impossible to give guidance here but whatever approach is taken should not be based upon an individual's judgment and decision but should be open and transparent and agreed in advance within the business.

Increasingly bribery is taken seriously the world over. Training in anti-bribery for those who hold office has become more preventative than punitive. In parts of Africa for example, meetings and negotiations between suppliers and officials representing public bodies now take place in special meeting rooms where all proceedings are video recorded. It would therefore be easy to assume that with this global strengthening of bribery legislation and arrangements that bribery is becoming less prevalent. This is not the case and according to the 2013 Global Corruption Barometer, corruption on a global scale is on the increase.

If a supplier pushes a Rolex across the table or slips a fat, cash-stuffed envelope into our hand then clearly we are being offered a bribe. Most buyers are typically unprepared for such things and this ill-preparedness can easily lead to an individual making the wrong decision, one that is regretted later, and one that then puts them in an impossible position. However, in my experience, such open bribes are rare; instead, inducements are typically made in a much more subtle way, and often those involved may feel they are not doing anything wrong. Perhaps attending a golf day or a sporting event at the invitation of a supplier is acceptable under the company's policy, but what if that event then takes place at a very expensive venue, with the chance to meet celebrity players, and prizes of value are won, apparently for playing well? What if this is one of many events? The hospitality is now much more than a simple golf day.

Its not just golf days that can cause a buyer to wind up in a position where they accept high-value hospitality. Having lunch or dinner with a supplier may be necessary or appropriate to our relationship, and essential to developing social interaction. However, lunch at high-end restaurants entirely at the supplier's expense on a regular basis is perhaps more of an inducement than building good relations. If both parties believe that social interaction is necessary to the relationship then it follows that both parties should recognize this and share the cost or perhaps take turns picking up the tab. It seems there is a, somewhat outdated, commonplace culture of 'getting whatever you can from a supplier', and viewing it as good practice for suppliers to buy lunch as if another small concession is being secured. In my experience of procurement people having dinner with a supplier, more often than not the bill/check is left untouched on the table for the supplier to pick it up. It is rare for the buyer to intervene and say something like 'No, please can we split this?' or 'Only if I can get it next time'. It remains, even in the most important of relationships, something the supplier is still expected to do. However, if we are serious about building the right relationship with important suppliers then even policies around lunch and how this can be fair and transparent are important.

With a few exceptions, it is not typically bad people who end up taking a bribe, often it is good people who end up in a situation they hadn't planned to be in. After all it may be in a supplier's interests to put the buyer in that position and they may have a range of approaches and tactics designed to take an inexperienced buyer by surprise. It is therefore essential for any buyer dealing with a supplier that they anticipate what could happen and are ready with a response and course of action to deal with it. This means clearly understanding any company policy on what is and is not acceptable as well as having in mind a clear set of personal boundaries and being ready to stop proceedings whenever things drift outside these. It helps to have some pre-prepared lines and courses of action in mind, these might include:

- Where a supplier appears to be suggesting something inappropriate, say 'Could you please clarify for me precisely what you are proposing here?'

- Where a supplier makes an offer of something that might be marginally appropriate: 'I'm sorry but I'm not able or willing to accept this as it might fall outside our policy on such matters and it is imperative that there is nothing within our dealings that would not bear scrutiny.'

- Where a supplier clearly offers a bribe, clearly decline what is being offered, stop proceedings, end the meeting, report what happened as quickly as possible internally to a line manager or a nominated individual for such matters and seek advice on how to proceed. The question to then be answered here is how appropriate it is to proceed with a company who has attempted to bribe us.

Bribes from suppliers are rarely as obvious as them producing envelopes of cash. Such things only happen if the bribe has been previously agreed. Instead a corrupt supplier attempting to offer an inducement will work up to the offer of a bribe. This is a bit like courtship where they need to gauge interest, gauge personality (those who are naive or inexperienced can be more susceptible to a bribe), establish personal circumstances of potential need and establish what the other party might want or be tempted to accept. This could be money but could also be sex, power or fear driven (the promise of safety against the suggestion of unfavourable consequences). It is therefore important to watch for any signs that a supplier might be working up to some sort of bribe and cut it off before it gets anywhere. Things to watch out for might be a supplier using phrases like:

- 'We see this as more of a give and take situation.'

- 'If you scratch my back I will scratch yours.'

- 'OK, so that's the deal, but what can we do to help *you?*'

- 'What would it take to make this easier for you?'
- 'There is nothing wrong here, it is part of what is expected.'
- 'Everyone does this, now its your turn.'

Watch out too for euphemisms used to suggest something extra is called for. For example in India a supplier might offer 'chai pani', literally meaning tea and water, but actually suggesting a bribe.

Buying in the public sector

Before we finish it is worth touching on buying in the public sector as there are some important differences between how buying works here when compared with commercial organizations. The underlying principles and the methodology outlined in this book are just as relevant in the public sector as in a commercial organization, but the *Power Buying Process* does need to be applied slightly differently or it will fail to deliver.

Whereas a commercial organization might have aims around maximizing profit, market share, competitive advantage and so on, public sector organizations tend to have quite different aims, perhaps guided by such needs as being able to demonstrate value for taxpayers' money, transparency of spend or improving outcomes for the resident, patient, passenger, etc. Furthermore, in the public sector procurement approaches are required to operate within a regulated framework that invokes strict rules around how contracts are awarded, designed to demonstrate transparency in all engagement with suppliers, to minimize corruption and to drive fairness to suppliers. Sometimes governmental legislation will demand positive discrimination towards suppliers in certain minority groups. In the United States, a programme of 'Supplier Diversity' demands that a certain percentage of spend by public sector organizations is with minority suppliers. In the EU, similar programmes can be found with government targets to place a certain amount of business with SMEs (small- and medium-sized enterprises) or minority-owned businesses. In the UK, the Social Value Act 2012 requires that the public sector opens up more opportunities for social enterprises (not-for profit organizations with primarily social aims) to win bids for delivery of pubic services and to consider how what is bought might improve the social, economic and environmental well-being of the area.

Different regulation exists the world over and each is an entire specialism of its own so further reading is recommended here. In Europe, legislation defines the requirements for procurement in public bodies.

Directives and regulations collectively known as *EU procurement legislation* are founded upon the four pillars of EU Law. These are: subsidiarity (the principle of needs and problems being dealt with at the most immediate or local country level, typically through local supporting, not subservient, bodies that are part of the whole); transparency; equal treatment; and proportionality (ensuring the correct balance of the different but related needs that must be satisfied). At the same time it seeks to ensure that the public sector is pursuing simplification, value for money, sustainability, innovation, efficiency, opportunities for SMEs and growth whilst maintaining the single market and complying with WTO (World Trade Organization) rules.

EU procurement legislation governs any governmental or public purchasing entity for expenditure above certain, published thresholds. In this case the opportunity must be advertised in the OJEU (Official Journal of the European Union). Prospective suppliers can then register their interest and potentially be invited to participate in some form of competitive bidding exercise according to one of a number of set procedures.

The *Power Buying Process* will deliver great buying outcomes in a public sector buying environment but it needs to be deployed slightly differently. This is primarily about spending more time early on to be certain about what we want to buy, to have a precise definition of our *Needs and Wants* and to determine in advance how we are going to *Contract* for it so at the point we approach the market we can clearly set out our requirements so all those interested can have equal opportunity. In a commercial organization it is often normal practice to engage with suppliers at any stage of the process to solicit information or ideas that might contribute to the formation of a sourcing strategy, prior to the market being formally approached. Whilst there is still provision for this in public sector, it must follow a strict procedure in order to manage this competitive dialogue to ensure fairness and transparency to all.

The areas where we need to adapt our deployment of the *Power Buying Process* are as follows (based primarily upon EU procurement legislation provision):

- *Needs and Wants* – our definition of requirements must be absolutely clear and final before we approach the market, or we must follow a strict 'competitive dialogue' process. Here any dialogue with suppliers must be fair and transparent to all, with no scope to favour a supplier, and this extends to discussions around capabilities or what might be possible. An engagement with one supplier must be replicated identically with all other suppliers under consideration, as if all were in their own swim lanes progressing forward individually, but identically in terms of discussion and engagement. *Needs and Wants* may need to provide for specific aims of the public sector body such as alignment with broader social objectives or diversity requirements.

- *Power Boosters and Power Buying Plan* – in the commercial buying world we might select *Power Boosters* and develop a *Power Buying Plan* based around *Competition,* perhaps involving running a competitive bidding process and selecting a supplier. In the public sector what happens here is guided by strict procedures set within the legislation.

- *Negotiation* – hard 'dog-eat-dog' negotiations can be standard practice for many commercial companies. It may be 'fair game' for a competitive bidding process to be followed by additional negotiation until the most favourable outcome is secured; suppliers might even be played off against each other. There is little to prevent extreme negotiations, with what is appropriate tending to be determined only by corporate policy or culture, the personal beliefs and ethics of the individual or the degree to which a future relationship is needed. Many negotiation approaches found in the commercial sector would fall foul of historic public sector procurement legislation as they are in conflict with the underpinning pillars of equal treatment, transparency and proportionality. However in 2014, changes in EU procurement legislation have moved some way forward with the introduction of new negotiated procedures.

- *Select Supplier(s)* – how we select suppliers might need to go beyond commercial and implementation concerns but may need to include selection criteria based upon meeting certain diversity thresholds.

- *Contract, Supplier Management and Performance Check* – there are subtle differences in the nature of the contract we agree and how we manage the supplier and performance in the public sector. The contract must reflect what we went to market to source, and supplier and performance management must be only in response to this. In the commercial sector we might manage the supplier by seeking to drive improvements going forward or even develop the relationship further with some suppliers, whereas in the public sector, things cannot easily change from that which was bid for. Therefore the concept of driving ongoing improvements or building a future supplier relationship is at odds with the legislative provision. Instead things must remain arm's-length and fair, so if we need to drive a performance improvement or we want some sort of collaborative relationship, the nature of this and way it will work and be measured must be defined from the outset so all suppliers can bid to have a chance of being part of a defined way of engagement. It cannot build and become different from that defined when suppliers bid for the work.

Some of these may seem to be quite burdensome. Opponents here might argue that public sector legislation restricts best practice procurement and drives sub-optimum results, making it harder to create a competitive tension between suppliers. However, advocates for EU procurement legislation would counter that it has a much bigger agenda than the needs of an individual entity and seeks to balance good procurement with a wider social and country progression. In other words, it is a necessary part of the bigger picture.

It is in fact possible to balance both here and deliver highly effective procurement whilst complying with public procurement legislation. However, an advanced level of capability is required, so those doing so can be confident in ensuring compliance. It also means those leading public sector buying functions need to guide teams to think more about the most effective route through, how to make the legislation work for them and working to prevent buyers only following the safe route through. For example, it is easy to default to use of a contracting approach based upon running a tender or competitive bid process instead of maximizing the opportunity using the full range of compliant contracting approaches available.

The power buying professional

To conclude we will touch on how we can develop as a *Power Buying* professional. There are many ongoing development options here including professional buying qualifications, degree or master's level qualifications and the raft of literature and learning options out there. Indeed, I have mentioned my three other books (*Category Management in Purchasing, Supplier Relationship Management and Negotiation for Procurement Professionals* – all published by Kogan Page) at key points throughout this book from which core concepts and tools in the *Power Buying Process* are derived. These publications, individually and collectively, provide the complete exposition with full supporting advanced methodologies and toolkits, for highly effective strategic procurement. They are written as a trilogy and designed to complement and work together to form the whole approach. If you are serious about advancing your capability further then securing and reading these is recommended.

If you have read to this point then you are now well equipped to be a *Power Buying* professional and hopefully this chapter has begun to expand the horizon of the world of procurement and what is possible if we can buy really well. Becoming equipped with the *Power Buying Process* and the tools contained in this book provides anyone with everything they need to buy effectively whether buying as an individual or professionally.

We started this journey back in Chapter 1 with the simple fact that buying is really not that complicated and something we all possess great skills for already. We cannot regard buying as one single thing, but as a broad spectrum of different approaches we can choose, so being good at buying means we need to think about *how* we choose to buy, shaped by factors such as the value, risk, how much choice we have, what relationship we need with the seller and how we will contract for what we buy. If we buy well we can secure dramatic benefits and not just around reduced price and cost, but also greater value, less risk, more innovation and improved effectiveness. Despite the great benefits on offer, many fail to realize them either by a sub-optimum buying approach such as not doing the homework, a skills disadvantage compared with the seller or an organizational structure that positions buying as tactical and reactive, or supply-driven factors such as relationships suppliers build with buyers to gain advantage, being conditioned by suppliers that we have the best deal, or making the area of supply too *Proprietary*. By learning, following, adopting the 5D *Power Buying Process* it is possible to overcome these obstacles and realize the benefits possible.

Our onward *Power Buying* journey is a constant quest and the best learning and development comes by doing it for real, by working to apply the principles and tools in this book and drawing on the learnings from each experience. If you put into practice everything I have covered through all the chapters that bring us to this final point then you are poised and ready to be highly effective at buying and achieve great buying outcomes.

Summary

The key learning points from this chapter:

1 The 5D *Power Buying Process* provides a means for highly effective buying by organizations and individuals.

2 The modern procurement function is strategic and is effective when the organization connects through cross-functional working procurement

'sourcing' with the 'satisfying' of the end customer and both informing and being informed by corporate 'strategy'.

3 The modern procurement function is positioned so it can add value to the organization, supporting talented practitioners using key tools and approaches including the ability to buy globally, outsourcing, category management, SRM, modern sourcing tools such as eAuctions, supply chain management, and sustainable buying.

4 Sustainable buying seeks to ensure what we buy, and how we buy it is sustainable, not just for us but for the people and companies that supply it, for each step of the supply chain and for the environment and the world at large. This means being able to understand and take action where there are detrimental impacts such as child labour, forced labour, unsafe or poor working conditions, social impacts, inequality (gender, age, race, etc), environmental damage, pollution and obligations such as being a good neighbour and so on.

5 Anyone in a buying role who has a dealing with suppliers is at risk of bribery and corruption. It is therefore good practice for buyers to understand how such circumstances might come about and be prepared.

6 The *Power Buying* process can be applied for public sector buying but with some subtle adaptations to ensure buying aligns with the relevant procurement legislation.

7 Becoming equipped with the *Power Buying Process* and the tools contained in this book provides anyone with everything they need to buy effectively, whether buying as an individual or professionally.

APPENDIX

This appendix provides the 15 tools and templates that make up the 5D *Power Buying Process* within this Buyer's Toolkit. Each tool and how to use it is explained in Chapters 5 through 9.

How you may use these templates

The *Power Buying Process* is © Positive Purchasing Ltd included and reproduced under licence in this book. If you have bought this book, you may make copies of these templates for your own personal use providing the uncompleted template is not modified and the copyright designation is preserved. Copies may not be distributed and these templates may not be used commercially without licence: for more information regarding licensing the Buyer's Toolkit and 5D *Power Buying Process* for organization-wide and commercial use, contact team@positivepurchasing.com.

The Power Buying Process

5D Buyer's Toolkit

Steps	1 Define — the need	2 Discover — our position	3 Determine — how to buy	4 Deal — Secure the best deal and make a contract	5 Deliver — Ensure we get what we agreed

Tools

Step 1	Step 2	Step 3	Step 4	Step 5
1 Define Objective	4 Power Check	7 Supplier Fact Find	10 Select Supplier (or solution)	13 Implementation
2 Consult and Engage	5 Price Check	8 Market Assessment	11 Negotiation (where possible)	14 Manage Supplier(s) (where appropriate)
3 Needs and Wants	6 Power Boosters	9 Power Buying Plan	12 Contract	15 Performance Check

Refine needs and wants

©Positive Purchasing 2017

5D Buyer's Toolkit

Stage 1 | Tool 1 — **Define Objective**

Gather background information then clarify and define the overall objectives that are driving the need to buy. Decide if we have influence over the purchase.

Date

What do we know?

What is the need?

What are we going to buy?

How much, how many, how often, by when, to where etc?

Have we bought this or something similar before? ☐ Yes ☐ No

If yes, what do we know (eg from whom, what exactly did we buy, was it a success, might we repeat this)?

Key considerations

Specification or preferences. Any preferences (eg suppliers, brand, products, solutions, timing etc), defined specification or details of what to buy?

Where/how is this defined/where does it come from?

Are there any risks if we get this wrong?

Is this a single purchase or will there be a future repeat requirement? ☐ One-off ☐ Repeat

How do we want to pay for this?

Primary objectives

What are the primary objectives behind this purchase? (tick those that most apply)

☐ None/don't know yet
☐ Lowest price/cost
☐ Best value for money
☐ Best quality or service
☐ Just to buy the specified goods/brand or service
☐ From the specified supplier
☐ Certainty of supply/lowest risk
☐ _____

What is driving these objectives?

☐ Own assessment
☐ Company policy
☐ Instruction by others
☐ It's specified

Budget/cost objectives or aspirations

Scope to consider alternative solutions that may not meet the objective(s) but might deliver better outcomes? ☐ Yes ☐ Unsure ☐ No

Sustainability objectives

☐ None
☐ Nice to have but at no or marginal additional cost
☐ Want even if small uplift in cost
☐ Essential and primary objective

Details

2 Consult and Engage

| What are we buying? | | Date |

Identify all the people or groups to consult or engage with, tick why we need to engage with them and determine how (and when) we will engage with them.

List the people (or groups) we should engage with	Interest/engagement needed				How we will consult and engage
	R	A	C	I	
1					
2					
3					
4					
5					
6					
7					
8					
9					
10					
11					
12					
13					
14					

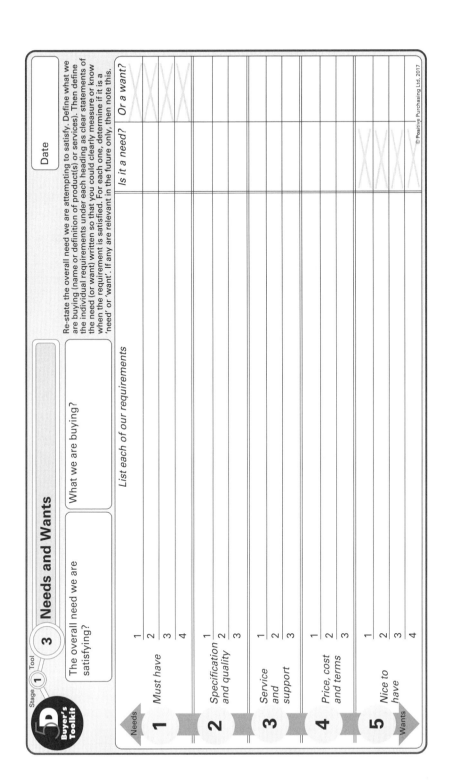

Buyer's Toolkit

Stage **1** Tool **3**

Needs and Wants

The overall need we are satisfying?

What we are buying?

Date

Re-state the overall need we are attempting to satisfy. Define what we are buying (name or definition of product(s) or services). Then define the individual requirements under each heading as clear statements of the need (or want) written so that you could clearly measure or know when the requirement is satisfied. For each one, determine if it is a 'need' or 'want'. If any are relevant in the future only, then note this.

List each of our requirements

	Is it a need?	Or a want?

Needs

1 Must have
1
2
3
4

2 Specification and quality
1
2
3

3 Service and support
1
2
3

4 Price, cost and terms
1
2
3

5 Nice to have
1
2
3
4

Wants

© Positive Purchasing Ltd, 2017

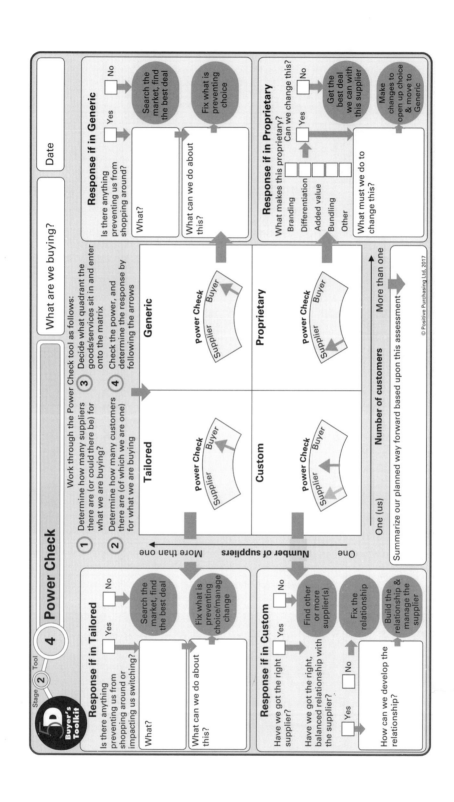

Stage 2 · Tool 4 — Power Check

5D Buyer's Toolkit

What are we buying? | **Date**

Work through the Power Check tool as follows:

1. Determine how many suppliers there are (or could there be) for what we are buying?
2. Determine how many customers there are (of which we are one) for what we are buying
3. Decide what quadrant the goods/services sit in and enter onto the matrix
4. Check the power, and determine the response by following the arrows

Number of suppliers — One / More than one

Number of customers — One (us) / More than one

Matrix quadrants:
- Tailored — Power Check: Supplier / Buyer
- Generic — Power Check: Supplier / Buyer
- Custom — Power Check: Supplier / Buyer
- Proprietary — Power Check: Supplier / Buyer

Summarize our planned way forward based upon this assessment

© Positive Purchasing Ltd. 2017

Response if in Tailored

Is there anything preventing us from shopping around or impacting us switching? Yes ☐ No ☐ → Search the market, find the best deal

What?

What can we do about this? → Fix what is preventing choice/manage change

Response if in Generic

Is there anything preventing us from shopping around? Yes ☐ No ☐ → Search the market, find the best deal

What?

What can we do about this? → Fix what is preventing choice

Response if in Custom

Have we got the right supplier? Yes ☐ No ☐ → Find other or more supplier(s)

Have we got the right, balanced relationship with the supplier? Yes ☐ No ☐ → Fix the relationship

How can we develop the relationship? → Build the relationship & manage the supplier

Response if in Proprietary

What makes this proprietary? Can we change this? Yes ☐ No ☐ → Get the best deal we can with this supplier

- Branding
- Differentiation
- Added value
- Bundling
- Other

What must we do to change this? → Make changes to open up choice & move to Generic

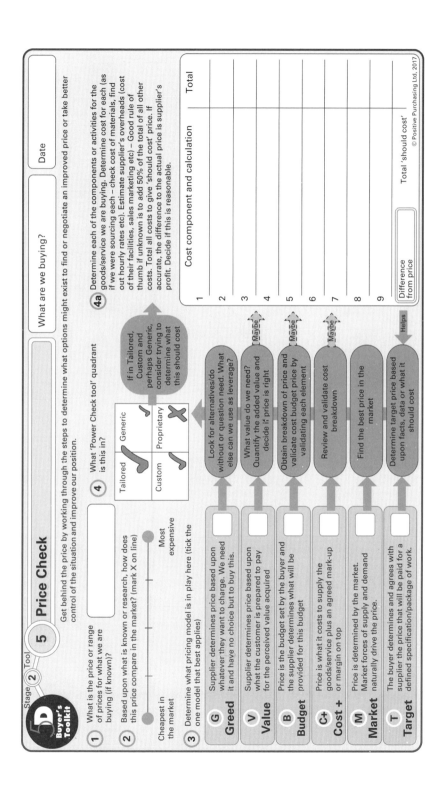

Price Check

Buyer's Toolkit — Stage 2, Tool 5

What are we buying? _____ Date _____

Get behind the price by working through the steps to determine what options might exist to find or negotiate an improved price or take better control of the situation and improve our position.

① What is the price or range of prices for what we are buying (if known)? _____

② Based upon what is known or research, how does this price compare in the market? (mark X on line)

Cheapest in the market ———●———————●——— Most expensive

③ Determine what pricing model is in play here (tick the one model that best applies)

G Greed	Supplier determines price based upon whatever they want to charge. We need it and have no choice but to buy this.	☐
V Value	Supplier determines price based upon what the customer is prepared to pay for the perceived value acquired	☐
B Budget	Price is the budget set by the buyer and the supplier determines what will be provided for this budget	☐
C+ Cost +	Price is what it costs to supply the goods/service plus an agreed mark-up or margin on top	☐
M Market	Price is determined by the market. Market forces of supply and demand naturally drive the price.	☐
T Target	The buyer determines and agrees with supplier the price that will be paid for a defined specification/package of work.	☐

④ What 'Power Check tool' quadrant is this in?

	Tailored	Generic
	✓	✓
	Custom	Proprietary
	✓	✗

If in Tailored, Custom and perhaps Generic, consider trying to determine what this should cost

- Look for alternatives/do without or question need. What else can we use as leverage?
- What value do we need? Quantify the added value and decide if price is right — *Maybe*
- Obtain breakdown of price and validate cost budget price by validating each element — *Maybe*
- Review and validate cost breakdown — *Maybe*
- Find the best price in the market
- Determine target price based upon facts, data or what it should cost — *Helps*

④a Determine each of the components or activities for the goods/service we are buying. Determine cost for each (as if we were sourcing each – check cost of materials, find out hourly rates etc). Estimate supplier's overheads (cost of their facilities, sales marketing etc) – Good rule of thumb if unknown is to add 50% of the total of all other costs. Total all costs to give 'should cost' price. If accurate, the difference to the actual price is supplier's profit. Decide if this is reasonable.

Cost component and calculation	Total
1	
2	
3	
4	
5	
6	
7	
8	
9	
Difference from price	Total 'should cost'

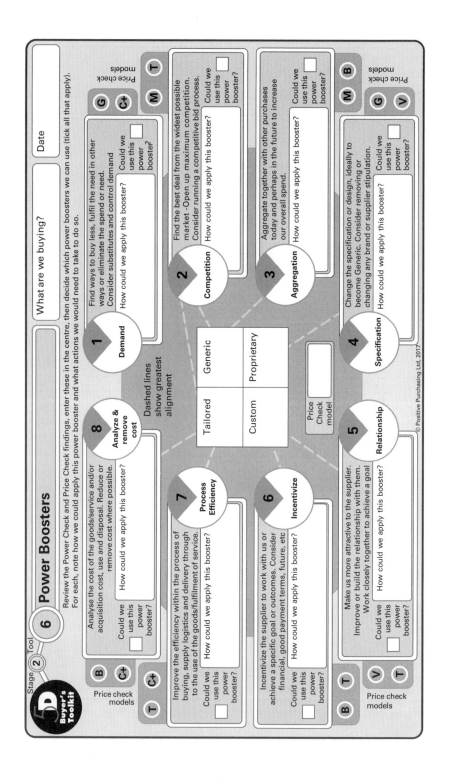

Stage 2 Tool

5D Buyer's Toolkit

6 Power Boosters

What are we buying?

Date

Review the Power Check and Price Check findings, enter these in the centre, then decide which power boosters we can use (tick all that apply). For each, note how we could apply this power booster and what actions we would need to take to do so.

1 Demand
Find ways to buy less, fulfil the need in other ways or eliminate the spend or need. Consider substitutes and control demand
How could we apply this booster?
Could we use this power booster?

Price check models
G   C+

2 Competition
Find the best deal from the widest possible market - Open up maximum competition. Consider running a competitive bid process.
How could we apply this booster?
Could we use this power booster?

M   T

3 Aggregation
Aggregate together with other purchases today and perhaps in the future to increase our overall spend.
How could we apply this booster?
Could we use this power booster?

Price check models
G   V

4 Specification
Change the specification or design, ideally to become Generic. Consider removing or changing any brand or supplier stipulation.
How could we apply this booster?
Could we use this power booster?

M   B

8 Analyze & remove cost
Analyse the cost of the goods/service and/or acquisition cost, use and disposal. Reduce or remove cost where possible.
How could we apply this booster?
Could we use this power booster?

Price check models
B
C+
T

Dashed lines show greatest alignment

Tailored	Generic
Custom	Proprietary

Price Check model

7 Process Efficiency
Improve the efficiency within the process of buying, supply logistics and delivery through to the use of the goods/fulfilment of service.
How could we apply this booster?
Could we use this power booster?

6 Incentivize
Incentivize the supplier to work with us or achieve a specific goal or outcomes. Consider financial, good payment terms, future, etc
How could we apply this booster?
Could we use this power booster?

5 Relationship
Make us more attractive to the supplier. Improve or build the relationship with them. Work closely together to achieve a goal
How could we apply this booster?
Could we use this power booster?

Price check models
B
V
T

© Positive Purchasing Ltd, 2017

Supplier Fact Find

What are we buying?	Date

As part of our supplier fact find, determine the suppliers who could do this along with a summary of what we know or have found out about them. Then based upon initial suitability check, determine if they might be suitable or should be excluded at this stage. Skip this step if the supplier is the single source or is specified and we cannot challenge this.

Pre-qualification criteria we will use to exclude unsuitable suppliers (if relevant)

Pre-qualification 1	Pre-qualification 2

Supplier 1
Summary of what we know

Potentially suitable? ☐ Exclude this supplier ☐

Supplier 2
Summary of what we know

Potentially suitable? ☐ Exclude this supplier ☐

Supplier 3
Summary of what we know

Potentially suitable? ☐ Exclude this supplier ☐

Supplier 4
Summary of what we know

Potentially suitable? ☐ Exclude this supplier ☐

Supplier 5
Summary of what we know

Potentially suitable? ☐ Exclude this supplier ☐

Supplier 6
Summary of what we know

Potentially suitable? ☐ Exclude this supplier ☐

Supplier 7
Summary of what we know

Potentially suitable? ☐ Exclude this supplier ☐

Supplier 8
Summary of what we know

Potentially suitable? ☐ Exclude this supplier ☐

Supplier 9
Summary of what we know

Potentially suitable? ☐ Exclude this supplier ☐

Supplier 10
Summary of what we know

Potentially suitable? ☐ Exclude this supplier ☐

Buyer's Toolkit

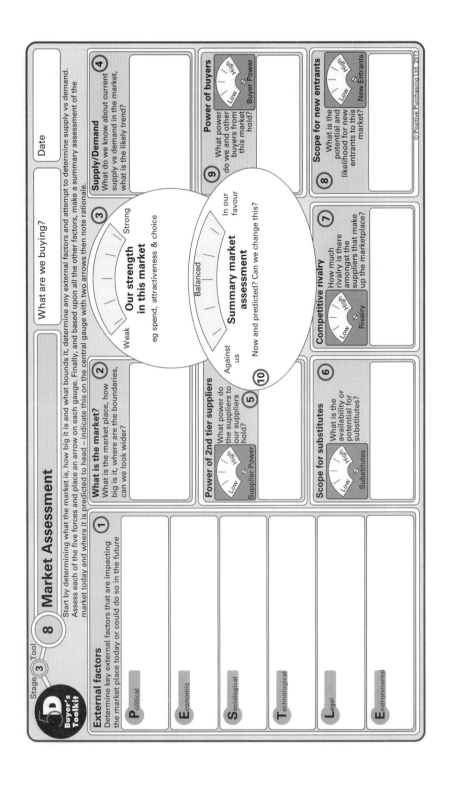

Stage 3 · Tool 8 — Market Assessment

5D Buyer's Toolkit

Start by determining what the market is, how big it is and what bounds it, determine any external factors and attempt to determine supply vs demand. Assess each of the five forces and place an arrow on each gauge. Finally, and based upon all the other factors, make a summary assessment of the market today and where it is predicted to head – indicate this on the central gauge with two arrows then note rationale.

What are we buying?

Date

External factors ①
Determine key external factors that are impacting the market place today or could do so in the future

Political

Economic

Sociological

Technological

Legal

Environmental

What is the market? ②
What is the market place, how big is it, where are the boundaries, can we look wider?

Our strength in this market ③
eg spend, attractiveness & choice

Weak — Strong

Supply/Demand ④
What do we know about current supply vs demand in the market, what is the likely trend?

Power of 2nd tier suppliers ⑤
What power do the suppliers to our suppliers hold?

Low — High
Supplier Power

Summary market assessment ⑩
Now and predicted? Can we change this?

Against us — Balanced — In our favour

Power of buyers ⑨
What power do we and other buyers from this market hold?

Low — High
Buyer Power

Scope for substitutes ⑥
What is the availability or potential for substitutes?

Low — High
Substitutes

Competitive rivalry ⑦
How much rivalry is there amongst the suppliers that make up the marketplace?

Low — High
Rivalry

Scope for new entrants ⑧
What is the potential and likelihood for new entrants to this market?

Low — High
New Entrants

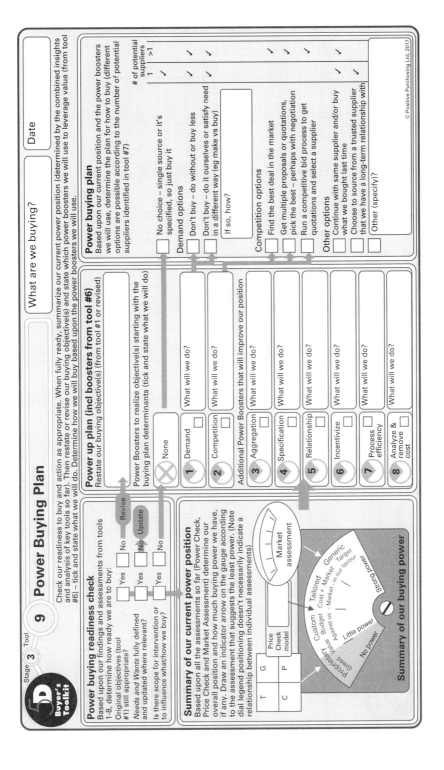

Stage 3 | **Tool 9** — **Power Buying Plan**

5D Buyer's Toolkit

What are we buying? | Date

Check our readiness to buy and action as appropriate. When fully ready, summarize our current power position (determined by the combined insights and analysis of key tools so far). Then restate or revise our buying objective(s) and state which power boosters we will use to leverage value (from tool #6) – tick and state what we will do. Determine how we will buy based upon the power boosters we will use.

Power buying readiness check

Based upon our findings and assessments from tools 1–8, determine how ready we are to buy:

Original objectives (tool #1) still appropriate? ☐ Yes ☐ No → Revise

Needs and Wants fully defined and updated where relevant? ☐ Yes ☐ No → Update

Is there scope for intervention or to influence what/how we buy? ☐ Yes ☐ No

Summary of our current power position

Based upon all the assessments so far (Power Check, Price Check and Market Assessment) determine our overall position and how much buying power we have, if any. Draw an indicator arrow on the gauge according to the assessment that suggests the least power. (Note dial legend positioning doesn't necessarily indicate a relationship between individual assessments)

Market assessment

T | G
C | P
Price Check model

Proprietary · Great value · Custom · Budget · Tailored · Cost + Market · Generic · Market – Against us – in our favour · Target · Strong power · Little power · No power

Summary of our buying power

Power up plan (incl boosters from tool #6)

Restate our buying objective(s) (from tool #1 or revised)

Power Boosters to realize objective(s) starting with the buying plan determinants (tick and state what we will do)

⊗ None

1 ☐ Demand | What will we do?
2 ☐ Competition | What will we do?

Additional Power Boosters that will improve our position

3 ☐ Aggregation | What will we do?
4 ☐ Specification | What will we do?
5 ☐ Relationship | What will we do?
6 ☐ Incentivize | What will we do?
7 ☐ Process efficiency | What will we do?
8 ☐ Analyze & remove cost | What will we do?

Power buying plan

Based upon our current position and the power boosters we will use, determine the plan for how to buy (different options are possible according to the number of potential suppliers identified in tool #7)

	# of potential suppliers	
	1	>1
☐ No choice – single source or it's specified, so just buy it	✓	

Demand options
☐ Don't buy – do without or buy less	✓	✓
☐ Don't buy – do it ourselves or satisfy need in a different way (eg make vs buy)	✓	✓
If so, how?		

Competition options
☐ Find the best deal in the market	✓	✓
☐ Get multiple proposals or quotations, pick the best – perhaps with negotiation		✓
☐ Run a competitive bid process to get quotations and select a supplier		✓

Other options
☐ Continue with same supplier and/or buy what we bought last time	✓	
☐ Choose to source from a trusted supplier that we have a long-term relationship with	✓	
☐ Other (specify)?		

Select Supplier

5D Buyer's Toolkit

| What are we buying? | | Date |

List each of the potential or shortlisted suppliers below. If single sourced supplier is specified, and we cannot challenge this, then skip this step. Note a summary of the evaluation for each supplier, then complete the selection matrix and select the supplier(s) we will use.

Supplier 1

Summary evaluation

Supplier 2

Summary evaluation

Supplier 3

Summary evaluation

Supplier 4

Summary evaluation

Supplier 5

Summary evaluation

Needs & Wants	Selection criteria	Weighting N/A Yes/No	Max score N/A	1	2	3	4	5
1 Must have	1 *Will satisfy our defined needs? (Yes/No)*							
2 Specification and quality	2 *Want...*							
3 Service and support	3 *Want...*							
4 Price, cost and terms	4 *Want...*							
5 Nice to have	5							
Other relevant criteria, eg	6							
• *Internal factors* • *Ability to switch to this supplier* • *Future factors*	7							
	Totals							

Determine the selection criteria, start with the *needs* from Tool #3. This is a 'yes/no' evaluation (exclude supplier if needs cannot be met). List key *wants* and other criteria, determine a weighting relative to importance then score each supplier. Calculate totals to select supplier(s).

Selected supplier(s)

Selected supplier 1

Selected supplier 2

Selected supplier 3

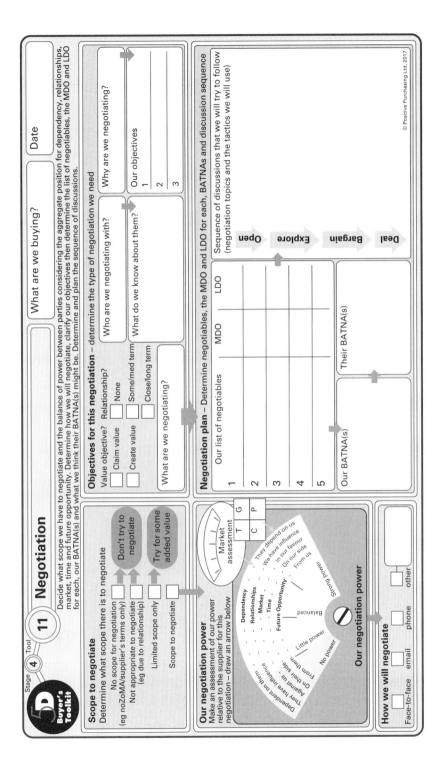

Negotiation

Decide what scope we have to negotiate and the balance of power between parties considering the aggregate position for dependency, relationships, market, time and future opportunity. Determine how we will negotiate, clarify our objectives then determine the list of negotiables, the MDO and LDO for each, our BATNA(s) and what we think their BATNA(s) might be. Determine and plan the sequence of discussions.

| What are we buying? | Date |

Scope to negotiate

Determine what scope there is to negotiate

No scope for negotiation (eg noZoMA/supplier's terms only) → Don't try to negotiate

Not appropriate to negotiate (eg due to relationship)

Limited scope only → Try for some added value

Scope to negotiate

Our negotiation power

Make an assessment of our power relative to the supplier for this negotiation – draw an arrow below

Market assessment

Dependency
Relationships
Market
Time
Future Opportunity

They depend on us
We have influence
In our favour
On our side
From us

Strong power
Balanced
Little power
No power

Dependent on them
They have influence
Against us
On their side
From them

Our negotiation power

How we will negotiate

Face-to-face ☐   email ☐   phone ☐   other ☐

Objectives for this negotiation – determine the type of negotiation we need

Value objective?   Relationship?
☐ Claim value   ☐ None
☐ Create value   ☐ Some/med term
                ☐ Close/long term

What are we negotiating?

Who are we negotiating with?

What do we know about them?

Why are we negotiating?

Our objectives
1
2
3

Negotiation plan – Determine negotiables, the MDO and LDO for each, BATNAs and discussion sequence

Our list of negotiables	MDO	LDO
1		
2		
3		
4		
5		

Our BATNA(s)

Their BATNA(s)

Sequence of discussions that we will try to follow (negotiation topics and the tactics we will use)

Open → Explore → Bargain → Deal

© Positive Purchasing Ltd. 2017

5D Buyer's Toolkit

Stage **4** Tool **12 Contract**

What are we buying?	Date

Determine what scope we have to influence contract terms, if any. Where there is scope, determine how we will agree the contract. For oral, simple written, or by conduct, determine the requirements or terms that must form part of the contact and communicate these as part of making the agreement. Where reviewing or drafting a full written contract or set of terms work through the checklist to ensure everything is provided for.

Scope to influence contract terms

Refer to *Power Check Tool* and overall current power position (from *Power Buying Plan*) and determine what scope we have to influence the contract and terms

- [ ] No scope – only option is to buy on the supplier's terms → *Review and decide whether to proceed*
- [ ] Some influence over contract and terms proposed by the supplier → *Review, proceed or agree changes*
- [ ] We determine the contract form and set the terms

How we will agree the contract

Determine the best way to agree the contract based upon complexity, risk, spend and relationship needed with supplier

- [ ] Full written contract → *Determine new or review and agree existing terms*
- [ ] Purchase order
- [ ] Written instruction (eg e-mail, letter or other) → *Include some conditions as part of the contract? If so decide what they are and include*
- [ ] By action (making payment regularity or other inference)
- [ ] Oral (verbal) agreement

Specific simple requirements, qualifiers, terms or conditions that we want to make part of the contract

Contract and contract terms checklist

Work through the following check list and use it to help guide the development of a new contract (eg using a boilerplate or model form of contract) or to review and check the suitability of existing terms and conditions. Any areas that we feel are not adequately provided for, or we are not comfortable with, are things to check, challenge, negotiate and agree.

Tick if OK

1. Are the parties to the agreement adequately defined? ☐
2. What exactly is to be provided? Is it adequately defined in a clear, definite and unambiguous way? ☐
3. Have any pertinent requirements from our *Needs and Wants* been included? ☐
4. Price or fees (consideration) and how they will be paid. Check terms for currency, payment terms, etc. ☐
5. Are all the terms and conditions included and clearly referenced? ☐
6. Are any schedules or additional information included and clear? ☐
7. Are the liabilities and limits of liability acceptable and appropriate to us (acceptable balance of risk) ☐
8. Are indemnification clauses acceptable and appropriate so to protect us/not leave us exposed? ☐
9. Are arrangements for how each party may terminate the contract (other than for breach) appropriate? ☐
10. Can the contract be terminated other than for breach? If so is the provision appropriate? ☐
11. Are any insurance provisions we require the supplier to hold adequately specified? ☐
12. Are our confidentiality needs adequately defined? ☐
13. Is any process or requirement for renewal of contract adequately defined? ☐
14. Are any required performance levels, standards, specification compliance etc adequately defined? ☐
15. Is it well drafted, clear, unambiguous, precise...is it absolutely clear what everything means and does? ☐

Tick if OK

16. Are goods/services required at a specific time or to a schedule? if so when and is this defined? ☐

    Required timing or schedule

17. What contract duration do we need? ☐

    Single | Short term fulfilment (eg 1 year) | Med term (eg 3 year) | Long term (eg 5+ year)

18. What payment terms do we need? ☐

    Payment terms (eg immediate, net 30, etc)

19. How will we manage this contract? ☐

20. Is there a need to state how the relationship will work and if so is this agreed and defined? ☐
21. Are the arrangements for dispute resolution/ arbitration appropriate for what we are buying? ☐
22. If intellectual property is an important consideration does the contract adequately provide for this? ☐

© Positive Purchasing Ltd. 2017

5D Buyer's Toolkit

13 Implementation

What are we buying?	Date

List all of the specific actions or activities to support any change for what we are buying/new buying arrangements. Agree and assign owners and required completion dates. Manage each until complete. Decide what needs to be communicated (key messages), how we will do this and to whom. Decide if this is the same as our *Consult and Engage* list and use this. If not, or if there are others to communicate to, list these. Manage communications until complete.

What do we need to communicate (key or central messages)?

What (action or change required)	Who	By When
1		
2		
3		
4		
5		
6		
7		
8		
9		
10		
11		
12		
13		
14		

How will we communicate this (media or approaches we will use)?

Who will we communicate this to? ☐ *Consult and Engage* list + . . .

Buyer's Toolkit — Stage 5 — Tool 14

Manage Supplier(s)

Start by determining how we will manage the supplier(s) and what sort of relationship we need with them. Tick the relevant box on the pyramid. Work down through the relevant section and all other sections that link to levels below that selected on the pyramid.

What are we buying?	Date

Ongoing supplier management

How will we manage this supplier?

- ☐ Manage the supplier to the agreed contract
- ☐ Monitor and manage risk with this supplier (determine Likelihood (L), Severity (S) and action)
- ☐ Conduct progress review(s) with the supplier

Supplier/supply risks to manage

Risk	L	S	Action
1			
2			
3			
4			
5			
6			

Review topics

1
2
3
4
5
Review frequency

Collaborative supplier management

Determine and agree with the supplier how this relationship should build and develop moving forward

Our long-term vision for this relationship

Key joint objectives

Agreed objectives	Target date
1	
2	
3	
4	
5	

How we will work together and collaborate

Pyramid (tick)

- Strategic — Long term, joint collaborative relationship
- Important Ongoing — Ongoing, repeat business relationship
- Important short term — Relationship management to support fulfilment
- Non-important suppliers (vast majority) — No or minimal relationship

Fulfilment check

Actions to have confidence this purchase will be fulfilled as expected?

- ☐ No specific action or intervention
- ☐ Basic check goods/service fulfilled on-time, in full, as agreed
- ☐ Performance check(s) needed

Relationship management

List key roles in the relationship and the agreed points of contact for each side against each role

Our team	Relationship Role	Supplier's team
1		
2		
3		
4		

Any agreed relationship rules

How to deal with/escalate problems?

15 Performance Check

Buyer's Toolkit

What are we buying?	Date

Where some sort of check of performance is required, complete the relevant sections. If a single purchase then determine if supplier performance is adequate or note any issues. For ongoing areas of supply, identify the different things that need to be monitored, what must be achieved and how this will be done. If there are issues or a supplier is underperforming, work through the bottom section.

Supplier scorecard (for ongoing performance monitoring of regular supply/longer term relationship)

Determine the requirements/measures and what must be achieved, check performance regularly to these.

Performance requirement, measure or KPI	Target	Results for each period 1 2 3 4
1		
2		
3		
4		
5		
6		

Fulfilment check (single purchase)

Determine if the supplier has fulfilled what was agreed or how the supplier has performed.

Goods delivered or service fulfilled:

- In full ☐
- On time ☐
- To specification/standard ☐
- Satisfactory quality/performance ☐

Any issues?

Supplier improvement

Response to a supplier-related problem or action required

☐ Do nothing
☐ Fix problem – corrective action
☐ Corrective & preventative action
☐ Continuous improvement
☐ Work together towards a mutual goal

S Study the situation

T Target outcome for improvement

P Plan to get there

D Do – implement the plan

R Review – verify and actions to make any changes stick

© Positive Purchasing Ltd, 2017

GLOSSARY

Category Management A methodology that enables organizations to take a strategic approach to their entire third-party spend by segmenting it into groups of products or services, or 'categories', that mirror how marketplaces are organized.

Continuous improvement An approach to drive in ongoing incremental improvement in one or more aspects of performance.

CSR (Corporate Social Responsibility) A strategic organization-wide initiative for the firm to consider the impact of its actions on society, the environment and the world at large and to identify actions to minimize or eliminate detrimental impacts.

eAuction An electronic, online reverse auction where suppliers bid to supply individual lots representing defined goods or services, usually for a defined period or for defined values. Supplier bid against other suppliers and in doing so the price (usually) falls until the auction ends when the winner is the supplier with the lowest bid. Whether this supplier then gets the business or progresses to further negotiation, or if lowest bid wins or not, depends upon the rules set within the eAuction.

e-bidding The term used within eAuctions where suppliers bid against each other to supply a defined lot of product or service to a customer.

ERP System (Enterprise Resource Planning System) An organization-wide system that enables an integrated, real-time view of core business processes using common databases of information and can track business resources.

First tier supplier A supplier with whom we have a direct contractual relationship, who is immediately next to our company in the supply chain.

Gantt Chart A visual planning tool developed by Henry Gantt in the 1910s to help project planning and management. The Gantt chart represents each individual activity that makes up a project as a horizontal bar positioned on a timeline according to when the activity starts and finishes and the width according to the duration of the activity. The visual representation allows dependencies between activities and resource loading to be identified more easily.

Graey Market An unofficial market or trade in something, especially controlled or scarce goods.

JIT (Just-In-Time) A production strategy that strives to reduce inventory and the costs of moving goods using a system of information and action to coordinate internal and supplier operations so the required materials arrive at the point they are needed when they are needed and the waste associated with storage and double carrying are removed or reduced.

Lead Time The time it takes from placing an order with a supplier to delivery being made (or services provided).

NPD (New Product Development) A process or function concerned with the development of new products or services for an organization.

OTIF (On-Time, In-Full) Checks or a measure of performance for goods delivered or services performed by a supplier.

OTIFIS (On-Time, In-Full, In-Specification) An extended version of OTIF.

Project Charter A document used at the outset of a team-based project as a basis to define and agree key aspects of the project including scope, targets, membership, roles, responsibilities and timings. May also be called a Team Charter.

RAQSCI Business Requirements A framework for developing and defining business requirements under the headings of Regulatory, Assurance of supply, Quality, Service, Cost (and commercial) and Innovation.

R&D (Research and Development) A process or function concerned with the research into potential new products and the development of new products or services for an organization.

RFI (Request for Information) A solicitation tool to request various pieces of information from a supplier or many suppliers, perhaps as part of market research or data gathering. RFIs can be paper-based questionnaires but these days are more commonly electronic – run online using one of the many proprietary e-sourcing platforms available.

RFP (Request for Proposal) A solicitation tools to request a specific supplier to make proposals for a defined area of supply, eg defined goods or services for a particular business unit and or period of time. RFPs may ask supplies to make proposals against very precise defined requirements or may invite free form creative ideas. They may be conducted in written form, e-mail or most typically online using a proprietary e-sourcing tool.

RFQ (Request for Quotation) A variant of the RFP but where the suppliers are asked to make a price proposal or provide firm quotes. May be an extension to an RFP or a further stage. Sometimes RFQs are referred to as RFPs.

RFx The generic suite of RFI, RFP or RFQ tools.

eRFX Electronic, online RFI, RFPs or RFQs.

Second-tier suppliers Suppliers who supply first-tier suppliers with whom we have no direct contractual relationship with.

Team Charter A document used at the outset of a team-based project as a basis to define and agree key aspects of the project including scope, targets, membership, roles, responsibilities and timings. May also be called a Project Charter.

Vertical integration A style of management control (from economic theory) that describes a situation where companies in a supply chain are united through a common owner. Each member of the supply chain produces a different product and these come together to satisfy a common need.

REFERENCES

Anderson, C and Thompson, L L (2004) *Management in Teams and Groups*, Vol 7, Greenwich, CT, Elsevier Science Press

British Institute of Facilities Management UK facilities management sector reports surge in confidence in economic outlook (2015) [online] http://www.bifm.org.uk/bifm/news/7363 [accessed 31 May 2017]

Crystal, G The Law of Contracts (2016) [online] http://www.contractsandagreements.co.uk/law-of-contracts.html [accessed 31 May 2017]

Granovetter, M (1985), Economic Action and Social Structure: The Problem of Embeddedness, *American Journal of Sociology*, 91(3), pp 481–510

Greenaway, J (2011) Deloitte – Bribery and corruption in Africa: Getting on the front foot. Downloaded from www.deloitte.com December 2013

Greenhouse S and Clifford S, 'US Retailers Offer Plan for Safety at Factories', *New York Times*, 10 July 2013 [online] http://www.nytimes.com/2013/07/11/business/global/us-retailers-offer-safety-plan-for-bangladeshi-factories.html

Gwartney, J D, Richard, S, Dwight R L (2005), *Common Sense Economics*, New York, St. Martin's Press, pp 8–9

IndustriALL, Global brands pull together on Bangladesh safety deal [Press Release] 23 May 2013

International Monetary Fund (2000) Globalization: Threats or opportunity, IMF Publications

Kaplan, R S and Norton, D P (1996), *The Balanced Scorecard*, Harvard Business School Press

Mauss, M (1925) Essai sur le don. Forme et raison de l'échange dans les sociétés archaïques [An essay on the gift: the form and reason of exchange in archaic societies], originally published in *L'Année Sociologique* in 1925. Later translated into English in 1954 by I Cunnison, downloaded from https://archive.org/details/giftformsfunctio00maus [accessed 31 May 2017]

O'Brien, J (2016) *Category Management in Purchasing*, 3rd Edition, Kogan Page

O'Brien, J (2016), *Negotiation for Purchasing Professionals*, 2nd Edition, Kogan Page

O'Brien, J (2014) *Supplier Relationship Management – Unlocking the value in the Supply Base*, Kogan Page

Open University Information Literacy Toolkit Advanced Internet Searching (2013) [Online] http://www2.open.ac.uk/students/iltoolkit/pages/advanced-internet-searching.php [accessed 31 May 2017]

Pollitt, M (2014) Unfinished abolitionists: Britain returns to the frontline of the war on slavery *New Statesman,* 16 October

Porter, M E (1985) *Competitive Advantage*, New York, Free Press

Porter, M E (1979) 'How competitive forces shape strategy', *Harvard Business Review*, 57(2), pp 137–45

Safire, W (1993) On language; Words left out in the cold, *New York Times*, 14 February

Sahlins, M (1972) *Stone Age Economics*, Chicago, Aldine-Atherton

Tam, D Is there a global chocolate shortage coming? (2016) [online] http://www.marketplace.org/2016/06/07/world/theres-global-chocolate-shortage-and-its-getting-worse. [accessed 31 May 2017]

Transparency International (2013) [accessed 31 May 2017] Global Corruption Barometer [Online] https://www.transparency.org/whatwedo/publication/global_corruption_barometer_2013.

http://www.building.co.uk/top-40-contractors-in-services-and-maintenance-ranked-by-turnover/5058203.article [available only to registered users]

Other sources and articles

'Bangladesh building collapse death toll passes 500' [accessed 31 May 2017] BBC News (2013) [online] http://www.bbc.co.uk/news/world-asia-22394094.

'Bangladesh Factory Safety Accord: At Least 14 Major North American Retailers Decline To Sign' [accessed 31 May 2017] The Huffington Post (2013) [online] http://www.huffingtonpost.com/2013/05/17/bangladesh-factory-safety-accord_n_3286430.html?ncid=txtlnkushpmg00000029#slide=2463111

INDEX

Italics indicate a figure or table in the text.